Rights and Responsibilities
International, Social, and Individual Dimensions

Steering Committee for the Conference on
"Rights and Responsibilities"

Nelson T. Horn, *Associate Dean of the Graduate School, University of Southern California; Chairman of the Committee and Editor of the Proceedings*

Norman R. Fertig, *Dean for Honors and Advisement, College of Letters, Arts, and Sciences, USC*

Charles A. McClelland, *Professor of International Relations, USC, and 1978-79 Annenberg Scholar-in-Residence*

John R. Schmidhauser, *Professor of Political Science and Chairman of the Department of Political Science, USC*

RIGHTS AND RESPONSIBILITIES

INTERNATIONAL, SOCIAL, AND INDIVIDUAL DIMENSIONS

*Proceedings of a Conference
Sponsored by the Center for
Study of the American Experience
Annenberg School of Communications
University of Southern California
November 1978*

University of Southern California Press
Transaction Books — Rutgers University

The Center for Study of the American Experience seeks to trace the evolutionary development and examine the future prospects of selected threads drawn from the unique fabric of American life, and to perform analysis and engage in creative thought on problems and opportunities that have been most influential in shaping America's past and present and will be most likely to define America's future.

The objectives are pursued through the assembling of conferences at the highest level of objectivity and expertise, the production of edited audio and video tapes and publications from these conferences, and the support of visiting distinguished Scholars-in-Residence.

The Center is a joint educational project of the University of Southern California and The Annenberg School of Communications located on that campus. It welcomes the intellectual involvement of the University's faculty and students, as well as leaders from the nation at large.

Topics for conferences are selected to stimulate awareness of the various aspects of the American experience, the potential benefits of future opportunities, and the possible solutions to existing and emerging problems for America.

Simon Ramo, *Chairman*   **John C. Weaver,** *Executive Director*
Center for Study of the American Experience

Published 1980
University of Southern California Press
Los Angeles, California 90007

Series Editor, Joyce J. Bartell
Designer, Robert W. Giese

Distributed by Transaction Books 🄶 Rutgers University
New Brunswick, N.J. 08903 (U.S.A.) and London (U.K.)

Library of Congress Cataloging in Publication Data

Main entry under title:

Rights and responsibilities

  Includes bibliographical references
  1. Civil rights—Congresses.   I. Annenberg School of Communications, University of Southern California, Center for Study of the American Experience.
JC571.R529   323.4   80-15054
ISBN 0-88474-095-1

CONTENTS

Rights and Responsibilities
International, Social, and Individual Dimensions

Individual Rights, Social Responsibility

by Barbara C. Jordan

Rights and Responsibilities; Rights and Responsibilities of the Individual; Individual Rights and Responsibilities—my subject will not be any of those phrases. My subject is "Individual Rights, Social Responsibility."

After accepting an invitation to participate in this conference, I speculated about the meaning of these concepts, "rights" and "responsibilities," to the American people. I opined that we do not consider the two in tandem, not unlike the Constitution. We emphasize rights almost to the exclusion of responsibilities, be they designated individual, political, human, simple, natural rights. They're something we've got. "I've got my rights": that is a declaration that transcends demography. Were we to ask a representative sample of the people the source of their rights, what would they say? Among the sources they would cite, they would probably include the first ten Amendments to the Constitution; perhaps the Fourteenth Amendment; maybe the Declaration of Independence. Least likely would they cite decisions of the Supreme Court of the United States.

My subject, "Individual Rights, Social Responsibility," emerged as an overview of the influences that contributed to the national shift from a predominantly exclusive focus on individual rights to the emergence of a concept of social responsibility in the nation's consciousness. The moral and legal ethos was middle-class individualism. Individualism was the ethos of that class which in Europe reacted against the hereditary privileges of the feudal aristocracy. And it was against the notion of class privilege and class rule that the American Declaration of Independence declared that all men are created equal. Individualism is that philosophy according to which the determining principle of society is our right to be free of external restraint in order that we may make of ourselves what we will and what we can. Given that view of individualism, external restraint upon the individual should be no more than is necessary to safeguard the same freedom for others.

Individualism as a philosophy emerged only with the advent of the experimental method of science. Technological innovation made it possible for individual initiative to transcend those communal bonds that previously were necessary for human survival. The basic right—and this is the key—the basic right that gave rise to the very notion of individual rights was that of property. Property is an object belonging exclusively to one who has made it. Regarded in this way, property is an extension of individual identity.

Gary Wills notwithstanding, it is generally agreed that John Locke exercised considerable influence on the framers of the Constitution. Locke authored *The Second Treatise of Civil Government* to justify the glorious Revolution of 1688 whereby the English Parliament, in effect, declared its supremacy over the Crown. John Locke based his conception of government upon the antecedent right of private property. He explained that the origin of property was the work of the owner himself. Locke said: "The labor of his body and the work of his hands are properly his, whatsoever then he removes out of the state that nature has provided it and left it in, he has mixed with his labor and joined to it something that is his own and thereby made it his property." For Locke, it was for the one purpose of protecting private property that individuals associate themselves into society and set up a government. Locke further said that "the chief and great end of men's uniting in the Commonwealth and putting themselves under government is for preservation of their property."

Thomas Jefferson's conception of government was similar to that of Locke. Here's what Jefferson said: "The true foundation of republican government is the equal right of every citizen in his person and property and in their management." James Madison said government is instituted to protect property of every sort. "This being the end of government," Madison said, "that alone is a just government which impartially secures to every man whatever is his own."

In an individualistic society based upon the principles of private property, the social nexus will be regarded as that of a contract of agreement between individuals for the exchange of what is their own property. An individualistic society will place a high value on the right of individuals to enter into contractual agreement free from external restraint, free from external condition. Indeed, the battle of individual rights against legislative interference on behalf of social purposes has been fought primarily over the liberty of contract. Where does that fight take us?

Chief Justice John Marshall was a very strong defender of liberty of contract against any legislative action that would abridge or modify the obligations of a contract. The point of view of Chief Justice Marshall was exemplified quite clearly in the *Dartmouth College* case. You will recall that this case involved a struggle between two factions for control of Dartmouth College. The former trustees of the college had held control as trustees of the original donors and by virtue of the charter from the English Crown. The other faction opposing the old trustees on the basis of religion and politics had an ace; they had the New Hampshire Legislature. The New Hampshire Legislature by legislative enactment abrogated the original charter of Dartmouth College and reorganized it in a manner such as to ensure control by the factions favored by the Legislature. Justice Marshall, delivering the opinion of the Court, found that the attempt to abrogate by legislative enactment the original contract between the donors who gave the money and the trustees, was a violation of Article I, Section 10 of the Constitution, which says, "No state shall pass any law impairing the obligation of contract."

In the Court's dissenting opinion in *Ogburn v. Sanders,* a case involving the validity of a state bankruptcy law which operated to relieve the debtor of all liability under a contract, Marshall again reasoned on the basis of a more or less absolutist construction of the contract laws, and he concluded that no legislative enactment of any state may abridge the obligation of contract, because this obligation, said the Chief Justice, derives from the right of the individual as a free agent to contract with another.

The majority of the Court upheld the validity of the state law. Justice Washington, delivering the majority opinion, said that the common or moral law, which obligated each party to perform a contract, is subordinate to legislative enactment. The logical conclusion of Justice Washington's argument is that the contract clause of the Constitution is no bar to legislation affecting an obligation of contract; that is, legislation designed to achieve social purposes transcending those rights of the individuals who are parties to the contract. Marshall vigorously dissented, and the Chief Justice's dissent could be read as a page from Locke's *Second Treatise.*

The rapid industrialization of the country after the Civil War gave rise to a reordering of society which generated a severe conflict between capital and labor. In this context, the issue of liberty of contract proved to be of crucial importance. An absolutist's conception of liberty of contract would allow capitalists to exercise that enormous power without restraint. This enormous power allowed capitalists to determine wages, hours, and conditions of work as they wished.

After passage of the Fourteenth Amendment in 1868, arguments in defense of liberty of contract shifted. They shifted from the contract laws of the Constitution to the due process law of the Fourteenth Amendment, which provides that no person shall be deprived of life, liberty or property, without due process of law.

Now those that argued for liberty of contract against legislative interference interpreted the term "liberty" in a substantive rather than a procedural sense.

In *Lockner v. New York,* the majority of the Supreme court based its decision squarely upon the substantive interpretation of liberty in the due process clause of the Fourteenth Amendment. Liberty of contract meant here that legislation could not modify the terms of a contract on which the individual parties to the contract had freely agreed. The case involved the validity of a New York State law which set maximum hours for employees in the baking industry. The majority opinion of the Court said in part that the statute "necessarily interferes with the right of contract between the employer and the employee, concerning the number of hours in which the latter may labor in the bakery of the employer. The general right to make a contract in relation to this business is part of the liberty of the individual, protected by the Fourteenth Amendment of the Federal Constitution. Under that provision, no state shall make any law to deprive any person of life, liberty, or property without due process of law." The right to purchase or sell labor is part of the liberty protected by this Amendment.

Justice Holmes wrote a dissenting opinion that has become a classic. He said, in part, "A Constitution is not intended to embody a particular economic theory, whether of paternalism or the organic relation of the citizen to the state or of *laissez faire,* but I think that the word 'liberty' of the Fourteenth Amendment is perverted when it is held to prevent the natural outcome of the dominant opinion, in this instance the opinion of the Legislature—unless it can be said that a rational and fair man necessarily would admit that the statute proposed would infringe fundamental rights, fundamental principles, as they have been understood by the traditions of our people and our law. It does not need research to show that no such sweeping condemnation can be passed upon the statute before us."

Justice Holmes was saying that the Constitution allows government to act not only to protect individual liberty but also to ensure human well-being. Throughout its history, the Court had upheld liberty of contract in order to guarantee each one's right to be free, to make of one's self what one could and what one would. Holmes was saying that the government may also assume the responsibility for what becomes of individual persons as a result of social factors. Holmes' argument in *Lockner* was vindicated several decades later.

In the *West Coast Hotel Company v. Parish* case, the principle involved was the constitutionality of a law of the State of Washington establishing a commission to set a standard for minimum wages for women and children in industry. It was argued against the statute that it violated the liberty of contract protected by the due process clause of the Fourteenth Amendment. In delivering the opinion, Chief Justice Hughes said, in part, "The principle which must control our decision is not in doubt. The constitutional provision invoked is due process of law; that clause of the Fourteenth Amendment governing the states. The violation alleged by those attacking the minimum wage regulation for women is deprivation of freedom."

Justice Hughes asked the question, "What is this freedom?" The Constitution does not speak of freedom of contract. It speaks of liberty, and prohibits the deprivation of liberty without due process of law. In prohibiting the deprivation, the Constitution does not recognize an absolute and uncontrollable liberty. Liberty in each of its phases has its history and its connotation, but the liberty safeguarded is the liberty of a social organization that requires the protection of law against the evils that menace the health, safety, morals and welfare of the people. Liberty under the Constitution is therefore necessary, but only within the context of due process.

In 1968 in the case of *Green v. County School Board of New Kent County*, the Supreme Court faced a very clear-cut choice between individual liberty and the responsibility that society and the government have for the negative effects of community conditions. In 1965 New Kent County adopted a freedom of choice plan, trying to satisfy an obligation for the desegregation of public schools. The school system consisted of two schools: one all black, one all white. Under the plan, each student could choose each year either to attend the all-black or the all-white school. Students who did not choose at all would attend the school they had attended the prior year.

The plan did not work. During the first three years, with freedom of choice operating, no white students chose to attend the all-black school and 85 percent of the black students chose to remain in the all-black school. The plan did not work, and the Court told New Kent County so. The Court stated that the sole purpose of any school desegregation plan is to achieve a non-discriminatory school system. The Court found the freedom of choice plan ineffective; it did not desegregate the school system and was therefore not acceptable.

But the Court also found in that same case that the exercise of individual liberty, in this instance freedom of choice, had the effect of negating the value upon which the Court had decided the case of *Brown v. Board of Education of Topeka*. What was that value? The personal development of black students. In *Brown*, the Court held that segregated schools are intrinsicly unequal and that a segregated school system is therefore in violation of the equal protection clause of the Fourteenth Amendment.

The Supreme Court's decisions in *West Coast Hotels* and in the *Green* case should not lead us to conclude that the Court has eliminated consideration of what belonged immediately to the individual and has replaced it with consideration of individuals once they have their rights as members of social groups. We know the Court has not done this because we have only recently experienced the *Bakke* case *(Regents of the University of California v. Bakke)*. The Court attempted in *Bakke* to achieve a balance between the rights of the individual and the rights of individuals as members of social groups. The Court divided 5-4 on the issue, finding that the special admissions program of the University of California was a quota system and therefore in violation of individual rights guaranteed by the equal protection clause of the Fourteenth Amendment.

Delivering the opinion of the Court, Justice Powell said, in part, "The guarantee of equal protection cannot mean one thing when applied to one individual and something else when applied to a person of another color. If both are not accorded the same protection, then it is not equal."

Powell continued, if the individual is entitled to judicial protection against classification based upon his racial or ethnic background because such distinctions impinge upon his individual and personal rights rather than because of his membership in a particular group, then constitutional standards may be applied consistently. Powell said also that the fatal flaw of the University of California's program is its disregard of the individual's rights as guaranteed by the Fourteenth Amendment.

A majority of the Court (and this was a different majority from that majority which invalidated the special admissions program) upheld the use of race as one element among others that could be considered in selecting individuals for admission to school, in order to reach out in an affirmative way to applicants from racially and economically disadvantaged backgrounds. Some special consideration could not eliminate competition among individuals. Race could be taken into account, but not in such a way that it eliminates competition among individuals. Justice Powell was a member of both majorities, and he said that in such an admission program, race or ethnic background may be deemed a plus in a particular applicant's file, yet it does not insulate that individual from comparison with all other candidates for available seats.

So we have gone from *Dartmouth College* to *Bakke*. And in the interim, the Court has grappled with the issue of the rights of the individual vis-à-vis social responsibility. Civil rights has been a front page issue but too many of us continue to consider civil rights in a vacuum. Too many of us consider civil rights in abstraction from concrete conditions, conditions that may prevent the exercise of civil rights.

The meaning or purpose of rights in America in equality of opportunity. That is what it means. Equality of opportunity is not a new idea. It was the formative idea of America. Individuals do not have equality of opportunity, however, if their way is blocked by economic and educational disadvantage. If their way is blocked by prejudice and discrimination, then equality of opportunity cannot be. To consider civil rights in abstraction from concrete conditions is really to be unaware in a total way of civil rights at all. Those who are interested in maintaining our free society must assume responsibility for enlarging the freedom, but concrete freedom, not merely the abstract freedom. We must try to enlarge this freedom, not for a few, but for all individuals.

When individuals here and elsewhere have been enabled to assume full responsibility for their own lives, when individuals can no longer justifiably blame society, or hold society responsible for living unproductive lives, what will they do then? We can hope they will have greater concern for the common good, for the public interest.

If people take responsibility for their own lives and assume a share of the responsibility for the common good and the public interest, the union will indeed be more perfect. The *we*, the we in "we, the people" will indeed be more inclusive.

The Individual
in Society
East and West

by Robert S. Ellwood, Jr.

Comparison of the meaning of the individual in society throughout various cultures is a treacherous enterprise. Few operations lend
themselves more readily to stereotyping, romanticizing, and premature judgment. Yet few are more important to human understanding, for the basic poles of human existence are the individual and the
social matrix. Human life as we know it is inconceivable without
both; the interaction between them is the key to the dynamics of
most individual and social processes.

First we must be clear on exactly what it is we are comparing. We
must be sure that we are not, as so often happens in ambitious
undertakings of this sort, comparing a traditional, classical or ideal
version of one society with the modernized version of another. For
in these times we can hardly help being aware that the question of
the role of the individual in society is hardly one of a timeless
symposium between great but static cultures or social philosophies,
each representing some sort of eternal Platonic idea. Rather, the

meaning of the individual in society in nearly all societies in changing rapidly in the wake of war, revolution, political turmoil, and socio-economic development.

Ancient cultures are being shaken down or even swept away in their traditional forms; new social classes with new experiences of individual existence are emerging in once-peasant societies; increasing literacy, world-wide exposure to new lifestyle ideals communicated by radio and TV—the so-called revolution of rising expectations and increasing mobility—as well as often increasing hunger and poverty which seem cruelly to defeat these promises, are all working havoc on the well-honed lifestyle patterns of many cultures, including our own. I would urge you to bear in mind that intercultural dialogue is hardly a leisurely intellectual activity taking place in a vacuum, and that our concepts regarding it are struggling for breath to keep up with the changing realities out there in the real world.

What I shall do first is present some apertures to traditional meanings of the individual in society in India, China, and Japan, remembering these represent stages of development that should be compared with medieval or early modern society in the West, not with the modern society in its many forms that these countries in quite different ways are increasingly sharing today. Then we shall look at the changes wrought by modernization East and West in a summary way; and finally canvass some of the problems and prospects for the individual in society suggested by this overview.

India

India is one of the most complex and most often misunderstood societies on the face of the earth. How do we understand the meaning of the individual in a society in which the caste system rigorously predetermined the occupation, marriage choice, residence, social contact, possible dining partners, and probable standard of living for each individual from birth? A society in which "panchayats" or local caste councils had far more real impact on the daily lives of most people than the relatively ephemeral empires and states of maharajahs which rose and fell in this ancient land—yet in which wandering or eremetical spiritual seekers seemed to exhibit a rarely-equalled inner freedom? A society highly structured in interpersonal and intergroup contact, yet noted for the lushness of its sacred/erotic art, and for the exuberant variety of its gods?

Betty Heimann, in one of the deeply insightful essays in her book *Facets of Indian Thought,* has suggested that it is to the profoundly *biological* nature of the Indian understanding of human life and society that one must turn really to comprehend it. Hindu society is not a contractual state on the model of the Western "social contract" theories of Hobbes, Locke, or Rousseau, or even of Western feudalism, in which the state is, in theory, an agreement between the autonomous individual to surrender certain rights in exchange for certain benefits only the power of the state can afford. Rather than a legally defined entity, the Indian society is a great organism.

Betty Heimann observed that even the borders of ancient Indian states were amorphous rather than precisely defined, more like the customary range of a species of animal than the frontiers of a legalistic state. By means of the caste system, every individual found his or her place through the biological process of birth, and contributed to the whole like a cell in a body. The Hindu temple, like the Indian street, is alive with riotous organic life, human, animal, and plant. The Western church is usually dead except for cut flowers; but through feast, sacrifice, and offering, and because of the freedom such animals as monkeys and cows customarily have in sacred places, the throbbing and dying life of the universe flows in and out of the Hindu temple like a vast tide of monkeys, cows, birds, flowers, and fruit.

The Indic paths to ultimate inner freedom, such as yoga, also reveal deep contact with the biological roots of human life. Yoga requires a skillful and persistent combined engineering of physiological and psychological forces. It says the two are ultimately one; that ultimate salvation or liberation is on the profoundest level not achieved by a dualistic separation of something spiritual—a soul— out from the flesh, but rather by pressing the potentials of biology to unimaginable reaches where the flesh's own capacity for ecstasy or equilibrium can be harnessed.

The caste system, too, is really a social expression of a biological view of human nature. Caste, contrary to what many in the West seem to think, is not really occupational, based on the division of labor principle carried to some grotesque extreme. Its essence is instead a more primordial purity/pollution syndrome—an expression of a sense that certain groups and certain activities are less pure than others, and that the more pure will be polluted by contact with the less. There is and always has been a certain pragmatic flexibility about occupation so long as lines of purity/pollution are clearly marked. True, some occupations are inherently more polluting than others. Anything having to do with the wastes of the human body, such as barbering or washing clothes, is by its nature done by low-caste people; only brahmins, of course, can perform the Vedic religious rites. But on the other hand some brahmins have been farmers without losing status, and some shudras or peasants have become kings, served by brahmins who nonetheless would not touch them.

The purity/pollution syndrome, with its suggestion of a basic social metaphor being keeping oneself and one's own gene pool free of infection or disease—reinforced by the characteristic Hindu, especially upper caste, attention to personal cleanliness even in the midst of communal squalor—supports the idea that basically modes of conceptualization are at work in the Hindu social mind. So is the basic myth from the ancient Laws of Manu rationalizing caste. It tells us that the brahmins came from the head of the primal man, the kshatriyas from the arms, the vaisyas from the belly, and the shudras from the legs and feet.

It needs to be pointed out, though the point may be obvious, that a caste-centered society means a family-centered society. Despite a few exceptions and the fact that the concept of karma theoretically implies an individual determination of caste and destiny, the practical working of caste overwhelmingly implies a hereditary, and hence familial, determination. Just as it is inseparable from biological life, so is caste life inseparable from family life. Marriage, worship, and occupation in traditional India are all essentially family matters whose parameters are ordinarily determined not by the individual, but by the family in concert under patriarchal leadership and deeply conditioned by the family's caste status. The really important worship of a Hindu is that in the home, at the household shrine, not in the temple; and what a brahmin family does there will be quite different and much more elaborate than the casual presentations of a flower or ochre paste in a low-caste home.

China

The family is also very important in China, the next Asian society to be considered. But the tone of traditional Chinese society, and so the meaning of family and individual within it, is somewhat different in China than in India. Without a larger unit like caste powerfully shaping individual lives with less religious emphasis on individual determination of destiny through karma and more on the power and significance of ancestors, the family was the unrivalled center of traditional Chinese life. Yet, particularly as it is interpreted in the immensely influential Confucian philosophy and way of life, the Chinese social mind is more interested in relationships than genes.

If the fundamental paradigms of Hindu society are biological, in China they might be called, in a very broad sense, sociological. For to Confucianism the supreme good is a good society. It is through society that the Tao—the Great Way of the universe—preeminently expresses itself on the human level. Of this society the family is the Confucian cornerstone. And while Buddhism and Taoism have deeply affected other areas of Chinese tradition—art, philosophy, literature, personal religion—when it comes to the role of the individual in family and society, Confucian values have generally triumphed to provide the basic models. It is through the family that the individual finds his or her identity. A person isolated from family and social relations was hardly a human being, certainly not one that Confucian society could "handle."

Basic to the Confucian order were the Five Relationships: ruler and subject, father and son, husband and wife, elder and younger brother, friend and friend. One's identity was based on the place into which one fitted in the grid of these relationships. In all five, proper behavior, *li,* was required to give what is simply biological or spontaneous the structure that makes it into good human society, calm and enduring for the benefit of all. In the immense emphasis given to making what starts as a biological relationship—the family—into the building blocks of a good human society, we see why the Chinese mind might be thought of as sociological rather than biological in its root metaphors.

The cornerstone relation is the second—father and son. A son was expected to negate his own feelings and individuality in deference to the wishes of his parents in "filial piety," though the parents had obligations to the child as well. It was in this relationship, which is (at least according to Freudian psychoanalysis) the most feeling-laden and difficult of all, father and son, that the fundamental attitudes of *jen* (virtue), *li* (propriety), and social orientation were to be learned. It was as though to say: If love and virtue are to be learned truly, they must be learned at home and by making this hard but all-important relationship—father and son—the pivot. Father-son becomes the primal model of an interpersonal relationship, and in Confucianism it is in interpersonal relationships that humans are humanized and Tao is manifested in the human order. If this relationship can be rectified, then all other relationships will also fall into place.

One might ask, why is the father-son relation the key, and not mother and child? Perhaps it can be looked at in this way: The mother-child relationship is essentially biological, fraught with deep feelings and instincts which humankind shares with many animals. The father-son relationship, on the other hand, is more social in nature.

This is not to say, of course, that the father does not have a biological role, and some instinctual equipment to go with it, or that there is not a great deal that is socially learned about motherhood. But in many archaic societies, the father's biological role does not in itself establish social responsibility for a child. Rather, the crucial factor is the father's taking responsibility for the child *in his social role* as head of the household. The role may be defined by his picking up the child, giving him a name, and recognizing him in some socially recognized way as his ward and heir. In other words, the father-son relationship may be seen as the most basic relationship inextricably intertwined with the social as well as biological components of human culture, such as language (giving a name), moral responsibility, family as a legal entity, and the combinations of privilege and repression that make learned behavior—all that flows into virtue and propriety—possible.

It is therefore significant that in Confucianism, with its emphasis on human society as the key bearer of the Tao for human beings, the father-son relationship—the primal social, structured relationship—should be central; but that Lao-tzu, whose Taoism emphasized the natural and biological and spontaneous as better than the social order in manifesting Tao, and indeed saw society as generally corrupting, should several times use the mother-child relationship as metaphor for the relation of individual with Tao.

Traditional China, then, can be thought of as a society in which the individual is basically defined as member of a family and one component in a set of relationships centering around the family. Even the relation to the state was thought of in this way. Confucian moralists were clear that if a situation arose in which one had to make a decision between loyalty to family and loyalty to sovereign and state, the family came first. For one's loyalty to the emperor went through the heads of one's family, and the sovereign was not an immediate ruler of each individual but the patriarch of the entire nation as a family of families. Family-ism, a barbarous but appropriate term, has been used to sum up the traditional Chinese social order.

Japan

Another society deeply tinctured by Confucianism is Japan. Here the fundamental unit of society, as in China, is in principle the household or extended family, called *ie* in Japanese. Within a household or *ie,* traditionally the eldest son and his wife would live with the son's aging parents, carrying on the traditional family farm, business, or estate. Younger sons would set up branch houses. But the senior line of this extended family would constitute the *honke* or "main family," which would have primacy of honor and a certain authority over the branches. Branch families visit the *honke* at New Year's, the main holiday for affirming traditional relationships, and assist it in such half-ceremonial ways as helping to clean its cemetery at Ōbon. The *honke* may keep ancestral tablets of the *ie* at its Buddhist temple, and may maintain a family Shinto shrine apart from the village or community shrine.

Having said this, another important reality—one that has not always been fully appreciated by outside observers of Japanese society—needs to be noted, to understand rightly the role of the individual in society in Japan. For the individual's social role is not really conditioned by Confucianism and the biological family in quite the way the model would suggest. For Japan, while using Confucian language, moves even further from its roots in the biological family than China, and in a way that suggests a facile management of Confucian forms to validate a society that was never quite as Confucian as appears on the surface, and much more feudal.

In traditional Japan, a father-son relationship with all the privileges and responsibilities this implied in Confucianism could easily be created by adoption when biology did not function as was desired. Filial piety and loyalty were and are easily transferred from actual parents to feudal lord or his modern equivalent, the heads of one's corporation or university or whatever, and to emperor and state. For the major loyalty of Japanese, especially working males, is, according to such perceptive sociologists as Chie Nakane, not to family as such, but to one's work or activity group. To this the family is secondary, save when it is also the major economic and activity unit, the operators of the family farm or family shop—a very common case in the past, less so in today's Japan of great corporations and industries. At New Year's, calls by subordinates upon superiors are more frequent than between collateral kin—married brothers, sisters, cousins—though the *honke* call remains important.

The work group may be the modern office or corporation, which is more paternalistic and more strictly ordered by seniority than its American counterpart. In a real sense it replaces the medieval *daimyō* or feudal lord and his retainers, or the spiritual master and his disciples, and even the ancient *uji* or clan head by an *uji no kami* or chieftain.

Very often, as already noted, the extended family is an *uchi* or familial economic unit, a farm or mercantile house, so the two loyalties are convergent. But this is not necessarily the case. Despite the influence of Confucianism, family loyalty beyond the point of mere courtesy is actually weak in Japan except when reinforced by economic cohesion. Unless they live or work together, relations between adult siblings, or adult children and their parents, are probably less intimate and more perfunctory than in America.

For this reason, Japanese Confucian thinkers have long tended to rationalize the transference of the central Confucian virtue of loyalty to parents to other objects of absolute devotion: the feudal lord, more recently the emperor and the state.

Today, family loyalty is still easily and quite explicitly transferred. Corporations like to speak of themselves as a family, and frequently have a partriarchal elder statesman in a paternal role. Formerly, as we have seen, feudal lords explicitly adopted promising successors as sons to maintain a fiction of familial continuity, and abbots made a family of their novices. In Japanese universities, graduate students generally make themselves followers of an *oyabun*, literally "parent substitute" or "one in the parent's social role," a professor who is like a parent. The student, even when he later becomes a junior professor, serves his *oyabun* assiduously in both scholarly and personal ways, and certainly does not criticize the senior's work before anyone else. One can change *oyabun*, but that is a serious matter. The same pattern obtains in business, government service, and even the underworld.

Japanese society, shaped by this family model and driven by the dynamics of *giri* or obligation, is preeminently a society of vertical relationships. This reality, rather than caste or family in the Chinese sense, fundamentally shapes the meaning of the individual in society in Japan; rather than biological or sociological, we could call it hierarchical. In any encounter, Japanese instinctively see themselves as superior or subordinate. (This understanding will shape the tone and govern the language of a conversation, for Japanese has many verbal and grammatical modulations appropriate to different types of relationships. For this reason, it is in interpersonal conversation that the marvelous range and subtlety of the Japanese language comes into its own; conversely, Japanese often find addressing a group, in which persons of several different types of relationship to the speaker may be present, an awkward task; public rhetoric is not a particularly well-developed art in Japan.)

Japanese tend to assume that really important decisions are made through interpersonal relations structured as all are by the family model—though not necessarily really *family* relations—and by patterns of obligation and hierarchy. In a society of vertical relationships, Japanese have trouble accepting anyone as actually an equal, except in relationships going back very far, as of schoolmates of the same age, who may remain equal friends for a lifetime.

Because loyalty is to a relationship and its structure rather than to abstract principles, Japanese ethical values, like the understanding of the individual in society, tend to be situational rather than absolutistic. There are no absolute rules; rather, the relational and human nature of each situation calling for decisions about behavior has its own rights and wrongs which must be perceived. Japanese society, then, is one in which the individual is in a matrix of many relationships and obligations which have highly structured responses they demand of him or her, but in which he or she must sometimes face baffling choices between conflicting obligations, and perhaps face the ultimate shame of having failed a relationship—conundrums that are the stock in trade of Japanese literature.

Death as a Key to Life

We have glanced briefly at the way the individual is set into three Asian societies. It is time now to move this discussion to another stage that will allow comparison of the individual in society in the West, and enable perception of the dynamics of the matters. For, as we indicated at the beginning, patterns such as we have described for the three Asian countries are not eternal realities, but subject to flux and change as is anything human.

In this next stage I hope to do something else as well: to suggest that the meaning of the individual in a society is to be grasped not only from its overt rules, rhetoric, and higher philosophy, but also from its entire web of symbols and practices, some of which are not at all deliberately intended to make such a statement.

I do not intend to undertake here the mighty task of trying to

describe the role of the individual in Western society in philosophical or descriptive terms, and to trace the vicissitudes of that
role down the centuries. Rather, I wish to present just one set of
symbols that I think speak powerfully of attitudes toward the meaning of the individual in society: those connected with death and
funerals. For it would seem that if anything could communicate the
deep, unspoken, underlying attitudes of a society toward the life of
the individual, it should be the way it attends to his or her passing
out of that existence and the physical remains that now symbolize
the individual he or she was.

In India, for example, the body is normally disposed of by cremation, the funeral pyre being lit, if possible, by the eldest son of the
deceased. The ceremony is relatively simple, consisting basically of
a few chants recited by the small group of mourners, scriptures read
by *mahabrahmana* priests, circumambulation of the pyre and, if possible, casting the ashes into the holy Ganges River. Fire fits the
underlying biological paradigms, for fire is considered both purify-
ing and emblematic of the Vedic fire-sacrifices that enacted models
of the universal life-processes of conception and consumption, both
engendering heat and oxydation. The disposal of the remains into
the stream that has received so many millions of other sons and
daughters of India without monument also suggests a facing of the
final realities of life and death unveiled by cultural pretensions; in
the end, one's physical envelope returns as ashes to the mud like an
animal, or a fire that has burned down.

In Confucian China, death was attended by far more mourning
and ceremony. A son was supposed to mourn three years for a
parent, indicating the extreme gravity with which a rupture in the
family unity was regarded. At the same time, every symbolic effort
was made to manifest the continuing spiritual presence of the parents and other deceased members of the family. Tablets bearing
their names would be enshrined in the home. At the patronal temple
of the extended family, large tablets might be set up rank on rank on
ascending steps, each level representing a generation, the whole
display vividly indicating the weight of multiplying ancestors
watching the living. Periodically, the tombs of the ancestors would
be visited—for bodies were buried in graves very carefully plotted

and aligned with cosmic forces by geomancy—to receive offerings and be cleaned.

Particularly in the south of China, graves would be placed on higher ground near the family homestead. A peasant farmer like Lung in Pearl Buck's *The Good Earth* might till the fields his house had tilled for innumerable generations, see the graves of his parents and more distant ancestors peacefully resting on the hill above him as he labored, and know that one day his own grave would be there beside them as his sons and grandsons toiled below. It is hardly necessary to spell out how all this brings forth the central reality of "family-ism"—the family as the sovereign reality in individual identity, and the long line of ancestors as the mediators through whom one is linked to the ultimate parents, Heaven and Earth.

The complexity of Japanese funeral and burial practices typifies the complexity of that culture and the diverse, seemingly contradictory forces that often appear to animate it. Funerals and the subsequent memorial services are commonly Buddhist, but ideas surrounding burial are often affected by archaic Shinto notions. Very basic to Shinto mentality is the separation of purity and pollution, and nothing is more polluted than a corpse. In many parts of Japan, this has led to a double burial system, in which the body is buried in one tomb, the *ume-baka*, which subsequently, at least for a period, is impure. Another grave marker, the *mairi-baka*, is set up some ways distant to serve as the site of visitations and memorial services; the spirit is believed to have moved there and is itself pure; sometimes the body itself is moved when reduced to a skeleton. But many Japanese, especially Shinshu Buddhists, prefer cremation, which in itself accomplishes through fire the act of purification, so the double grave system is not necessary; it is also obsolete in the larger urban areas.

Nonetheless, it seems that something in this intricate pattern reflects the hierarchical, situational Japanese way of being in society. It suggests a sharp distinction between the impure, decaying biological self, which after disposal is pretended no longer to exist (Japanese words for burial have such harsh meanings as "to throw away," "to abandon"), and a fictive spiritual self made up of one's nexus of obligations and memorial services owed one by relatives, friends, and associates. Often these are simply perpetuations of the visits and respects owed the deceased in terms of the intricate hierarchy of his family, business, and profession. Even when the double grave system no longer literally exists, its spirit seems to live on in the double existence, biological and socially constructed, of Japanese. This split exists everywhere there is society, of course, but rarely does it seem more deeply driven or deeply determinative than in Japan.

Death in the West

Turning to the European and American West, the distinguished French social historian Philippe Ariès has traced death through several stages from the early Middle Ages to the present. Early medieval death he speaks of as matter-of-fact dying—"tamed death." For most people it was marked by little ceremony save the routine sacraments of the church after the conversion of heathendom, little anxiety apart from ordinary instinctive aversion to destruction, and little individuality. Judging from, say, Anglo-Saxon literature, Christian teaching provided more confidence than fear before the last crossing, and knights and yeomen died whether from sword or sickness with little more than resignation to the common fate of humankind. Bodies were buried in common graves around the village church; no individual markers were employed for most people.

In the high Middle Ages, however, death became "my death," a lonely, anxiety-laden affair. The earlier vast Christian eschatological perspective turned to an emphasis on personal judgment after death. Art concerning death showed the soul transiting nervously to the other world holding his "passport"—a small book with a ledger of his merits and demerits, which he expected to be carefully scrutinized before a decision that could go either way. Funeral rites, with the singing of the dolefully melodious *Dies Irae*—Day of Wrath, Day of Mourning—reiterated the same mood.

As Europe moved into modernity, death evoked another mood—one of sentimental feeling on the part of the survivors for the dear departed—"thy death." The charnel house and common grave gave way to the well-tended cemetery with its neat individual tombstones. Much emotion was spent on grieving over the loss, much sentiment attended visits to the grave, much energy was devoted to preserving the memory of the loved one. This attitude grew with the growth of bourgeois culture, with its regard for the neatly structured home, city, and commercial or industrial plant— reflected as in a mirror image in the green modern cemetery with its neatly arranged rows of headstones, and in the rise of the warm nuclear family, in which deaths came as genuine losses and sorrows.

The point, I think, is clear. The history of death in the West is a history of the growth of a sense of individuality from out of tribal and communal consciousness. The individual emerges in anxiety, as one who experiences anxiety before awareness that he himself, by his own decisions, determines his ultimate destiny. Later, as the culture gains confidence in its emerging values, it expands to embrace awareness of the unique individuality of others—ideally, of all—an individuality worth preserving in funeral symbol and memory.

A similar narrative regarding the dynamics through history of the understanding of death could be done for our Asian cultures, and has been done recently in the case of Japan by Professor Whalen Lai. Some broad similarities to the European pattern appear, for medieval and early modern forms of religion and culture in Asia and Europe are broadly comparable. Time, however, does not permit us to undertake that task here. It is time to move beyond the discussion of death to indicate that what Europe discovered in medieval anxiety and modern bourgeois confidence (very oversimplified ideas, of course)—the individual as a center of ultimate decision and destiny—has become a universal discovery.

Modern China has left behind the Confucian family-centered society for a state in which individuals, ideally, become equal units within that society; in which family, or at lest all but the nuclear family, fades away before the demands of centralized planning and an ethic of "Serve the people"—all equally, without regard for family first as Confucius would have had it.

India, shaken by the shocks to traditions of colonialism, the independence movement, and the anti-caste reforms that accompanied independence, and now by a new upsurge of democratic awareness in the revulsion against the Indira Gandhi regime, is familiar with tension (though tension not as thoroughly resolved in one way as in China) between its old values and the technological age. So is Japan, which has managed to incorporate very thoroughly its old social patterns into the forms of modern political and economic institutions, which needless to say have been no less successful for that, though substantial tensions are beginning to emerge.

Modernization

The situation everywhere is that people find themselves with old though not changeless social forms, and also a new experience of individuality induced by the network of factors called modernity.

The concept of modernization has rightly come under criticism when it has been oversimplified to suggest that recent changes in human thought and society are totally without precedent, or to suggest that all changing societies are following the same course, presumably one modelled on the rise of industrialization and democracy in Europe and America. There are many paths through the changes the world is undergoing, and no particular final goal is in sight; we don't know where we are going, and we're going there in many different ways.

The basic external component of modernization—the development of large-scale industrial and technological systems by which problems of production and distribution are solved through mechanized means based on scientific knowledge—seems to be possible in several kinds of societies and political orders, democratic or authoritarian, so long as stability, a labor force capable of being mobilized for new tasks, and a reasonable freedom for innovation obtain.

More significant for our particular purpose, the understanding of the individual in society, is the subjective component of modernization. Here the danger of overgeneralization is even greater, for the variables are as many as the billions of people on this planet. Nonetheless, it cannot be denied that most of those people in some manner experience the world and their own being in it differently than did their premodern ancestors. In some cases their lives and thoughts may be more regimented, in others less so; some may be happier and others less happy, but inward changes have emphatically occurred as reflexes of the immense changes in means of production and distribution.

For our lives are made up of a thousand details of how we work, shop, eat, read, travel, live, get the news, are entertained, learn, and meet others, whether to socialize or establish families. The means and results alike of all these processes are internalized to provide the categories by which we perceive and understand other processes. Only a generation like ours, for example, which is so used to computers it thinks of the human mind itself in computer language, could use a term like "deprogramming" for a process another age might have called "exorcism" or "mesmerism."

What has been the upshot of all this in terms of the individual in society? Increasingly it has been, I think, a sense of the isolation of individual subjectivity, and a realization—stated or not—that one must take responsibility for one's own subjectivity; that the comforts, supports, and conceptualizations subjectivity needs to maintain its equilibrium and happiness will not be automatically provided by a society whose apparent primary interests—mechanizing, technologizing, distributing, and producing—do not seem directly geared to the deepest needs of subjectivity as were the traditional matrices of caste group, family, and social hierarchy, which gave one a place surrounded by rituals and symbols directly relating one to ultimate cosmic order and meaning.

Now, I am not a Luddite or anti-technologist with some romantic view of premodern life. I am well aware that modern means of production and distribution have on very important levels eased the subjective life of millions through solving problems of disease, poverty, hunger, and narrow horizons that could only have disturbed subjectivities. I am also aware that much remains to be done in these areas, and that the means the future may call for in solving the problems may be very different from those of the industrial and technological phase of modernization.

Nonetheless, the fact remains that the deepest level of subjectivity, the individual's understanding of his or her ultimate nature and destiny, remains an area for which, in a different kind of society one must increasingly take responsibility oneself. That does not mean it cannot be done, or that in millions of instances people have not done so in a way satisfactory to them, whether through religion, philosophy, devotion to art or science, or some other way. The point is, one must now do it for oneself; society will not provide an overarching symbolic matrix on this level; and there are also millions who seem not to have the inner resources to do it for themselves. This is then the ultimate, though perhaps not always initially apparent, result of industrialization, technologizing, colonialism, and socialist or communist revolution.

It might seem that at least in some cases this would not necessarily be so. What about the sense of unity and common purpose so much promulgated by nationalism, communist states, or the great corporations of the West? The problem is that before they can make their new appeals to solidarity, they are parts of a process that has tended to break down the subjective viability of traditional family and community, and make the individual simply that—an individual whose relation to production and distribution is essentially as an individual, a worker, a consumer. Family and community are not basic producers or consumers in a modernized society, though they may have been in the premodern.

Only on the heels of this fundamental fact—which atomizes the individual into a separate producing and consuming unit so far as the message imparted by the apparent concerns of the social, economic, and political order is concerned—comes the next message, that one can after all find a symbolic matrix larger than self in nation, political or economic cause, or a commune like those of the People's Republic of China.

Quite apart from the question of whether these are really ultimate enough to take the place of the old spiritual cosmos, it seems thus far that they are antibodies engendered by the disease, rather than preventives prior to it working so subtly that twinges of symptoms would never be felt. They may offer genuine alleviation, yet they too are parts of the situation insofar as they also must be appropriated by a conscious or unconscious act of taking responsibility for one's own subjectivity; they are rarely bought apart from the concurrent anxiety caused by the fundamental message of a civilization whose bedrock structures of production and distribution do not fully engage subjectivity.

Increasingly, the growing isolation and autonomy of the individual is a root condition—inevitably, a root problem—of the modern world shared by East and West alike. The real divide is not between East and West, but between modern and premodern.

The growing awareness that the individual is fundamentally isolated is bespoken now, in the seventies, by all sorts of signs: the "me generation;" voter apathy or single-issue commitment which makes politics not a truly communal enterprise but a projection of one's own ego-structures; the end of the "cultural revolution" in China and an apparent return to emphasis on individual education and standard of living rather than causes of the collective psyche; the almost total breakdown of more than token communist fervor in the Soviet Union; the gradual decline of caste in India and growth of individualized politics and enterprise.

In some places the new individualism in society has meant a growth of democracy and prosperity, in others of corruption and apathy; more often an intricate combination of both, no doubt confusing to the moralist and the ideological purist. For much of what is spoken of as the decline of morality and the prematurely heralded end of ideology is really this decline of communal structures and values, and the individual grappling without many guidelines to take responsibility, if only by default, for his or her own subjectivity.

We value this new inner autonomy and freedom sometimes, and in any case we know instinctively in some mysterious way that it is now ours and we can't get rid of it even if we want to, that we are somehow only fooling ourselves when we try. The modern means of production and distribution, of communications media and technologized knowledge, which gave it to us almost as an industrial by-product, are too well in place with an ongoing life of their own to be dislodged except in illusion. The new autonomy has advanced surprisingly far in only some thirty-five years. It is remarkable how many people who were on opposite sides of World War II—Russia, Japan, the United States—for all the uncountable horrors of that era, harbor a strange nostalgia for those days of drama, darkness, and glory, as though it were a time of living myth, the last time we felt a truly great sense of national purpose and solidarity, and of being a part of a great cause of undoubted, unambivalent righteousness. In India, there is a similar feeling for the unequivocal idealism and passion of Gandhi's independence movement of the same era.

Yet, while yearning, we usually support most of the individual freedoms and choices that make up the contemporary crisis of a society of increasingly atomized subjectivities. One wonders how much inner isolation of its members from each other and from any common purpose—a pathology the opposite of the "ant-hill society" we always say we fear—a nation or world can take before it collapses like a house of cards.

Perhaps some new kind of individual-in-society pattern, one in which both sides are equally strong and mutually supportive and which is genuinely accessible in an age like ours, will appear before it is too late.

If so, it will probably have learned something from both traditional East and West, and be available equally to the East and the West, which share alike this modern or postmodern world; for whatever happens to us from here on out, will happen to all of us.

Comment

Gordon M. Berger

What Dr. Ellwood has been discussing here is the secularization of modern society and social relations, and the dilemmas of self-definition for the individual autonomized and atomized in a new matrix of social relationships unvalidated by divine will or, more simply, moral imperatives.

Dr. Ellwood's paper sets the problem before us very well. If man is stripped of matrices that embody God's will or moral imperatives, how can he define his ultimate destiny, his ultimate nature, his identity? Can there be anything like a concept of individual responsibility in such a situation? Does man not need some external transcendant referent, a viable spiritual cosmos? Does he not need it even to consider the problem of individual responsibility, and if he does, are the divinely sanctioned and morally imperative referents of old totally bankrupt? And if they are, can he hope to find new ones?

Is social responsibility rapidly becoming an ideal of the past? I submit emphatically that it is not. For even in modern society, a society of "do your own thing," an existentialist vision of social intercourse in which we are responsible, we are totally responsible, for ourselves, the need for self-definition remains paramount and inevitably carries with it a definition of our relationship and responsibilities to others than ourselves. What I wish to do is to share some of my own reflections on this issue as they came out of Dr. Ellwood's paper. First I would like to take a couple of concrete examples of what I hope to summarize at the end.

I begin with a brief parable. It is by that great helmsman, Mao Tse Tung. Mao found himself in somewhat the same position I find myself: I go for a story to Mao, he went to T'ang China of a thousand years ago. He said, right at the end of the war with Japan, in Ancient China there was a fable. How can you remove the mountains? An old man in North China by the name of Hua Gung of the North Mountain, had a house facing south and its doorway was obstructed by two big mountains. With great determination, he led his sons to dig up the mountains with pick-axes. Another old man witnessed their attempts and laughed, saying, "What fools you are to attempt this; to dig up two huge mountains is utterly beyond your capacity." Hua Gung replied, "When I die there are my sons, and when they die there will be their own sons, and so on through infinity. As to these two mountains, high as they are, they cannot become higher. But on the contrary, with every bit dug away, they will become lower and lower. Why can't we dig them away?" Thus, Hua Gung refuted the other old man's erroneous view and went on digging at the mountains day after day without interruption. Mao says, "God's heart was so touched by such perseverance that he sent two celestial beings down to earth to carry away the mountains on their backs. Now, there are also two big mountains lying like dead weight on the Chinese people: imperalism and feudalism. The Chinese Communist Party long ago made up its mind to remove them. We must work persistently and ceaselessly so tha we too may be able to touch God's heart. This god is no other than the masses of the people throughout China. And if they rise and dig together with us, why can't we dig up these two mountains?"

Now Mao here is quite plainly making a case for the power of the human will operating in a social matrix. His allegory transformed the lesson of the T'ang China of a thousand years ago, in which a context of social matrices composed of family and heaven provided the individual with his definition of self identity, ultimate purpose, and social responsibility, to a secular one in the twentieth century in which the new god and family are the Chinese masses.

The first point to make about this allegory is that it's told by someone who is totally committed to destroy the old matrices that Professor Ellwood was talking about, in order to mobilize the individual sense of responsibility and identity in the process of creating a new modern society. Not only is the commitment to destroy the old order strong, but Mao is equally committed to and engaged in the process of establishing a new society, a modern society, based on new sources of power and new moral imperatives: the new moral imperatives of the collective will. There's not the slightest hint of neutrality in Mao toward the individual's task of defining himself. This is one of the salient lessons of Mao and one that has meaning for the present discussion. There is no sense of neutrality at all about the individual's problem in modern society, of defining himself and his responsibilities. Indeed that definition, even after Mao's death, awaits final resolution in the context of an endless debating China.

The second point that I want to make about this allegory is that Mao's new god, the collective power of human will, is not totally new. The Chinese family in the story knew of the collective power of that family over generations. It had a consciousness of identity transcending the finiteness of individual existence. That family knew about it, so did the nineteenth century Chinese families into which Mao and his contemporaries were born. And one might well argue that without the earlier consciousness of the moral imperatives of heaven and the multi-generational family, Mao's new god could never come into existence conceptually.

Another thing that struck me as I read Dr. Ellwood's paper is the situation in which the Japanese state found itself in 1940-41. As a modernized society, Japan felt compelled to intervene in the life of the individual in order to prevent the weakening of the fabric of society, even society's atomization, in a time of great national crisis. It was necessary to provide a new god, new moral imperatives.

I want to quote here from a pamphlet that Japan distributed to its citizens in order to let them know what the new god was. (Not that they hadn't discovered it over the course of the previous decade or so, but this was the final statement on the subject.) The statement is from a 1941 pamphlet called *The Way of the Subject.* It was issued by the Ministry of Education and declares, "Imperial subjects look up to the Imperial household as their head of family and live as a nation comprising a single household. Since the days of old, there have been in our country those who have come to serve the throne from among other peoples, having been attracted by the benevolence of our Imperial household. And these amiable people, too, have all come to enjoy the munificence that comes to those who are Japanese subjects under the august virtue of His Majesty. And with the passage of time, they become completely united, both spiritually and in blood and have served their parts amply as subjects. The august Imperial virtues are vast and boundless."

The nation embraces and assimilates all peoples so that there has been more and more realization of the idea of a single national unit constituting a single household; and the glorious state in which ruler and subject are united in one has prospered endlessly. Heaven and earth render service to the Emperor under the influence of his graciousness by which he cares for the well-being of all peoples; this indeed constitutes the essential quality of an imperial subject. This way in which one follows and serves the emperor is "the way of the subject."

When this document was submitted to the Diet, the Japanese parliament, someone was impertinent enough to ask why it was needed. Among the reasons given by a Ministry of Education official was "to abolish the concept of self-centered utilitarianism."

The point I draw from *The Way of the Subject*—the content of the ideal, the conceptualization as well as the motive behind its issuance—is that we again see here the compulsion to provide a new god, in this case a newly defined divine emperor who was master of the world; and the use of old paradigms from old social matrices, namely the family, ancestor worship, the ancient imperial state.

These two examples, Mao's allegory and *The Way of the Subject*, lead to a couple concluding general remarks about these subjects that have been raised in Professor Ellwood's paper.

First, consider the new social matrices for individual existence that Dr. Ellwood rightly contends are as much a manifestation of as they are an amelioration of the individual's dilemma in a secularized society. Unless neutral on the matter of individual subjectivity, we might fear or hope that they must inevitably seek to facilitate something we might call with Erich Fromm "The Escape from Freedom," or alternatively, "Our Flight from Atomization to Meaningful Commitment—Social Purpose and a New Sense of Social Responsibility."

Excepting for a moment the assumption that the new matrices of modern society are primarily concerned with mechanizing, technologizing, producing and distributing, they must still, for the sake of the stability and the freedom to innovate requisite to their own survival, seek to integrate the atomized individual with a sense of identification, a oneness of purpose with himself. If the old gods and moral imperatives do not possess sufficiently compelling force to achieve this end, and cannot provide meaningful definitions of modern man's responsibilities to those beyond himself, I have little doubt that new ones will be sought.

The second point that strikes me is that the process of developing the external reference for the definition of responsibility, even in revolutionary situations such as Mao's, is bound to be an organic one, growing out of old social matrices, old moral imperatives, and old gods. This is true, not simply because rumors of God's death have proven to be premature, but because the subjectivities of both modern individuals and the collective management of the new social matrices are, in part, products of the past and bearers of its legacy as well as victims or beneficiaries of their own liberation from that past to modernization. Thus, what appears to be new and totally divorced from the past is not necessarily so, and what will succeed in re-integrating energies in common social purpose cannot be so.

In short, I am perhaps a bit more optimistic than Dr. Ellwood in my belief that we have not been cast irrevocably adrift by modernization as atomized individuals who must swim ourselves off to totally unknown shores to save ourselves; that there are out there others who need us and, it is to be hoped, will guide us back to what they at least regard as the safety of their own harbors; and that whether we are rescued by others or swim ourselves to land, eventually we will not find ourselves in totally unfamiliar terrain.

Comment

William J. Goode

As we ponder the complex fabric of rich thought that Professor Ellwood has presented to us in comparing three great Eastern culture patterns with that of the West, with reference to their traditional views of the individual in the society, I think it is inevitable that we are moved to consider what will happen next in our history. Now we are all participants in and witnesses of global changes that are unique in world history. They can be characterized in a very particular way that has a high relevance for the individual in his or her relation in society whether East or West. I believe these changes can best be described by saying that at no period in world history have we had such gigantic resources to bring to bear on our problems, while the problems themselves have been growing at a much more rapid rate than the resources. Thus, there is at most class levels in most societies a growing feeling of individual helplessness in the face of difficulties whose causes and whose cures seem impossible to imagine.

Three of these massive complex sets of forces are urbanization, population growth, and industrialization on a world scale. All these phenomena have occurred before but never in all countries simultaneously or at such a rapid rate. With reference to these great forces, we must agree with the judgment made centuries ago by Montesquieu that great events do not necessarily have great causes. In spite of the efforts of scholars to disentangle the causes of these phenomena, I do not believe that we understand them fully yet, and we certainly do not understand all their consequences.

Some additional changes come closer to the theme of our discussion. One is the transition from kings to dictators, and four changes associated with that move. First, there is the increasing power of national governments and second, the decline of the communal network relative to the increasing influence of national pattern. Third, there is the loss of personal privacy, and fourth, the loss of authoritarian deference once possessed by group leaders.

Another great change is that everyone everywhere is under the threat of the atomic bomb in one form or another, and this has great social consequences. Most central is the idea that individual identities become meaningless before this threat. We all share the same fate. Another great change whose solution may require a far more radical step than we have yet been willing to face is pollution and the exhaustion of natural resources. Again, this is a problem that has no individual solution. A final great change, much easier to understand in some ways, although its effects have been both benign and lethal, is the growth of science.

I suggest that these have been occurring on a global scale and that they are a threat or an actual occurrence in the experience of most of the population in the world. I do not see at present any likelihood that that pattern will be altered much in our lifetime. All these changes have, as is evident, an immense impact upon the ways in which the individual can think of himself or herself as a person, attempting to establish his or her own identity within the surrounding society.

In the West we have moved, as sociologists have reminded us for generations, from some kind of community, usually called the *Gemeinschaft* to some type of larger society, usually referred to as the *Gesellschaft*. In other words, a move from a group or communal life to one in which the individual is permitted or encouraged to express his or her own personality, aspirations and even selfish interests, if they do not clash too much with the power or legal rights of others.

It is only a seeming paradox that the near victory of that latter set of forces, in the more developed sectors of the world society, has revealed to us deficiencies, even its destructiveness; and it has begun to generate increasingly strong forces toward a new type of communalism. To be sure, only a few supporters seriously hope that communalism will embrace the world and make it into one real community, a world village. Nevertheless, an increasing number of thoughtful people are coming to believe that the costs of unbridled individualism are too much to bear in a world marked by the set of great changes just mentioned.

The peculiarity of the great changes I have noted is that although they brought great material benefits to the nations that took part in them and even a flowering of intellectual and artistic creativity, they have left the individual so vulnerable to massive threats that people may find it necessary even for survival to impose far more collective control, to become much more communal in the sense of demanding concern for the community as a whole against the private individual claims of unique persons.

Whether we can make that transition without simultaneously experiencing a great loss in freedom and even a loss in authenticity in personal growth, is not yet clear. Indeed, we do not even know whether we can make the transition before we destroy ourselves. We shall not be close to knowing the answer perhaps even within our lifetime. We shall, on the other hand, certainly witness some part of this drama being unfolded over the next few decades, if we survive them.

In the industrialized countries of the West, the praise of individuality of the unique person set against, or at least independent of, the larger population, was expressed in its most extreme form in the aesthetic philosophy of nineteenth century Romanticism, which viewed the artist as embodying its ideal. However, without question, its most extreme forms have appeared in our own generation, the "Me Generation" of some commentators. One form that it took during the 1950s and '60s was the philosophy that it would be better simply to drop out, to stop participating in the larger society at all and to deride or attack tradition or authority in all forms.

However, and perhaps a much more destructive expression of that philosophy, was to be seen in corporate behavior which stubbornly refused, decade after decade, to take responsibility for its waste products, for the carcinogenic foods and chemicals sold or spewed forth into the air and waters, to protest any attempts to force communal responsibility by asserting that any such efforts would be far too costly, and to claim against all the facts that what was good for the individual corporation would necessarily be good for the society. That individualistic philosophy asserted essentially that whatever costs were imposed upon other people by one person's acts or by a corporation's activities could be ignored entirely.

One result of a growing awareness of that glorification of the individual decision means, in all of its ramifications, an expanding set of social movements that aim at persuading all of us that we are all sisters and brothers to one another; that even strangers who are downwind from our factory smoke ought to be our concern; that this is the only world we have and we must be diligent in our stewardship of it. It argues that we should be thoughtful, not only of our own wages but the wages of workers in other countries who may be building products we may ultimately consume. It argues that we should try to preserve some of the beautiful wild areas of the world for later generations though they are not part of our group and may not even be of our own nation. It proclaims that corporations should not corrupt even citizens of other countries, and they should bear all the costs of manufacturing their products, including the destructiveness they engender.

All these arguments and social movements, supported by a diverse array of people in many countries, form a social political program that has to be viewed as radical in the political context of high individualism. They suggest that since we are in one world, we must also become one community. That program suggests that whatever material benefits there may be from individual effort, including free individual artistic creativity, the group as a whole should not be willing indefinitely to bear all the cost of further extension of the traditional Western philosophy of individualism.

We should see the supporters of such programs as a sign of hope for the future.

However, such supporters are only a minute fraction of the total population in most countries. The larger part of the population, especially in the United States, has moved in a somewhat different direction. Seeing that people in power are either helpless or simply do not care for them as members of the society, and since those leaders do not seem to offer solutions for their present concerns, people move away from participation in political action and toward a distrust of government generally, as well as of high officials in the corporate life and labor movement.

In this country that trend has been visible and measured since the late 1950s. People feel increasingly dominated by a system they cannot understand, one that seems to reward people who care primarily for themselves and not for communal welfare. Thus, in an age where more people are committed and even encouraged to participate politically to make their voices heard, fewer people are willing to bother because their leaders do not offer programs that focus on their communal concern. In retreating from those larger problems that they cannot solve and their leaders do not bother to solve, they continue to drift toward a self-interested set of purely personal activities in which they do not have to bother much about the difficulties other people face. Whether we can reverse that trend is not yet clear, but it is certain that failure to do so will undermine the society.

An additional source of the increased concern of communal welfare may be found in the answer to what seems to be a rhetorical question. Which things have become harder to do in modern life with its high technology? A moment's thought will tell us, almost everything, except the things machines and bureaucracies can do when they function well. Among these might be included rearing children in cities, dropping in on friends with the sure expectation of being welcome, obtaining adequate servicing of the machines we use in our homes, keeping efficient domestic help, putting on an election campaign, maintaining friendships or marriages, generating community loyalty, cooperation and safety. These and other matters tell us that in pursuing the achievements that an individualistic philosophy facilitates, we have made it difficult to obtain many personal and social goals.

If we move now from the smaller world, noted in that set of difficulties, to larger spheres, we would encounter these things: protection for the mass consumer from shoddy or dangerous goods, getting clean air and water, conserving natural resources, obtaining influence and decisions about one's community or even national life. More precisely, a wide variety of goals requiring the conscientious or responsible cooperation of other people seems to have become much more difficult, except when people are paid individually to give attention to those matters.

We now understand better than did the analysts of the past four great troubling truths about this great drama of world change which Professor Ellwood has described, in which the relationship of the individual to the larger society has altered fundamentally. These truths apply, I believe, to all the great societies of the world, both East and West, now engaged in facing the challenge of the future.

The first of the great troubling truths is that the landed gentry and aristocrats who once deplored the social destructiveness of capitalism and industrialism were correct. That change did erode or undermine respect for authority, loyalty, concern for the communal welfare. People gradually came to consider their individual fate and needs more important than that of their village, their group, or their fellow citizen. They were encouraged to do so by an economic philosophy that assured them that this self-interested behavior would nevertheless be good for the society despite the loss of ties among individuals; that the feeling of responsibility for other members of the society and the human cost of development is simply a necessary cost of modernization.

Second, the brash profit-hungry capitalist who led the forces toward industrialization were also correct. Their entrepreneurial daring fueled by selfishness did in fact improve material benefits for most people and not alone for the rich. By almost any standard we have to conclude that, though indeed the poor are always with us, they are not so poor as in the past. Many diseases have been conquered or controlled, the length of life has been extended, and higher production in industrialized countries has in fact given greater comforts to more people than at any time in the past.

Third, in the most bureaucratic urban and industrialized settings, social pressures toward communal links or group loyalties continue to grow and they are not simply remnants of some ancient customs or outmoded psychological dependencies; they are the natural, spontaneous expressions of human needs that must be satisfied if these large social organizations are to continue at all. The most advanced of social machinery, like the most advanced physical machinery, always fails to take care of fundamental human tasks that must be done. Consequently, and contrary to the preachings of the economist who wishes to allow market forces to be completely free, guided only by the individual's conception of what is best for himself or herself, such a system cannot in the long run even be efficient. The purely autonomous person's concern only for his own needs may well exist, but no society as a whole or even a profit-driven corporation can continue to function effectively if it has only that kind of human material with which to get work done.

Fourth, unfortunately the efforts of communist systems to create a national communality or group that would retain the old concern of the village for its members though now on a much vaster scale, also recreate some of the hurts and losses those village systems imposed upon their inhabitants: constant surveillance, lack of freedom, and even economic inefficiency. These somewhat unhappy aspects of communal life are, once more, not merely remnants of ancient customs; they inevitably appear when any group attempts to face the crisis of a challenge by organizing intensely, subordinating the individual to group needs, and channeling all human energies toward one set of larger group goals. We can admire that effort, as well as some of its results, without averting our eyes to the great cost the members of that system must endure.

Moreover, we must also accept historical change that makes this last truth more painful—to emphasize Professor Ellwood's point. Modern members of such systems are no longer naive or innocent villagers. They know what is happening to them in communist countries. They have had enough contact with modernizing influences to know that there are alternatives to group thinking or enforced unity. Most important, they have become aware, as most villagers of the past probably were not, of their own potential individuality and they become restive or dissident under the continuing social pressures. This is a central message of Professor Ellwood's description of the changes in India, Japan, and China with reference to the place of the individual in modern society.

As participants we have thus been making a gigantic world experiment of possible societies over the past several centuries: from sets of small communities to a larger society made of people seeking their own individual goals with little thought of others; and now perhaps moving toward some new version of a larger communality. We move toward a recognition that we cannot survive without building into all our modern societies far more communal concerns. In other words, we recognize a need to return consciously to some kind of communal life. Nevertheless, the contemporary experiments in reinstating communal life on a national scale bring costs that most of us view as too great.

To be participants in a world-wide, inadvertent experiment makes us all subject animals, and their fate even in these days of newly discovered ethics of human experimentation has never been very attractive. Are there ways of transforming our situation so as to make the outcome somewhat more desirable?

I do not think there are any solutions by which we can ensure a proper balance between the driving urges of an imperial self and the less immediate but no less necessary need of a communal fold. What we do know is that we must, as in all situations, try to make virtue pay off a little bit better and destructiveness pay off a little bit worse while trying to develop ways of distinguishing one from the other in this and any other social system. We have to make personal investments in communal welfare at least seem to have a fair chance of being rewarded by success, and that applies to the gigantic communal experiments in Russia and China, as well as it does to Western democratic polities.

We have never, as a species, been in this situation before. If we do not solve the problem of balancing communal and individual needs better than we are now doing, we may end up without having a world to live in.

The Roots of the American Commitment to the Rights of Man

by Adda B. Bozeman

Part I: Concepts, Words, and Realities

The destiny of each linguistically and morally unified community depends in the final analysis upon the survival of certain primary or structuring ideas—ideas, namely, that carry the fundamental values around which successive generations have coalesced and that thus symbolize the society's continuity in time.

THE DEVELOPMENT OF CONCEPTS IN DIVERSE CULTURES

Philology, philosophy, and history instruct us that different speech communities and cultures have brought forth different types of such life-sustaining conceptions. For example, India and China could preserve their identities throughout millennia and despite the heavy incidence of political turbulence, natural disasters, and poverty because they held fast to a life-sustaining confidence in the perennial harmony and order of the cosmic universe.

51

According to the intricate metaphysics of Hindus, Buddhists, and Jains, all things, including humans, come into being as aspects of a single world manifestation: the phenomena of past and future, time and space, life and death present no problems here since they are concerned with mere elements of this one great transcendent form of which every part is in accord with all. In this context no particular importance can be attached to biography or ideas of the self. The aim of existence for a believing Hindu is rather to carry out the caste role assigned him at birth; for only selfless performance of *dharma* can assure maintenance of cosmic harmony.

Similar beliefs in the need to subordinate individual life to the unchanging demands of the heavenly order controlled traditional Chinese society. Taoism thus teaches that one must erase all traces of free will from one's consciousness and renounce the attractions of secular life, while Confucianism insists that the person is, above all, a function of the family or other association to which he belongs. The logic of this comprehensive world view thus requires that he must be held to strict compliance with all duties attendant upon his particular station in life.

In each of these two literate civilizations of the East, then, the focus had traditionally been not on the individual but rather on society viewed as a conglomerate of multiple groups.

Some of the typically Oriental mental preoccupations with transcendental truths have also been cultivated in European philosophy and religion, but it cannot be said that Europe ever accepted either of the great Indian or Chinese beliefs as a ruling measure of life on earth. In fact, Western civilization, which is rooted in the heritage of classical antiquity and Christianity, brought forth quite different, indeed contrary, sustaining conceptions.

Foremost among them is a strong commitment to the idea of individuation, whether in the arts, the sciences, religion or politics. This concern, as evident in the records of ancient Greece and Rome as in those of medieval Europe and the modern nation-states of Europe and America, is the source of the West's major norms of organizing society. And among these norms, again, none have exercised the Occidental imagination as consistently as those summarily described as "law." The efforts registered under this heading in civil law and common law countries are greatly various but they have converged on the following tasks: to identify the essence of law in counterpoint to other norm-engendering schemes such as nature, ethics, and philosophy; to cast human associations, including that of the state, in reliable legal moulds; and to emancipate the individual from the group by defining his rights and obligations not only as an autonomous person but also as a citizen of his state.

Numerous instruments and agencies evolved for the purpose of assuring these objectives, among them constitutions, charters of liberty and bills of individual rights. What is noteworthy today about all of these European models is the fact that they constitute severely abbreviated renditions of the general code of ruling values and beliefs. The highly complex yet pervasive understandings of what biography is all about and how political organization is linked to law, were not recapitulated in the documents. Indeed, they were seldom expressly mentioned because their existence in the minds of men was presumed secure.

Each of the world's culturally distinct orders of ideas may thus be said to rest upon the logic that is intrinsic to the culture. Thus, if *dharma* is a basic theme in traditional Indian life and thought, then it goes without saying that the Indian state, being the patrimony of the warrior caste, is rightly identified with the commitment to wage war and win power. And analogous relations between that which is expressed and that which is implied hold for the West. No one could have fathomed or explained constitutionalism as a form of government if he had not been able to assume that its core concept, namely contract, was clearly understood as a legal bond between free autonomous persons. Nor could the idea of a "law of nature" have evolved *before* "law" had been carefully set apart from "nature." And finally, such phrases as "the rights of man" or "the dignity of man" would surely be nonsensical if one did not remember that "man the individual" had been carefully singled out from such indeterminate generic references as "mankind" or "humanity" before his claims to "dignity" and "rights" were ever argued.

Reflections on the role of concepts in the history of civilizations thus suggest that primary or root ideas should not be confused with secondary or derivative notions, and that one ought to guard against joining unrelated ideas. Yet ideas do have adventures, many of them unplanned.

Integrity and Vitality of Concepts Not Assured

In a wonderful book on this theme, Alfred North Whitehead remarks that ideas are the long-lived actors on the human stage, and that once in history they are always there, "at once gadflies irritating, and beacons luring the victims among whom they dwell."[1] Conceptions, then, run risks in their careers, and so do the short-lived mortals who bank on them as the sustaining elements of their collective destinies. Whether their integrity and vitality can be assured is therefore an important question in the domestic and foreign affairs of any society.

The answer is probably affirmative in India where culturally strategic concepts have been firmly encapsuled for millennia in essentially unchanging social institutions, religious ceremonies, a sacred language and classical texts such as the Laws of Mani and the Mahabharata with which Indians in all walks of life have always been familiar. The norms and values thus passed on were therefore not readily susceptible to neglect or tampering within the civilization. Timeless and enduring in common understanding, they could also retain their intrinsic validity under politically various auspices. And, being fully meaningful to Hindus only, they did not lend themselves to wholesale export, thus avoiding misconstruction from without.

Similar factors combined to favor the maintenance of basic conceptions in the great literate societies of Southeast Asia, East Asia, West Asia and Northeast Africa. Only in Europe was the situation altogether different, and that—it is here suggested—for the following reasons.

As I. A. Richards has explained it in his analytical discourse on the difficulties of rendering Chinese modes of thought and meaning into English (and vice versa), there is first the linguistic and intellectual heritage, notably from Greece, which has provided the European mind with such distinct conceptual categories as objects, events, forms, substances, abstracts, concretes, organic wholes, classes, individuals, and so forth, thus equipping it to abstract universals from the maze of particulars amassed in either science, philosophy or politics.[2] The general phenomenon of the "individual man" could therefore become the subject of tireless speculation in the West, whereas it did not elicit such concern in China where thought dwelt equally intensely on "man the father" or "man the son," or in India, where thinkers were preoccupied with defining the qualities and attributes of "man the brahmin" or "man the sudra." In short, the Western propensity to formulate conceptually crucial propositions in such a way that culturally extended relevance or universal validity can be claimed in their behalf, invites intense communications with non-Western societies. But because it is not easy to control such intercultural relations, ideas are often transferred or interchanged too hastily, with the result that essential meanings either get distorted or are altogether being missed.

"Individualism" in Western Thought

Another set of factors promoting instability in the Occident's substratum of constitutive conceptions is of course implicit in its foremost element, namely individualism. In contrast to other systems of persuasion in which the stress is squarely on the survival of the community and therefore on resistance to change, this one must allow itself to be buffeted by individualized interpretations of what a given idea, indeed the entire way of life, is all about.

The possibility of intellectual and moral disunity or disorder is therefore always present, and it is accentuated by the peculiarly European perspective on time which insists that the present should not just repeat the past, and that the future should be the object of deliberate development on the levels of both biography and society. The customary measure of "achievement" in this culture world is therefore not merely perfection in carrying out established tasks but also, perhaps mainly, innovation rendered in terms of progress and reform. The prominence of this bent of mind accounts for the fact, persuasively stated by Redfield, that utopian and experimental modes of thinking—both unsettling to society—have here been cultivated more consistently than elsewhere in the world.[3] It also goes a long way toward explaining just why and how this civilization—always a market place of ideas—could be transformed into the battlefield of ideas that it has become in the twentieth century under the relentless onslaught of the culturally alien and aggressive ideology of Marxist-Leninist communism—an ideology, incidentally, that had been designed expressly for the purpose of knocking out the basic values of Europe and America.

The major question faced by the West in modern times is therefore this: how can the integrity of its basic constitutive concepts be safeguarded in both domestic and foreign affairs without impairment of the values implicit in freedom of thought?

The search for an effective answer, it is here suggested, must begin with the realization that the contentions of rival normative orders are everywhere enacted in the minds of men even though they are also always apt to be resolved by violent means, and that a society must assure orderly processes of thought and its communication if it wishes to endure intact. Compliance with such a mandate thus hinges upon insistence that each fundamental idea is clearly understood in the morally and politically unified community, and that words chosen to convey it really represent its meaning and purport. In other words, the issue turns in the final analysis on honesty in the relation between language and conception. It therefore stipulates two major specific tasks: on the one hand to defend the meaning content of basic norms or values against slippage, atrophy, misunderstanding and abuse, and on the other, to prevent the severance of words from the contexts they were meant to serve.

Words as Carriers of Concepts: Humanity, Man, Nature, Law, Rights of Man

The importance traditionally attached to established words and names is so fully borne out by the records of all literate and non-literate societies that it requires no special comment here. What deserves attention in the context of this paper is the effect of the twentieth century revolution in verbal communication upon the world's diverse vocabularies of words, values and ideas. This complex process was initiated by innovative Western developments in science and technology as well as in government, economics and international affairs that had the cumulative effect of narrowing distances between culturally and linguistically separate communities and therefore of supporting trust in the imminence of global accords on all major concerns of human existence.

Constitutionalism, a Failure in Cultural Borrowing

In respect of political organization, most nationally conscious elites thus agreed during the first half of the century that European and American patterns of constitutionalism were the proper models to be emulated everywhere. Apart from projecting the kind of power, prestige and stability which was then commonly associated with the politically dominant and economically successful Occidental states, these forms of rule appealed to Westernized African and Asian elites because the great causes of national independence and individual liberty were here encased in simple yet eloquently written texts that seemed addressed to everyone as old states were recast in modern moulds and new ones were established. Constitutions and other enactments of the rule of law, including bills of individual rights, thus mushroomed in scores of non-Western societies that had been kept going for centuries, even millennia, by principles of administration not bearing the faintest resemblance to "democracy" as first fathomed by the ancient Greeks.

Reflections upon the rapid conversion of newly established democracies into dictatorships lead to the conclusion that the transfer of Occidental concepts to Africa and Asia was precipitate, to say the least. Contrary to some earlier episodes of cultural borrowing as, for example, when the major concepts of Buddhism were carefully adjusted first to Chinese modes of thought and then to the Chinese language,[4] recent grafting operations proceeded rather mechanistically, especially after the close of the Second World War when Europe's colonial empires were dissolved and peoples everywhere were pronounced equally committed to democracy and equally entitled, therefore, to whatever material boons had come to be associated with this form of rule. In these altered circumstances it would have been illogical to engage in elaborate comparisons of the conceptual and semantic orders of the borrowing and the lending civilizations before deciding which blueprint for governance would provide the best auspices for political order and development.

In the absence of such analyses, drift became the general motto. It gradually carried the distinct majority of non-communist Asian and African states back to trusted pre-modern understandings of what political life and government were all about, but it was not instrumental in scattering the masses of constitutions, bills of civil rights, and other legal papers that had officially declared this past defunct. Emptied of their conceptual contents, these verbal references are now often enlisted to serve state interests in all foreign policy contexts in which it is considered important to deflect attention from the reality of domestic lawlessness or authoritarianism. Indeed, in extreme cases such as those recorded in some of the Black African non-communist states, governmental actions ordering mass massacres and mass explusions of human beings can remain unexplicated and therefore internationally irrelevant, whereas the same government's covenants and declarations assuring each individual of his rights to life and liberty are fully registered and counted on the credit side of the world's official ledgers.

These incongruities certainly mock the logic of the Western value language; however, it is important to bear in mind that they are not attributable to deliberate misconstruction but rather to fundamental incompatibilities between widely divergent cultural traditions.

Semantics of Governance in Communist Societies

The situation is altogether different in societies primarily committed to communism, foremost among them the Soviet Union. For here Marxist-Leninist doctrine—steadfastly maintained throughout the last half-century—insists that human destiny is the exclusive function of material circumstances, more particularly of the continuous struggle between economic classes representing contending methods of production; that law is but the will of the dominant class; that constitutionalism is therefore rightly defined as the dictatorship of the capitalist class, and that "individualism" with its corollary of individuated rights is a nonsensical aberrant conception, easily dismissible as a bourgeois entrapment. The only legitimate reference in this dogma is "humanity" but it would be concretized only, according to Marxian prophecy, when men had ceased to think that they were individuals with separate inalienable rights.

These negative understandings of what the West accepts as major positive norms condition all thought processes in the regnant circles of the Soviet Union and other fully established communist societies. However, the negatives are turned back into positives when it comes to the semantic aspects of the revolutionary struggle. Lenin's operational code thus stipulates that democratic societies are undermined best—at least in the preliminary phase of the ongoing conflict—by deploying psychological and diplomatic techniques of manipulation; and that such attack campaigns must be launched in the value language of the West if they are to reach, confound, and eventually win the minds of those in the nation—peasants in the '20s, students in the '60s—who are relegated to the status of "carriers of spontaneity" by the self-selected "carriers of class consciousness" in the communist leadership.

The Marxist-Leninist message that constitutionalism is ripe for overthrow, or that civil rights are the monopoly of the rich, is thus not propagated in terms either of Marxist-Leninist theory or of the foreign policy interests of the Soviet Union, but rather in those of European and American constitutionalism. What counts today is what has counted in the last half-century, namely success in persuading the impressionable, first, that ten identifiable human beings were denied due process of law or that one citizen had died in prison in unexplained circumstances, and last, that "law" is therefore tantamount to "police brutality," and that "democracy" actually is its opposite, namely "despotism."

Within established communist societies, meanwhile, the relations between word, concept, and reality are skillfully administered by guardian-commissars of semantic usage who prescribe when to use the Western, when, by contrast the revolutionary Marxist vocabulary; which words to pirate from the ideological enemy, and how to modify their meanings. The idiom of Occidental law and political organization has thus been conscripted to project the dictatorship of the proletariat as "the Union of Soviet Socialist Republics" and the latter's East European dependencies as "People's Democracies."

Notwithstanding all official Marxist-Leninist strictures against the state, law and individuality, the Soviet Union has yet supplied itself regularly with constitutions, law codes, and bills of right—all formulated on Western models. Stalin's constitution of 1936 (revised 1947) as well as the new 1977 charter thus enumerate the classical freedoms of speech, religion and assembly. But they also prescribe that these political rights are to be exercised by citizens only in order to strengthen the established order. They may not be advanced against the state or for that matter against the Communist party which is described in the 1977 constitution as "the leading and guiding force of . . . all state and public organizations."

Constitutional references to civil and political rights, then, are meant to be spurious and devoid of meaning in this system, and the same holds for their equivalents in the context of criminal law in which the great question of the individual's guilt or innocence, and therefore ultimately also of his life or death, is supposed to be resolved arbitrarily in the exclusive interest of the monolithic state.

The same overriding interest also inhabits legally worded assurances of social, economic and cultural rights, foremost among them rights to health, education and work, even though these stipulations—in contrast to those mentioned previously—are *prima facie* reasonable renditions of the major values with which socialism and communism are commonly associated. For example, implementation of the right to education certainly enhances literacy in the population, but it does not entitle a person to engage in independent intellectual quests for learning. After all, the entire domain of knowledge is preempted and policed by the state for the contrary purpose, namely that of controlling and, if necessary, suppressing thought. Similarly, there is nothing obviously suspicious about the phrasing of a "right to work," but in the absence of enforceable civil and political liberties, "work" also stands for slave labor, even for consignment to extinction.

In short, the Soviet Union and all other states created in its likeness are transvestites on the stage of world affairs. Wrapped in clothing taken from the West, they can dissimulate the actuality of their existence when to do so is expedient, while simultaneously continuing to shape the destinies of other nations in accordance with the dictates of the communist creed.

The United Nations and Human Rights

The careers of the West's great structuring concepts are thus clearly off course today. Deflected to the plane of mere semantics by the majority of non-Western governments and allowed to atrophy in their home civilization where universal validity was prematurely claimed in their behalf, the legal norms seem meaningless today.

Nowhere is this more apparent than in the context of the United Nations, an organization of states that had its origin in the military wartime alliance of the Western democracies and the Soviet Union and which consisted in August 1977 of 149 independent states representing quite disparate moral and political orders. However, these differences are officially cancelled by the UN Charter which presumes that all member states are peace-loving democracies and therefore committed to the precepts of the international quasi-federal constitution that had been drafted on American and European models.

The fact that a locally operative system of norms does not, perhaps cannot, either recognize or guarantee the individual citizen's life and liberty of thought, speech, movement, or association has thus not prevented that state's representatives from explicitly endorsing each of the thirty articles of the Universal Declaration of Human Rights (proclaimed by the General Assembly in 1948). This document starts with the proposition (for which no philosophical, religious, biological or historical justification is adduced) that all human beings are born free and equal in dignity and rights, and that they are endowed with reason and conscience. Therefore, the text continues, no one may be subjected to arbitrary interference with privacy, to slavery, torture, cruel punishment, arbitrary arrest, detention, exile, or deprivation of property. Everyone, by contrast, has the right to life, liberty, and security; to freedom of thought, religion, expression and peaceful assembly; to participation in government and trade unions; to social security, free choice of employment, work, education, rest and leisure; to standards of living and medical care adequate for the health and well-being of himself and of his family; to full development of the human personality; and to social and international order.

International Covenants: A Matter of Interpretation

These provisions were subsequently restated and amplified in fifty-three assorted articles strung together in the International Cov-

enant on Civil and Political Rights and in thirty-one articles of the
International Covenant on Economic, Social and Cultural Rights.
All were adopted in 1966 and have been officially in force since 1976,
though the majority of covenanting governments actually functions
in accordance with principles quite contrary to those enunciated
internationally. Some reasons for the general acquiescence in this
type of incongruity or deception have already been suggested in this
paper; others, specially relevant to the covenants, are the following.

Although the texts recognize, on the authority of the UN Charter
and the Universal Declaration of Human Rights, that each individual on earth has "equal and inalienable rights" which derive from
"the inherent dignity of the human person," they are quick to add
that no one can expect to be in possession of any of the scores of
listed freedoms before suitable conditions have been created in
which everyone *may* enjoy his civil, political, economic, social, and
cultural rights. Foremost among these conditions is the attainment
of the right to self-determination, a right not mentioned in the
Universal Declaration. Article 1, Section 1, of each of the two Covenants thus stipulates that

> All peoples have the right of self-determination. By virtue of that right
> they freely determine their political status and freely pursue their
> economic, social and cultural development.

This right, then, which inheres in "people," not in the person, is the
major control principle: as long as it is not concretized to the satis-
faction of those who represent "the people," individuals may have
to put up with (for example) torture, slavery, servitude, and forced
or compulsory labor—abuses of freedom carefully proscribed in
Article 8 of the Covenant on Civil and Political Rights.

In this connection one must recall, furthermore, that civil and
political liberties are viewed in Marxist perspectives as alienable,
secondary and limited rather than as inalienable, primary and fundamental rights.[5] And lastly it needs remembering that the United
Nations continues to be an association of sovereign states however
determined the thrust to convert it into a custodianship for the
citizens or subjects of these states. This means that each member
nation is in essence free to do as it likes when it comes to evaluating
the rights situation in another state. All findings having the UN

imprimatur are therefore in the final analysis political decisions that record the national interests of the voting majority.[6] This UN majority has long consisted of authoritarian and totalitarian governments, and thus it is not surprising to find that commitments to the twin causes of the individual and his rights are generally considered negotiable, to say the least.

Whatever the motivations for the intense and widespread espousal of "human rights" in contemporary world affairs—and the spectrum here is certainly variegated, ranging from shrewd calculations of state advantage to earnest concern with the moral condition of mankind and utopian dreams of an entirely new order for human kind—they cannot be investigated reliably. This is not so when attention shifts to the effects of this newly fashionable preoccupation with the rights of man.

Effects of World Preoccupation with "Rights of Man"

Contrary to such an explicit concept as civil liberties, which is persuasively explicated, for example, in the American Constitution, an implicit, not clearly defined notion like "human rights" can be sent roaming so as to make random attachments with all manner of conceptual contexts, some quite obviously alien to its apparent meaning. Two sets of consequences are likely to ensue from such wanton adventures. The idea itself, chameleon-like, may acquire attributes or come to serve functions which its original protagonists had not intended or foreseen, and in the process it may, in fact, disintegrate. Its new host context, meanwhile, is likely to become disordered as a result of the fortuitous acceptance of a new volatile and hence destabilizing element. Indeed, if the recipient order of ideas is already in a vulnerable condition, it may be totally devalued and corrupted by the impact.

This, it is here suggested, in what is now happening on the one hand to international law which was designed to provide norms for the conduct of inter-state relations rather than norms for the regulation of relations between governments and citizenry; and on the other to constitutional law and government with which international law is now confounded.[7]

Although the evolution of the human rights complex into a motley assemblage of legal rights, moral aspirations, policy objectives, and social welfare programs has obvious negative effects on established conceptual categories and orderly processes of thought, it is being celebrated tirelessly throughout the world as the advent of new and better times for mankind. A dizzying array of laws, resolutions, and treaties is thus today on record establishing the dignity of man and committing governments in each province of the globe to serve the cause of human liberty—"Now the one great revolutionary cause," as Archibald MacLeish had occasion to put it in 1976, during our Bicentennial celebration. Conventions on the elimination of all forms of intolerance and of discrimination based on sex or status, religion or belief, abound, as do decisions to liberate the A's from oppression or to punish the B's for acts of injustice.

A veritable Human Rights Industry[8] has thus evolved as men meet tirelessly in congresses, associations, special committees and seminars, all designed to mobilize action in behalf of rights, and as reams of print pour forth invoking human-ness, human nature, humanitarianism, humanitarian law, natural law, natural rights, and the rights of man. It is indeed as if some deus ex machina had just created or discovered MAN. The year 1968 was thus solemnly declared to be "The Human Rights Year." Other years were singled out in praise of "The Child" or "The Woman," and 1978—proclaimed as the International Anti-Apartheid Year—is officially dedicated to the cause of fighting the Republic of South Africa.

REALITIES OF NATIONAL AND INTERNATIONAL BEHAVIOR

What is the relation of all these words to the actualities of behavior within states, in international relations, and in the decision-making processes of the United Nations?

Attention has already been drawn to the distance that separates behavioral reality from laws and formal systems in communist countries where such incongruities are cultivated deliberately in accordance with precepts of ideology and statecraft, and in the majority of non-communist societies in Africa and Asia where obdurate cultural traditions do not favor individuated liberties. This distance between fact and its representation has greatly widened in recent years, and in that measure the sphere of freedom has contracted appreciably throughout the world.

Communist Totalitarianism Expanding

In respect of communism it is thus important to recognize first, that the camp of Marxist-Leninist totalitarianism has expanded significantly as a result of the takeovers of Vietnam, Laos, Cambodia and Ethiopia, and of several successful coups and military interventions, notably those in Angola, Mozambique, Afghanistan, and South Yemen (Aden); and second, that the totalitarian aspects of rule have become dramatically intensified. How to make people die was thus the declared genocidal program of the Cambodian regime as it proceeded methodically to massacre millions of its nationals, including women and children—all old grass that needed burning so that the new would grow.[9] How to extinguish whatever is left of the physical and cultural identity of the Meo community is one of the new Vietnam-backed Laotian government's major commitments; and how to break man's capacity and will to think independently remains the major social goal of communist Vietnam as it continues to herd men, women, and children into educational retooling camps and to consign tens of thousands of formerly non-communist South Vietnamese to hard labor in the distant "New Economic Zones."

The standards for this type of relation between government and citizenry had been set decades ago in the Soviet Union and communist China where millions of civilian lives have been terminated by the ruling establishments in similar manner; where no ethnically or culturally distinct people—be they Buddhist Tibetans in their vast Central Asian homeland or dispersed communities of Crimean Tatars and Volga Germans—is entitled to retain its identity; and where the war against the mind continues to be waged relentlessly not only in prisons, slave labor camps, psychiatric clinics specializing in the art of decomposing psyches, and other physically confining places, but also in the daily "normal" context of life in schools and professions, factories and offices, at home, and in the streets.[10]

If one agrees that elementary civil liberties consist in being free to think independently, to express oneself openly, to discuss public affairs without fear, and to belong to an independent private organization free of governmental control,[11] one would have to conclude that none of these freedoms exists anywhere within the communist realm. The only liberty within the reach of an individual living in either of these societies—and they hold over half of mankind today—is the one that beckons after one has decided to escape and after one has avoided death by shooting, drowning, starvation, or neglect by those from whom help or asylum was expected.[12]

In sum, the barest of incontrovertible facts throughout this world of totalitarian politics combine to lend sad credence to George Orwell's prophetic message ("Inside the Whale") that the autonomous individual is being stamped out of existence here.

Retreat from official national and international commitments to civil, political, and other rights has also been accelerated in many of the established states of Central and South America and in just about all new nations of Black Africa where the issues here under consideration are illustrated particularly vividly today. Indeed, developments in the last ten years certainly bear out Rupert Emerson's conclusion that it is a far cry from the provisions of the Covenant on Civil and Political Rights to the actuality of civil and political life.[13] It is interesting to recall, for example, that President Sékou Touré of Guinea (West Africa) proclaimed solemnly at the second Afro-Asian Conference in Conakry (1960) that

> Asia and Africa . . . have never colonised any people, nor hampered the process of development of any nation, any civilisation, have no bad conscience, no perfidious intentions, no unavowable schemes vis-à-vis the rest of the world. There is not a single one of our deeds which is not in keeping with the moral and material interests of social man, universal man.[14]

Yet it has been estimated that as many as one million citizens have fled the state and it was announced this year by Amnesty International that between 2,000 and 4,000 out of a population of about five million are being kept incommunicado in the grimmest of prisons.[15] Nor is Guinea an exception.

State Security Outweighs "Rights" in New African Nations

Reports gathered by trustworthy organizations tell us that deprivations of freedom and due process of law and inflictions of "cruel and degrading punishment" have become routine in all African states, however different the ideological auspices of their inception.[16] For example, Mozambique (which does not divulge figures on how many citizens it is holding in "reeducation" camps) and

Tanzania are today at one in disallowing basic human rights (Tanzania does permit freedom of religion) as well as public dissent from government policies and freedom of the press. The Tanzanian government has justified its actions by stating that it must subordinate all such rights to the demands of state security and to the task of achieving its socialist objectives. And this orientation was openly condoned in a UN-sponsored seminar (1973) on new ways of promoting human rights in the African context where delegates acknowledged that the protection of individual rights was secondary to the needs of the state. Yet no Black African government comes to mind—least of all Tanzania—which does not insist upon the absolute primacy of full constitutional rights including civil liberties when it comes to South Africa, Rhodesia or other white-ruled nations in the world—a set of incongruities that lends special poignancy to the relation between concepts, words, and actualities with which this part of the paper is concerned.

Genocide Ignored by U.N.

Less common than the above mentioned violations of human rights but more disturbing for an assessment of the likely future of human rights in Africa is the heavy incidence of genocide which has claimed millions of lives during the last two decades, mostly in Burundi, Rwanda, Uganda, and more recently in Equatorial Guinea where tens of thousands are reported to have been executed or to have simply vanished.[17] What is noteworthy in this connection is the fact that few if any of the mass killings have been subjected to debate either in the councils of the OAU or in those of the UN. The excuse or explanation, energetically pressed by other African governments, has been to the effect that the charters of the two organizations prohibit interference in the domestic affairs of member states. In fact, government representatives are now in the habit of arguing on the one hand that the norms of human rights as set out in UN documents are alien to Africa, and on the other, that UN standards for human rights cannot be met until all outstanding economic problems have been solved and until the exercise of the right to self-determination has conduced to the elimination of the remaining white regimes in Southern Africa.

Self-Determination: Prerequisite to Human Rights

Self-determination, then, emerges as the primary, perhaps the only "right" that Africans are really interested in, and much the same may be said about the majority of other non-Western nations.[18] Those assembled at Bandung in 1955 thus declared that the right of peoples and nations to self-determination is a prerequisite for the full enjoyment of all fundamental human rights—a view fully endorsed by numerous UN texts, among them the following: a Declaration on the Granting of Independence to Colonial Countries and Peoples (1953), which provides also that peoples have the right freely to pursue their economic, social, and cultural development, and that inadequacy of political, economic, social or educational preparedness should never serve as a pretext for delaying independence; Article 1 of each of the two Covenants,[19] and several General Assembly resolutions, among them one (1950) calling on the Economic and Social Council to request the Human Rights Commission to study ways and means for ensuring these rights effectively; another (1965) which stipulates that the dignity of the human person requires struggles for national liberation by all means at the disposal of the disfranchised; and a third (1971) which confirms the legality of the peoples' struggles for self-determination and liberation from colonial and foreign domination and alien subjugation. Singled out as particularly meritorious are the struggles of the peoples of Zimbabwe, Namibia, Angola, Mozambique and Guinea (Bissau) as well as those of the Palestinian people.

It is possible to derive a few general conclusions from the many different texts that chronicle the recent evolution of the right to self-determination.

As interpreted in the age of the UN, the right is definitely a group right. Contrary to the Wilsonian era,[20] in which a people's self-determination was generally perceived as the logical extension of an individual's concern with self-development, the "self" is exclusively communal now. Furthermore, the right is a strictly political proposition. Its formulation is so imprecise and the area of its applicability so loosely bounded that it does not qualify as a legal norm. One can therefore maintain that the concept's prominent presence in Article 1 of the Covenant on Civil and Political Rights is a mistake, all the more so as this "right" has no relation whatsoever to civil liberties. These attributes may be deficient, but they have made for the concept's successful international career. For since words mean what a UN majority says they mean, and since the majority of the UN has long been composed of non-Western and communist nations, "self-determination" was soon conscripted to serve the special interests of these groups. Under such auspices it could be used as the masterkey for interpreting Chapter XI and XII of the UN Charter and of Articles 1 Sections 3 of the two Covenants on Human Rights, all addressed to the duties incumbent upon Western European colonial powers; as the major instrument for speeding up decolonization through decision-making in the UN; and as an effective weapon in the resolution of other discords with Western governments; for "colonialism," too, is a word fit to carry new and alien connotations.

All discourse and decision-making in matters relating to self-determination are thus pervaded today by a strong partisan spirit rather than by efforts to apply legal or moral guidelines objectively. In this heavily politicized atmosphere in which besting a hated enemy is all that really counts, language—whether oral or written— is preferably weighted with vituperation, and resort to double standards in argument and action has become *de rigueur*, after a few pariah nations have been singled out authoritatively by the majority to serve as villains, scapegoats, or carriers of all accumulated evil. For most Black African governments and their supporters in world affairs, this role is being played today by South Africa and Rhodesia. The right to self-determination can thus be said to stipulate that the principle of "one man one vote" must be accepted in Rhodesia even if it is not assured in any of the Black African states; and that apartheid in South Africa must be terminated, even though it is a widely accepted arrangement in inter-tribal relations within most politically unified Black African nations.

Furthermore, and in line with internationally approved verbal statements, it is now clear that self-determination can, indeed should, be sought by resort to violence, terror, and war whenever a majority of states decides that it is an organic aspect of a "National

Liberation Struggle"—yet another composite of ideas which defies objective definition. In the United Nations we thus find the Economic and Social Council calling for more aid to National Liberation Movements and to the peoples of Zimbabwe and Namibia;[21] an ECOSOC Committee deciding to withhold financial, economic, technical or other assistance to the government of South Africa and the illegal regime of Rhodesia;[22] a Sub-Commission of the Human Rights Commission condemning South Africa for encroaching on the territorial integrity of Angola even though this country had allowed irregular guerrilla forces to violate the territorial integrity of South Africa; and the United Nations membership in general aglow with projects for "United Nations Humanitarian Armed Intervention" in South West Africa (Namibia).[23]

In Southern Africa itself, meanwhile, where liberation forces have long been operating freely across established territorial boundaries so as to gain power first in Mozambique and Angola and subsequently in Rhodesia and South Africa, acting presidents and would-be presidents of authoritarian one-party systems agree that "independence" must be achieved by armed struggle, not by negotiation; that elections and referendums, being nefarious tactics of the enemy, have to be prevented or disrupted if necessary by terrorizing the black citizenry; and that the heads of state of so-called "frontline" nations in this ongoing war do not violate either international law and UN Charter provisions or anybody's rights when they simply jail black citizens of other states on the ground that they are opponents or rivals of present guerrilla leaders whose personal causes the frontline presidents espouse.[24] In short, the right to go to war and to remain at war sums up all rights to freedom here and now.

Authoritarian and Totalitarian States Dominate United Nations

The norms and values with which the communist nations of Eurasia and the communist and non-communist nations of Africa identify are today the dominant norms and values in the United Nations. And because this majority consists of totalitarian and authoritarian states that are rated by Freedom House either as "Not

Free" or as "Partly Free,"[25] it is not surprising to learn that twenty-three of the co-sponsors of a draft resolution calling for amnesty for South African political prisoners have political prisoners of their own, and that sixteen of the co-sponsors of a draft resolution calling attention to the plight of political prisoners in Chile themselves belong in the category of nations holding such prisoners.

Likewise, it could not have caused much consternation—although it should have evoked forthright protests—that the Human Rights Commission refused to sponsor international investigations of the massacres perpetrated by the governments of Cambodia, Equatorial Guinea, and Uganda, and that no UN agency has been seriously concerned with the continuous and massive violations of human rights in the People's Republic of China, the Soviet Union, the East European communist dictatorships, Cuba, Tanzania, Zambia, Guinea, and other undisguised despotisms. What one finds instead in the voluminous records of the international organization is that accusatory resolutions have been directed year in, year out against the Republic of South Africa and Chile.[26]

The conclusion, then, is irrefutable that the Human Rights Commission has not performed its mandate under the Economic and Social Council's Resolution 1503; that the United Nations as a whole has made little if any progress toward the realization in practice of the high objectives enunciated by the Charter and the Universal Declaration; and that there is little reason for thinking that the situation will change in the foreseeable future.[27] Indeed, the overwhelming evidence of caprice in the application of moral and legal standards supports Daniel P. Moynihan's impression that it is not human rights at all that are being invoked, but simply arbitrary standards dressed up in the guise of human rights. From this perception, he continues, it is no great distance to the conclusion that in truth there are no human rights recognized by the international community.[28]

The short international adventure of the "rights" idea may thus be over, and it is even doubtful whether the now fractured concept—once a gadfly irritating and a beacon luring the victims among whom it dwells[29]—has a future in the civilization that was so long its house of life. What we are left with today are hollow discredited words—a situation which Goethe contemplated when he had Mephistopheles declare:

> For if your meaning's threatened with stagnation
> Words come in to save the situation:
> They'll fight your battles well if you enlist them;
> Or furnish you a universal system.

Part II: America's Commitment to Human Rights, in Policy and in Practice

The twentieth-century world has been shaped decisively by the United States. American thought and planning are thus largely responsible for the formulation of present principles of state behavior; the establishment of guide lines for the creation of new states; the building of a new international system in the service of world peace, law and order; and, above all, for projecting a design that would unify the destinies of all men and peoples in binding collective commitments to respect and further the rights of man.

This is a remarkable intellectual and moral achievement in the annals of international history, and inquiries into the origins of the country's deep concern with human rights should therefore always be on the agenda of citizens. They are particularly important now when it is clear that the world design is flawed when judged in the light of the purposes it was meant to serve; that the nation's own avowal of "the rights of man" is too shaky and confused today to be taken seriously either at home or abroad; and that too many American foreign policies have been seriously faulted in consequence of misperceiving moral, legal and political realities.

What then are the roots of the American commitment to "The Rights of Man"? When and why were the values implicit in this commitment brought into an explicit relationship to the conduct of the nation's foreign policy? And how should one evaluate this entire development in the American experience?

HISTORICAL AND PHILOSOPHICAL BEGINNINGS

The store of textual sources is rich in bills of rights, declarations of rights and other documents, each carefully drafted with a view to creating the kind of social and political order that would assure freedom and security for the new communities and their individual inhabitants. The settlers had thus drawn up a code of law containing a rudimentary bill of rights as early as 1636, the Puritans had followed suit, and William Penn's "Laws, Concessions, and Agreements" for the province of West New Jersey (published in 1699) had provided the people of that area with certain fundamental rights and privileges before the great constitutive documents were formulated in the last decades of the eighteenth century. This series, which includes the Virginia Bill of Rights and the Massachusetts and Virginia Declarations of Rights, culminated in the Declaration of Independence—the basic repository of American ideas about human rights—the Constitution, and the Bill of Rights.[30]

The founding charters converge on several shared themes, chief among them the concern to settle the relationship between power and liberty. Reflections on "power" had convinced the American Fathers that this was as natural and necessary a phenomenon as liberty, but that it could not be considered legitimate unless and until it had been securely harnessed by law. For as Samuel Adams had explained it, unrestrained power was everywhere generally known to kindle the worst passions of the human heart and the worst projects of the human mind "in league against the liberties of mankind."[31] But once power was securely lodged in voluntary compacts and mutual consent, one could safely conclude that it issued from the people. With society thus emergent from the state of nature, men could create a government that would act as the trustee and custodian of the mass of surrendered individual powers. Liberty, then, being bound up with the reservation of balanced and limited power, came to signify the capacity to exercise "natural rights" within the limits set by law. But "law" could not be arbitrary; the understanding was that it had to emanate from legislatures that were responsible to the people.

The second major preoccupation consisted in efforts to find proper definitions for two components or types of Liberty Writ Large that have subsequently been distinguished as political freedoms and civil rights. The former, which derived from the belief in popular sovereignty and relate to participation in government, cover voting processes, elections, political representation, and ways of choosing govermental leadership. They were designed in particular to protect democracy and guard the people against tyranny. The latter, which came to comprise the individual's rights to freedom of life, thought, speech, press, assembly, and property, were in essence the rights under English law with which the settlers had identified as Englishmen. That is to say, they were not conceived at that time as rights antecedent to government and law. Penn's statements on rights and privileges had thus provided already in the seventeenth century that no men have authority to rule over man's conscience in religious matters and that no one shall be deprived or condemned of life, limb, liberty, and estate or property without a due trial and judgment passed by twelve good and lawful men in the neighborhood.[32]

These two categories of rights were of course interdependent: the insistence on protection of life called forth a constitutional order, but no one could have claimed the rights assuring a secure and independent personal life, had the exercise of the political freedoms not resulted in a government under law. Furthermore, both sets of ideas supported the norm that men were, or should be, equal before the law. Indeed, this principle of "equality" soon became a dogma as Americans began to believe that since the possession of political rights gives self-respect and imposes responsibilities, it also makes all men equally fit to exercise those rights.

A third major theme which emerged slowly in the eighteenth century as the English connection weakened was the conviction that rights must be set out clearly and firmly in a written constitution.

Reflections on the early origins of the American commitment to the rights of man lead to the conclusion that we are dealing with two sets of different roots and therefore with two sets of assumptions and arguments. These were fundamentally incompatible and it does not appear that sustained efforts were made to clear up the resulting ambiguities in American thought and discourse.

Common Law and the Laws of Nature

Thus we find on the one hand pride in the acknowledgment that the common law was the colonists' birthright; that they as Britishers shared in a unique inheritance of liberty, and that their liberties were those concretely specified in the English common law, English charters and statutes, and in English judicial decisions. Moreover, almost everyone familiar with these legal records also knew the history of their development. Blackstone's commentaries and lectures on the laws of England had a secure place in American homes and libraries; Coke and other early English authorities on law were widely read; and numerous Americans in each generation crossed the Atlantic to receive training in the English Inns of Court. Two truths, both particularly relevant to the issue of rights, must therefore have been absorbed by those who were engaged in building the foundations for a new nation. One was to the effect that most English liberties, including the nation's constitution, are so deeply imbedded in the law of the land that they can be assumed and thus do not have to be enumerated. The second reminded the reader that all existing law was traditionally subject to amelioration under the impact of principles of equity as administered by the courts under the Lord Chancellor, an official long identified as the keeper of the King's conscience.

The other root system that was cultivated assiduously by thoughtful and influential colonists stemmed from a fervent conviction that the rights that Americans enjoyed as part of their British heritage were by no means "unique"; rather, they inhered inalienably in human beings everywhere. An eighteenth century spokesman for Pennsylvania thus proclaimed that the liberties of Pennsylvanians were founded on the acknowledged rights of human nature. Others in his generation maintained that no written laws, not even Magna Carta, could create liberties since all were mere declarations of existing law, and that legal rights are those rights which men are entitled to by the eternal laws of right reason. Neither of these and similar references was linked to equity even though this complex of ethical ideas had by that time been successfully transformed into legally operational rules.

This orientation gained momentum as the transAtlantic crisis in

relations with the mother country deepened. Few spokesmen for
the new America went so far as to cast out the entire British tradition, yet most followed Jefferson in wanting it clearly understood
that the true source of rights is to be found in the laws of nature, if
only because the ideal must be presumed to have existed before the
real. However, no one spelled out what "the ideal" was or explained
in precisely which ways existing positive rights were deficient. Nor
did any of the critics seriously check on the presence or absence of
"rights" in mankind's different provinces. Pessimism had actually
been voiced about the future of liberty in the world-at-large, as
when it was noted that the rulers of the East were "almost universally absolute tyrannies. . ."; that "the states of Africa are scenes of
tyranny, barbarity, confusion, and every form of violence;"[33] and
that despotism was rising too in continental Europe where "human
nature" had at one time been highly developed. But these impres-
sions were not brought into any relationship with the abstractions
that reigned supreme on the eve of independence. At that time
people seem to have agreed with Alexander Hamilton, who wrote in
1775 that "the sacred rights of mankind are not to be rummaged for
among old parchments or musty records. They are written as with a
sunbeam, in the whole *volume* of human nature, by the hand of
divinity itself. . . ."[34]

"A Perfect Constitution"

Americans, then, had begun to think of themselves as a new
people, and after their successful revolution they fancied their history to have begun in 1776, forgetting, as Bryce remarks in his
comparison of different Western democracies,[35] that they were actually "an old people, the heirs of many ages," and that their
character and institutions were due to causes that had been at work
for many centuries.

In this euphoric mood Thomas Paine declared that Europe was
incapable of bringing forth a perfect constitution, and most of his
politically conscious countrymen agreed that it was their mission to
produce one. Overlooked was the information that numerous
"compacts" on the order of Magna Carta had been recorded in
medieval Europe, among them the solemn covenant between the

three original cantons upon which Switzerland's democracy continues to rest securely; and the charter of liberties negotiated between King Alfonso IX of Leon (Iberian Peninsula) and the kingdom's princes and feudal assemblies, which confirmed a whole series of individual rights, among them the right of the accused to a regular trial and the right to inviolability of life, honor, home, and property.

Dropped from consciousness too was knowledge of classical Rome's legal and political history, which relayed the circumstances in which constitutionalism (the word's provenance is Latin, after all) had emerged from the early history of contract[36]—a complex set of precisely defined interlocking ideas without which eighteenth century theories of the contractual origin of the state and government cannot be fathomed readily. More important in light precisely of these theories is the fact that eighteenth century Americans did not make much of Rome's success in linking the state's positive laws— the *Jus Civile*—to the model system or theory of the *Jus Naturale*, which had originally been borrowed from the Stoics. This success was due to the clear-minded recognition on the part of Roman jurist-statesmen that natural law *underlay* existing law and must therefore be looked for through it. That is to say, it was not viewed here either as the opposite or as the superior reference. In contrast to opinions prevalent in revolutionary America and France, natural law had thus *remedial*, not revolutionary or anarchical functions.[37] And similar caution was applied by Rome in handling the idea of "happiness;" although it was accepted as the proper object of reformist legislation it was not allowed to become a freely floating abstraction divorced from the pleasures and demands of real life.

Americans, then, did not turn to history in their search of confirmation for the cause of mankind's rights that they espoused. Critical of what Europe actually stood for and determined to set things right for future times, they looked for guidance to some of the old world's philosophers. The founding generation was thus attracted to the English Levellers of the seventeenth century who had also legitimized their revolt by appeals to "the Laws of God and Nature" and who had held to the view that every man, whatever his learning, had a right to take part in all affairs of state because, they maintained, man everywhere has the same access to moral truth.

Another group of thinkers whose works appealed particularly to Jefferson was identified with the Scottish Enlightenment of the eighteenth century. The writings of Francis Hutcheson thus seem to have been particularly persuasive when the Declaration of Independence was being written. Not only did Hutcheson, too, stress the innateness of man's moral sense; he also dwelt intensively on the pursuit of happiness as one of man's main natural inclinations. His influence may thus have been ultimately responsible for Jefferson's assertion that the pursuit of happiness is an inalienable right and for the decision to substitute this right for that to "property" which had been emphasized by John Locke.[38] Yet the major sources of inspiration for the Declaration of Independence were doubtlessly Locke's theories on natural law and civil liberty as set forth especially in *The Second Treatise of Government* and *An Essay Concerning Human Understanding,* and Rousseau's ideas about "equality," "the State of Nature," and the "Social Contract."

The conviction holding sway in revolutionary France that "all men are born equal" was thus joined in the American Declaration with the assumption, more familiar to Englishmen, that "all men are born free." Both propositions were hypotheses that had become articles of speculative faith and thus did not require validation. And the same was true of the premise that man was natively good, disposed to follow reason, tolerant, virtuous, and therefore ideally equipped to function as a responsible citizen. The conclusion that Carl Becker reached after his study of eighteenth century philosophy also holds after reflections on America's politically most influential thinkers, namely that the principles they were looking for were already established in their minds: they knew what was just and what unjust and did not need to check on evidence.[39]

Independence and Individual Liberty

The main root of the commitment to the rights of man may well have been this determination that Americans must form an independent nation—"to assume among the Powers of the Earth, the separate and equal Station to which the Laws of Nature and of Nature's God entitle them." No argument or theoretical construction seemed necessary to explain away the fact that the "independence" of a state is conceptually unrelated to an individual's liberties, and that most states in history have not been anchored in foundations built on individual freedom. Nor was the actual American experience of "self-government" and "self-determination" on the plane of colonial, provincial or state existence officially presented as the logical extension of the norm of *individual* self-government or self-determination—gaps in rationalization that go a long way toward explaining why the American Declaration of Independence could become the main reference for countless claims to revolution and independence throughout the world, and why the foreign policies of the United States have remained deeply grounded in the Declaration's thought world.

Influence of Christianity

This dimension of the American thrust forward into time was clearly projected by the Founders as when they evoked images of America as "an asylum for mankind," "a lesson for mankind," and "a service to mankind." The will of "Providence," "Divinity," or "Nature's God" was cited as the ultimate sanction of this conception of the new nation's "manifest destiny" (a phrase invented later, in 1845). Yet the deeper springs of this messianic persuasion are found in Christianity, the religion of the settlers who really built the nation, and the order of moral values which together with that of the common law had sustained the American hope through successive generations.

America's self-selected role of "Redeemer Nation"[40] recalls that which Jehovah assigned to the Jews as his chosen people. However, it is the New Testament's commitment to the principles of brotherhood, the equality of all men, and the unity of the human race that went into the making of the nation and thus also, albeit implicitly, into the writing first of the Declaration and then of the Constitution.

Yet some fundamental Christian themes were certainly not developed in the climate of official atheism, rationalism and enlightenment in which the great announcement of America's independence was composed. Unacknowledged was the supposition that all men are imperfect even as each human being is unique and therefore different from the other. And unacknowledged too, therefore, was the Christian ethic which teaches that in Christ there is neither Jew nor Greek, barbarian nor Scythian, bond nor free;[41] that every man should love his neighbor and be his brother's keeper. Furthermore, the omission, perhaps even downgrading, of this entire realm of feeling may also explain why American leaders put the stress almost entirely on rights and did not follow Locke, who knew as a Christian and as an Englishman familiar with contract law, that no one could or should claim rights without accepting obligations.[42] Had some of these beliefs been integrated into the philosophy of the Revolution, it might not have been found necessary to subscribe so strenuously to the preposterous dogma that every man is by nature virtuous and good and that all men are equal—dogmas, incidentally, for which no educated person in the eighteenth century could have found a shred of supporting evidence in the natural sciences as these were then developed.

The substratum of essentially Christian values released another complex of sentiments that was to have decisive effects upon the American commitment to the idea of human rights, namely guilt. This psychological reaction to human failing and imperfection is of course a corollary of Christianity's severely demanding moral code and of its insistence that the human being must never cease aspiring.

In eighteenth and nineteenth century America, where the measure of human perfection was deemed to be "equality," guilt was experienced most acutely in connection with the reality of slavery in the land. The fact that slavery was a universally established institution sanctioned by most non-Western belief systems and thus did not elicit guilt or revulsion among either Asians or Africans was irrelevant to this American reaction. After all, it was one of numerous facts that had been screened from consciousness in deference to higher, allegedly universally valid causes. Expiation thus came through one of the bitterest and most tragic of wars—"the Ennobling War" in Tuveson's phrasing[43]—and through steadfastly pursued legislative actions in behalf of equal rights for the black citizenry of the nation. These domestic successes in the approximation of the Declaration's ideas about the rights of man naturally strengthened the general American commitment. In fact, they helped make for that posture of self-righteousness in which the United States presumed, from the 1920s onward, to determine patterns of race relations also in other independent societies of the world.

Rights for an Independent America: Some Conclusions

Reflections on the complex history of this country's great commitment lead to a few general conclusions.

The rights that really mattered in the first century of statehood were the civil liberties and political freedoms with which Americans were endowed as citizens and which were eventually listed in the Constitution and the Bill of Rights.[44] Some specific aspects of this particular European heritage had been jettisoned officially, among them certain traditional understandings of what Christianity, law, and history really meant when brought into relation to these rights. However, while the European settlers were presumed to have cut their roots so as to begin a new history in a new type of state, they actually continued to cling to them. That is to say, the heritage persisted.[45] Moreover, it continued to give direction to life and thought in subsequent decades since it was carried to the new world also by nineteenth century immigrants from Europe.

Next, economic and social rights were not recognized in either of the founding documents. Rights to education, work, health, social security and so forth were unknown to Locke and the natural rights theorists of the eighteenth century.[46] They were developed gradually in the United States as part of social legislation and in response to the demands of industrialization and educational philosophy, under the influence of utopian socialism, Marxism and different other theories of economic determinism, and in a steadily growing awareness of the needs of non-European immigrants whose linguistic and cultural traditions were at variance with those found in the settled American citizenry. Self-determination, self-development and self-reliance, being implications of the type of individualism associated with Europeanized America,[47] could not suggest biographical norms for the new waves of prospective citizens coming from non-European societies, and compensatory social arrangements naturally evolved in the course of time.

Lastly, it goes without saying that rights to culture were neither recognized nor envisioned. After the initial English settlement, the United States was re-conceived officially as a melting pot of cultures and of nations. Dedicated to the principle (borrowed from Europe's civilization) that "man" is an active pragmatic individual who is ready to cast off tradition in order to develop in his own right, this country thus stated its case as a nation-state by subscribing to the commitment to transcend ethnic, religious and linguistic particularities. In short, the United States has stood without qualification for the cause of overcoming culture. This theory or orientation was destined to disintegrate in the twentieth century, partly under the same diverse pressures that induced the emergence of social and economic rights, and partly in consequence of the development of Black consciousness among its Negro citizens. Yet another set of ambiguities was thus added to the ongoing already muddled discourse about the real meaning of the "rights" and "values" that ostensibly sustain America.

It has thus become clear in the last decades of the twentieth century that "Black" rights, "Latino" rights, "Chicano" rights, and "American Indian" rights are what really matter; for spokesmen of these so-called ethnic minorities—a term not often applied to non-English white members of the nation—go out of their way explaining that the rights of citizens belonging to these communities are functions not of the constitution in virtue of which the state exists, but rather of the collective mores that make it difficult for individual members of the minorities to qualify as citizens. It has thus become common "liberal" practice to accede to the principle of apartheid and separate development in the case of numerous American Indian tribes, even though doing so certainly denies aspiring individual Indians opportunities to education, material advancement, and access to leadership in the unified American nation. And these incongruities in official policy are totally confounded if one thinks of them in juxtaposition to some of the present Administration's major foreign policies, especially in Africa. Here we find the United States in adamant opposition to South Africa's "reactionary" policy of recognizing the separate cultural identities of the country's various Bantu-speaking peoples by granting these communities self-government in Bantustans along with the hope of eventual political independence.

Changes in the country's population, the world environment, and government policies are not the only factors responsible for the momentous shifts in orientation toward the rights of man within the nation. Due allowance must also be made for the fact that the drift away from individualism and the philosophy of basic individual rights has met with strong support from the country's intellectual leadership in the academic establishments, the media of communication, and the churches. Among current tendencies the following can thus be discerned: to overstate the case for universalism in human thought and conduct, and neglect or ignore evidence of difference, dissonance or conflict; to accept words at face value without finding out whether they continue to carry the meanings once invested in them; and to evaluate facts in light of preferred theories or ideologies without making sure that the theories are borne out by the realities.

"Levelling" has thus all too often become an end in itself. It proves attractive because it feeds moral certainty by lending support to optimism, utopian thought, and doctrines of equality, and because it makes it possible to avoid the study of history, an object of aversion also among many of the nation's founders.

AMERICA'S "RIGHTS" COMMITMENT AND U.S. FOREIGN POLICY

Two post-Revolutionary clubs meeting together in Philadelphia on May 1, 1794, drank the following toast:

> The Democratic and Republican Societies of the United States: May they preserve and disseminate their principles, undaunted by the frowns of power, uncontaminated by the luxury of aristocracy, until the Rights of Man shall become the supreme law of every land, and their separate fraternities be absorbed in one great democratic society comprehending the human race.[48]

And North Carolina democrats, meeting in 1796, toasted Thomas Paine's *The Rights of Man* and the Tree of Liberty, adding for the latter, "may its roots be cherished in this its mother land, until its branches shall extend themselves over the remotest corner of the earth.''[49]

The First Hundred Years

The hopes here enunciated pervaded American thought about the nation's foreign relations, and they also found expression in Jefferson's Sixth Annual Message (Dec. 2, 1806):

> I congratulate you, fellow citizens, on the approach of the period at which you may interpose your authority constitutionally to withdraw the citizens of the United States from all further participation in those violations of human rights which have been so long continued on the unoffending inhabitants of Africa, and which the morality, the reputation, and the best interests of our country have long been eager to proscribe.[50]

But governmental endeavors to substantiate the image of a morally unified world democracy or to put morally deficient members of the states system on the proper path were few and far between throughout the nineteenth century. After all, Americans had now acceded to the family of established states and therewith to the rules of the Law of Nations. And one of these as explained by de Vattel's *Law of Nations* (published 1759)—a volume widely read in America—was to the effect that nations, like men, are naturally free and independent of each other, except where a bonded relation has been incurred.[51] Both Washington and Hamilton had thus stressed the necessity of realizing that in foreign affairs each nation is guided by its own interests even as it must scrupulously observe treaty obligations. This principle was firmly endorsed also by President Monroe's Annual Message of 1823 (the Monroe Doctrine), but it was joined with the warning that European efforts to oppress or control populations in this hemisphere would seriously endanger "the peace and happiness" of the United States. And an earlier Message (1822) had reminded the nation that Americans

> owe to the world a great example, and, by means thereof, to the cause of liberty and humanity a generous support . . . There is no reason to doubt that their whole movement will be regulated by a sacred regard to principle, all our institutions being founded on that basis.[52]

The same sense of mission and futurist hope for the "melioration of man" pervades John Quincy Adams' Inaugural Address, which

holds special interest for this discussion because it contains one of
the earliest direct references to "human rights":

> It is a source of gratification and of encouragement to me to observe
> that the great result of this experiment upon the theory of human
> rights has at the close of that generation by which it was formed been
> crowned with success equal to the most sanguine expectations of its
> founders.[53]

The theme is followed up in his Message to the House of Representatives (March 15, 1826). After pointing to what may be "the
noblest treaty of peace," namely that by which the Carthaginians
were bound to abolish the practice of sacrificing their own children
"because it was stipulated in favor of human nature," Adams said:

> I can not exaggerate to myself the unfading glory with which these
> United States will go forth in the memory of future ages if by their
> friendly counsel, by their moral influence, by the power of argument
> and persuasion alone they can prevail upon the American nations at
> Panama to stipulate by general agreement among themselves . . . the
> abolition of private war upon the ocean.[54]

Group rights and rights to culture were not acknowledged in
those times, but the existence within the nation of American Indian
communities presented vexing problems. President Andrew
Jackson responded to them in his Third Annual Message (1831) by
noting that time and experence have proved that the abode of the
native Indian within the limits of the confederated states "is dangerous to their peace and injurious to himself."[55] The reasons for this
conclusion are explained in the following way:

> That those tribes can not exist surrounded by our settlements and in
> continual contact with our citizens is certain. They have neither the
> intelligence, the industry, the moral habits, nor the desire of im-
> provement which are essential to any favorable change in their condi-
> tion. Established in the midst of another and a superior race, and
> without appreciating the causes of their inferiority or seeking to
> control them, they must necessarily yield to the force of circumstances
> and ere long disappear.

The Administration therefore urged the tribes to move voluntarily
beyond the boundaries of the states. "The Chickasaws and Choc-
taws had accepted the generous offer of the Government" and
treaties were being drafted to that effect, the President explained,
and the Cherokees were expected to do likewise. But—the Message

continues—"those who prefer remaining at their present homes will hereafter be governed by the laws of Georgia, as all her citizens are, and cease to be the objects of peculiar care on the part of the General Government."

This particular orientation to an "ethnic minority" which was destined for reversal in the twentieth century, contrasts interestingly with the response of President Grant to certain problems implicit in the growing Chinese immigration to this country. Grant's Sixth Annual Message (1874) thus addressed the troubling issues by pointing to "a generally conceded fact" that

> the great proportion of the Chinese immigrants who come to our shores do not come voluntarily, to make their homes with us and their labor production of general prosperity, but come under contract with headmen who own them almost absolutely. In a worse form does this apply to Chinese women. Hardly a perceptible percentage of them perform any honorable labor, but they are brought for shameful purposes, to the disgrace of communities where settled and to the great demoralization of the youth of those localities.

The sympathy for the "right-less" newcomers is obvious, but so is the President's concern for the social and moral welfare of the American host society. And a similarly measured stance was taken by this Administration when unrest and revolt in Cuba compelled attention to the lack of liberty and self-government in an adjoining land. Grant's First Annual Message (1869) contains the following policy propositions in this regard:

> As the United States is the freest of all nations, so, too, its people sympathize with all people struggling for liberty and self government, but while sympathizing it is due to our honor that we shall abstain from enforcing our views upon unwilling nations, and from taking an interested part, without invitation, in the quarrels between different nations or between governments and their subjects. Our course should always be in conformity with strict justice and law, international and local.[56]

Here sentiment is balanced by the declared American interest in supporting local and international law.

The Cleveland Administration

The same determination to maintain respect for the principle of domestic jurisdiction while admitting to deep concern for the plight of aggrieved individuals or groups of persons was very marked also in Grover Cleveland's Administration. The matter of asylum illustrates the point. Two individuals in Chile who had just failed in an attempt at revolution and against whom criminal charges were pending, had been given refuge by the resident American minister. But Cleveland deemed this action unauthorized:

> The doctrine of asylum as applied to this case is not sanctioned by the best precedents, and when allowed tends to encourage sedition and strife. Under no circumstances can the representation of this Government be permitted, under ill-defined fiction of extra-territoriality, to interrupt the administration of criminal justice in the countries to which they are accredited.[57]

The same caution was employed also in relations with Salvador. Here the government had been overthrown by a popular outbreak and some of the military and civil officers, while hotly pursued by infuriated insurgents, sought asylum on board a U.S. warship. In this case the President explained that

> although the practice of asylum is not favored by this Government, yet in view of the imminent peril which threatened the fugitives and solely from considerations of humanity they were offered shelter.

Judicial hearings were promptly instituted as stipulated by a treaty of extradition with Salvador, and the ensuing ruling distinguished carefully between "political" offenders who were entitled to seek refuge, and criminals who were not.[58]

The Cleveland Administration also had occasion to deal with alleged violations of the rights of naturalized citizens. One case that related to an American who had been arrested in Russia on charges of unpermitted renunciation of Russian allegiance, was the object of diplomatic negotiations seeking his release when he died. Several other cases arose in this country's relations with Turkey, more particularly in regard to the problems faced by Turkey's Armenian population. Acting on a complaint from Turkey that its Armenian subjects often seek U.S. citizenship with the intention to go back to Turkey and preach sedition, the President took the following position:

> The right to exclude any or all classes of aliens is an attribute of sovereignty. It is a right asserted, and to a limited extent, enforced by the United States, with the sanction of our highest court. There being

no naturalization treaty between the United States and Turkey, our minister at Constantinople has been instructed that, while recognizing the right of that Government to enforce its declared policy against Naturalized Armenians, he is expected to protect them against unnecessary harshness of treatment.[59]

But the main concern to which the Senate gave full expression was "the alleged cruelties committed upon Armenians in Turkey, and especially whether any such cruelties have been committed upon citizens who have declared their intention to become naturalized in this country or upon persons because of their being Christians."[60] This matter was handled very carefully by the Executive because detailed information was lacking and also because credit had to be given to the statement by Turkey's grand vizier who had explained that it was necessary to suppress insurrections in the incidents under consideration.

Yet another "rights"-related issue in the Cleveland Administration's foreign policy was the "unsatisfactory state of affairs in Samoa"—then under the governmental supervision of three powers under the terms of the Berlin Treaty. This government, Cleveland explained, had been set up against the "inveterate hostility" of the Samoans; could be maintained only by the continued presence of foreign military force; did not provide any economic benefits to the United States; and was in every respect signally illustrative of "the impolicy of entangling alliances with foreign powers." Since "our participation in its establishment against the wishes of the natives was in plain defiance of the conservative teachings and warnings of the wise and patriotic men who laid the foundations of our free institutions. . .," and since there had been numerous insurrections, the President requested Congress to give its views about the propriety of an American withdrawal from its treaty commitments.[61]

"The White Man's Burden"

The ascendancy of American concern with the cause of "self-determination" in societies ruled by the West was already quite pronounced at the turn of the century, as was the conviction that the White Man had a special "Burden" to help and guide disadvantaged peoples. Selfish motives were not disguised either by European governments which were at that time beginning to become colonial governments, or by the United States. But they coexisted on both sides of the Atlantic with genuinely altruistic intentions that were deeply grounded in Christian belief and received steady confirmation from the overwhelming evidence of disease, ignorance, poverty, and "inhuman practices" such as cannibalism.

To develop the underdeveloped so that they might attain a new sense of human dignity thus became a strong commitment on the part of the government as well as of churches, missionary groups, and other private philanthropic organizations. The stress here was placed on providing schools and medical facilities, and the achievements registered under these headings included the founding of the American University in Beirut and of Roberts College in Istanbul and the establishment, by the Rockefeller Foundation, of a medical school in Peking. This place of learning and of service became known throughout the world as the outpost of modern medicine in the Far East; but it has been downgraded in recent times under the influence of communist ways of thought as just another typical manifestation of cultural imperialism.

Support of Self-Determination

The other major road toward the goal of improving the human condition was charted in the direction of self-government and self-determination. Neither was considered a "human right" before the advent of the Wilson era. Each was at best a guiding principle that the government was free to utilize or ignore in accordance with its perception of the national interest. The state of Liberia was thus founded for "humanitarian reasons," but the American South had not been allowed to secede. Sympathy was expressed for the oppressed Samoans, but the suggestion, made in 1897 by a Japanese minister, that a plebiscite be held in Hawaii in order to determine that population's wishes in regard to annexation by the U.S. was rejected.

The same deliberately pragmatic approach marked early American reactions to revolutions in its international environment. Up to the 1800s the U.S. refrained from giving militay and financial aid, confining itself to moral declarations of support for rebel causes it approved. Between the McKinley and Wilson Administrations, by contrast, military interventions became quite common, especially in Central America. However, it is interesting to note that the objective of almost all such moves was the establishment of order, not of liberty. And this remained true, by and large, after the pendulum had swung the other way again in the aftermath of the Bolshevik revolution in Russia, when it was being generally realized that the United States was not altogether successful as a tutor of the world.[62]

The Wilsonian persuasion that peoples and individuals had to be self-governing if they wished to enhance their self-respect and their status in the greater society of man, and that self-determination was the necessary means toward those ends, was nonetheless acclaimed within the nation. Toward the end of the First World War it was recognized also as a major peace objective among the contesting states in the sense that certain national religious or linguistic minorities of the multi-national continental powers were given the opportunity to determine their political allegiance once peace had come. And after the Second World War the principle received an extended range of meaning and applicability under the UN Charter and subsequent UN resolutions which provided, in essence, that peoples in the colonial possessions and trust territories of the European empires and the United States had a right not merely to self-determination and self-government but to political independence.[63]

The same certainty does not obtain in the context of American foreign policy, even though this nation has endorsed UN resolutions affirming "the inalienable right" of, for example, the Micronesian people and the Angolan people to self-determination and independence. What was being universalized in this and other ways were the values of "democracy" and "peace." The "Rights of Man," by contrast, did not become major issues in Wilsonian foreign policies. They came to the fore again in the Administration of Franklin D. Roosevelt, who included in his State of the Union Message (1944) what he called "a second Bill of Rights" that stressed rights to work, medical care, social security, and education. These New Deal initiatives were to receive considerable support from later UN activities in the fields of social, economic, and cultural rights, but their validity as constitutional rights was seriously questioned in the United States itself.[64] No claims were made in either of these two administrations that political rights and civil liberties were universally applicable. However, certain departures from international custom and national tradition deserve mention because they were to have profound effects on all conceptualizations of the state, the individual, and the basic rights of man.

Changes in American Attitudes

The source of these departures was the American government's deliberate administration of enmity for the peoples with whom it was at war. Although Wilson had declared that the German Kaiser's regime was the enemy in the First World War and that Americans had no quarrel with the German nation, the doctrine of collective guilt was allowed to stand in treaties and become established doctrine, thus invalidating important existing principles of ethics, law and international law. The precedent here set was followed by the Administration of Franklin D. Roosevelt at the occasion of the Second World War when, as Louis J. Halle put it in an important essay on "The Fallacy of Daemonic Enmity,"[65] the conception was advanced by the President that the German, Italian, and Japanese peoples were aggressors by their inborn nature, and that this should therefore be the basis on which the Atlantic allies would deal with them after their defeat. The notion of a "common humanity" which had supplied roots for the early commitment to the rights of man, was thus rather blithely disestablished.

Certain other long-standing norms were also seriously put into question. This was brought about when the United States decided in concert with its wartime allies to create an entirely new category of penal international law under the heading of "Crimes against Humanity." But the concern with humanity was selective, for these allegedly legal norms were made *ex post facto*, to be applied exclusively to the vanquished so as to cover abuses of humanity of which they had been found guilty by their victorious judges. Included in this group of international crimes was genocide, which the Convention on the Prevention and Punishment of Genocide (1948) has defined as an act committed in peace or war with intent to destroy in whole or in part a national, ethnic, racial or religious group. Such a crime, it was explicitly concluded, could be perpetrated by a government within its own territorial boundaries and against its own citizens. The twin principles of sovereignty and domestic jurisdiction—cornerstones of the international states system which the U.S. had also been instrumental in developing during the early '40s—were thus chipped away.

Neither these nor other incongruities in the nation's espousal of international law and order on the one hand, and of the rights of citizens within the independent sovereign state on the other, have been officially addressed by the government in the last decades. Up to the advent of the Carter Presidency, during which "human rights" was to emerge as the primary political cause, the Administrations, whether Democratic or Republican, continued to subscribe to both principles simultaneously, with just occasional shifts of accent from one position to the other.

President Truman had thus expressed himself at the San Francisco Conference in favor of developing an international bill of rights that "will be as much a part of international life as our own Bill of Rights is part of our Constitution," but his subsequent foreign policies cannot be said to have been mortgaged by the projection of this hope. And Secretary of State John Foster Dulles, who had explicitly endorsed the Universal Declaration of Human Rights in the early '50s, hoping that international standards would soon be developed in the field of human rights "in terms of laws which operate on individuals, not upon states, and which are enforceable by the courts and not by armies," reversed this stand decisively later on. Only non-governmental interest groups recognized the incompatibility of the two principles in that era, chief among them representatives of the American Bar Association and members of Congress under the leadership of Senator Bricker; and they succeeded at that time to frustrate American support for the Genocide Convention and other related texts.[66]

RECENT FOREIGN POLICY

Opposition to UN-sponsored Covenants and Declarations weakened in ensuing years and argumentations on the merits of conflicting norms and values ceased altogether as the U.S. allowed the human rights rhetoric of the United Nations to wash away whatever policy intentions it might have wished to develop. Under these auspices the United States came to propagate primarily group rights, foremost among them the right to self-determination, which has been discussed in earlier parts of this paper. What requires renewed emphasis here is the fact that this complex of ideas lacks precise legal definitions, that it has no ethically definable core, and that it is therefore essentially a political proposition. As such it has always invited excesses, as Clyde Eagleton remarked already in the '50s.[67]

But whereas this nation had the power and the interest in the earlier part of the century to prevent or curb excesses, as for example when it instructed the Taft Commission in the Philippine Islands to design a regime that would conform to local customs, even prejudices, so far as was consistent with the principles of good government, it now simply follows prevalent local trends as supported by the UN majority of the moment. This orientation has hardened into a policy under the Carter Administration, especially in regard to Africa. Here the government has been siding openly with Marxist guerrilla forces and liberation fronts that are intent on bypassing the principle of self-determination by election and on forcing the issue of independence in Rhodesia (Zimbabwe) and South West Africa (Namibia) through warfare waged from without with the massive assistance of the Soviet Union and Cuba.

The "Liberation Theology" that informs our foreign policy today can be traced to many sources, among them Christianity.[68] The fact that President Carter's personal world view was shaped decisively by the Protestant-Baptist faith as rendered in his native South is therefore not irrelevant. And the same holds for the related fact that this particular Carter policy has widespread support in some of this country's Christian establishments. But as one reflects upon such official Christian actions as the allotment of funds by the World Council of Churches to communist guerrilla forces in Africa, one cannot help but conclude that one of the mainsprings of American thought and action is critically muddied at this time. A discussion of the causes for this transposition of values cannot be conducted in the present paper, but some of the factors were set out by Gustave Von

Grunebaum by way of comment on American attitudes toward the modern Middle East in the following passage:

> Our traditional sympathy for the underdog, for liberation irrespective of the ruler to be cast out, and for independence irrespective of the level of the society that is to be lifted into statehood, has crystallized of late in the emotional doctrine that an underdeveloped country can do no wrong. We may object to the more flagrant excesses of the younger nationalisms, but we seem to feel that if we remove frustration from their path they will soon quiet down and be content to develop . . . and become as reasonable or as resigned as the maintenance of world peace will require.[69]

These explanations also hold for the second major American commitment in the field of group "rights," that, namely, which consists in helping underdeveloped nations satisfy their economic aspirations. Yet the roots here are clearly traceable also on the one hand to the Christian ethic of brotherhood and of guilt for failures of compassionate action, and on the other hand to the native American dogma of equality which rests on the unproven assumption that given equal opportunities every individual—and hence every nation—is equally capable of succeeding. The question whether economic development is possible without a strong commitment to specific moral and intellectual values, and in the absence of political and civil liberties that assure the investment of human inventiveness and determination, has not been seriously raised in the context of policy-making. The probable reason for this acquiescent uncritical disposition on the part of the government as well as of the public is the widespread acceptance today of theories of economic determinism, especially of materialist explanations of history and society, that had no decisive sway over the minds of the country's founding generations.

The cause of political freedoms and individuated civil liberties did not become operational in the foreign policies of the nation before the Nixon and Ford Administrations. At that time it was espoused officially in the limited context of negotiations with the Soviet Union and other states that aimed at the establishment of security in Europe and culminated, eventually, in the Helsinki Accord of 1975. That is to say, human rights issues were here distinctly subservient to the main policy objective of stabilizing what was called "détente" in our relations with the Soviets.[70] However, President Ford expressed himself satisfied with the Agreement's (the Helsinki Accord is not a treaty) stipulations regarding the exercise of freedoms in the different communist societies of Eastern Europe and the Russian motherland of socialism. Addressing the Helsinki Conference on August 1, 1975, the President carefully listed "the most fundamental human rights," namely, liberty of thought, conscience, and faith; the exercise of civil and political rights; and the rights of minorities, as constituting the main content of the so-called Basket III. However, it was to become clear in the ensuing years that neither of these commitments was redeemable in the countries ruled by communist regimes.

The Carter Administration and Human Rights

The Carter Administration's foreign policy team may not have had an electoral mandate for the different human rights adventures upon which it seemed determined to embark, but as McGeorge Bundy points out, neither was there a mandate against such a program.[71] In fact, President Carter inherited the détente and human rights policies of the preceding Republican administration, and aligned himself firmly with the policy statements of the Ford government even as he chose to transcend the Helsinki context so as to make the world-at-large the object of the American commitment to human rights. A heavy accent was thus placed in his Inaugural Address on the nation's moral duties and on "the quiet strength of noble truths and this country's absolute commitment to human rights."

In a subsequent address (at Notre Dame University in May 1977) the President extended this commitment by announcing the need for an entirely "new foreign policy that is democratic, based on our fundamental values and that uses power and influence for humane purposes." This policy, he explained, "is rooted in our moral values; it is designed to serve mankind"—a theme also stressed by Secretary of State Cyrus R. Vance on April 30, 1977 (during an address in Athens, Georgia), when he noted that "our concern for human rights is built upon ancient values. . . ," and that the philosophy of our human rights policy is revolutionary in the intellectual sense, reflecting our nation's origin and progressive values. But in defining what the Administration means by "human rights," the spokesmen place civil and political liberties third and last in the list. The foremost right is the right to be free from governmental violation of the integrity of the person, and the second right relates to fulfillment of such vital needs as food, shelter, healthcare, education and so forth.[72]

The Carter Administration has not set out its understanding of these "ancient values" nor has it explained its reasons for linking these values to its own insistence on holding other independent states to compliance with American constitutional stipulations on the subject of civil liberties and political freedoms. Since the history of American foreign policies would suggest contrary conclusions in this regard, we are left with the reference to our revolutionary philosophy, and this, as rooted in the Declaration of Independence, is not so much a philosophy as an ideologically and morally inspiring evocation of several *not* self-evident truths. These have supplied the underpinning also for policy statements by previous administrations, but none has been as messianic, doctrinaire and self-righteous in invoking them as Mr. Carter's government.

Words may be actions, as Mr. Carter says they are, but the vocabulary of civil rights and political freedoms is being used too carelessly today in our foreign relations, thus exacerbating the semantically and conceptually chaotic conditions set out in the first part of the present paper. Furthermore, reliance on ill-defined values and ideas favors dispositions to invoke "universal truths" arbitrarily[73] and to dispense with thorough analyses of the particular societies that are expected to comply with the norms of American constitutionalism. These failings were prominently apparent in the Administration's approach to the implementation of the Helsinki Accords.[74] They continue to mark our policies in Asia, where we seem determined to ignore the important difference between totalitarian and authoritarian regimes, thus penalizing such allies as South Korea and the Philippines; and in Africa, where the confusion between foreign and domestic policies has become an article of faith.

For what has become apparent here is the fact that most, if not all, political judgments are being made from the vantage point of the

American civil rights movement of the 1960s as this cause was understood by President Carter and Andrew Young, now his chief adviser on all African affairs. In a 1977 speech, the latter thus explained to his African audience how the civil rights movement evolved into the anti-war protest movement, which in turn created a "new approach to the problems we face everywhere in the world."[75] Thanks to this new approach, Mr. Young continued, the United States is finally getting on the right side of the moral issues in international affairs, ready to repair the damage that was done during the years when America became party to a "vast network of oppression" instead of siding with "oppressed peoples everywhere." Now, too, the audience was told, Americans are coming to acknowledge the past racism of their government and to recognize the truth that "the problem of the twentieth century is the problem of the color line."

In light of these preconceptions, it is not difficult to understand why neither Mr. Carter nor Mr. Young has ever bothered to study Africa south of the Sahara on its own merits. Uganda is thus described by Young as a Western problem, ". . .a result of the excesses of both colonialism and neocolonialism"; the guerrillas on Rhodesia's borders are said to be engaged in a morally righteous armed struggle, and people "who are engaged in negotiated settlements" have therefore no moral right to tell them "how to run their paths and determine their freedom."

As for South Africa, South West Africa, and Rhodesia, the Carter Administration sees them as just so many Georgias. Because they are ruled by whites, it is incumbent upon each of these regimes to institute the principle of One Man One Vote—a requirement not made in, for example, Ethiopia whose totalitarian government continues to receive substantial economic assistance without being reminded of its record of genocide and other stark violations of human rights.

In short, the Carter Administration's human rights policy is conceptually so flawed that it is now diffficult to develop foreign policies in support of the country's national interest.[76] More seriously, it has brought confusion and disorder into the nation's value system, and it has effectively severed present generations from their roots.

Notes

1. A. N. Whitehead, *The Adventures of Ideas*, Penguin Books, 1948, p. 27.

2. I. A. Richards, *Mencius on the Mind, Experiments in Multiple Definition*, London, 1932, p. 89.

3. Robert Redfield, *The Primitive World and Its Transformations*, Great Seal Books, Ithaca, New York, 1958, pp. 111-112. Redfield remarks in this connection that the West may be said to have invented progress and reform, and he also suggests that there was no Utopia prior to *The Republic*.

4. Adda B. Bozeman, *Politics and Culture in International History*, Princeton University Press, 1960, pp. 148 ff.

5. *Supra* p. 58 on the Marxist approach to individual rights.

6. Professor John Humphrey, the leading authority on human rights issues in the United Nations, thus notes the following in a recent report: "What must be disturbing to lawyers dedicated to the rule of law is that the choice of cases and the action taken on them is only too often determined by political considerations and the hazards of the voting majorities." The International Law Association, *Report on the Fifty-Seventh Conference held at Madrid, August 30th, 1976*, London, 1978, p. 514.

7. See Adda B. Bozeman, *The Future of Law in a Multicultural World*, Princeton University Press, 1971, for a comprehensive development of these conclusions.

8. This phase was used by Tibor Szamuely in his article "Partial Amnesty," *Encounter*, June 1970, p. 33.

9. The *New York Times*, May 13, 1978, relaying reports by refugees from Cambodia that district officials were more and more openly speaking of a need to kill great numbers of Cambodians. One of these, who had announced at a meeting in early 1977 that of the 15,000 people of the district 10,000 would have to be killed as enemies, and that 6,000 had already perished, added: "We must burn the old grass and the new will grow."

10. See Peter L. Berger, "Are Human Rights Universal?", *Commentary*, September 1977, p. 60, for the conclusion that massacring large numbers of innocent people; deliberately abandoning entire sections of a population to starvation; systematically using terror including torture; expelling large numbers of people; deliberately desecrating religious symbols and destroying institutions that embody ethnic identity are routine policies in modern communist Asia.

11. For this formulation see *Freedom at Issue*, February 1976.

12. Reports on the plight of refugees from the Soviet Union, Eastern Europe, China, and Southeast Asia are legion. On the outpouring of tens of thousands of boat refugees and land refugees from Indochina and their distress on land and at sea in overcrowded unseaworthy boats, see the Department of State, Bureau of Public Affairs, Office of Public Communication, no. 30, August 1978, *The Indochinese Refugees: A Status Report*.

13. Rupert Emerson, "The Fate of Human Rights in the Third World," *World Politics*, July 1975 (reprinted in Robert Woito, ed., *International Human Rights Kit*, Chicago, 1977, pp. 44-63).

For analyses of African forms of government, see Adda B. Bozeman, *Conflict in Africa: Concepts and Realities*, Princeton University Press, 1976, and authorities there cited.

One of the most recent illustrations of the growth of centralization is the program recently announced by the ruling Revolution Party of Benin (formerly Dahomey): Four organizations will be established for the purpose of centralizing control over young people from age 6 to 40; one for workers age 15-40; one for students, age 18-30; one for pupils, age 13-20; and one for children, age 6-15. Control over women is to be entrusted to a single national organization. See *Africa Report,* July-August 1978, vol. 23, no. 4, p. 30.

14. From Sékou Touré, *The International Policy of the Democratic Party of Guinea,* (Republic of Guinea (n.d.), VII, 121, as quoted by Rupert Emerson, "The Fate of Human Rights in the Third World," *World Politics,* July 1975.

15. The *New York Times,* June 22, 1978. On the refugee problem in Africa see the annual *Report of the United Nations High Commissioner for Refugees;* also Hugh C. Brooks and Yassin El Ayouty, eds., *Refugees South of the Sahara,* Westport, Conn., 1970.

16. See the Department of State's report on "The Status of Human Rights Abroad" (which includes reports on 105 nations made public February 1978 by the House International Relations Committee); for excerpts, see the *New York Times,* February 10, 1978.

17. The *New York Times,* February 16, 1978.

18. *Supra* p. 62.

19. For the history of this Article 1, see United Nations, *United Nations Action in the Field of Human Rights 1948-1973,* New York, 1974, pp. 24 ff. See this volume also for other relevant resolutions and declarations.

20. *Infra* p. 90.

21. United Nations Weekly News Summary, Press Release, July 28, 1978.

22. UN Press Release, WS/875, July 14, 1978.

23. UN Press Release, HR/299, September 12, 1975.

24. See the *New York Times,* August 1, 1978, for an account of the circumstances in which Mr. Sam Nujoma, President of the South West Africa Peoples Organization, prevailed upon Presidents Kaunda of Zambia and Nyerere of Tanzania to imprison approximately 2,000 of Nujoma's opponents and one-time supporters, chief among them Mr. Shipanga, head of SWAPO D, and his followers.

See UN Weekly News Summary, July 21, 1978, for a declaration by the representative of Nigeria at a Symposium in Lesotho on the Exploitation of Blacks in South Africa that there could be no peace or stability in southern Africa while the apartheid regime exists even if negotiated settlements were reached in Namibia and Rhodesia.

25. Freedom House ranks levels of political and civil rights in individual nations on a scale of 1 to 7 and then classifies nations as Free, Part Free, or Not Free. A nation in which individuals are imprisoned for political beliefs or activities of a non-criminal nature is considered Not Free. Barely a fifth of the UN membership can today be considered "Free."

See Raymond D. Gastil, ed., *Freedom in the World: Political Rights and Civil Liberties 1978,* Boston and New York, 1978, pp. 22 ff., for these measures of rating and comparison.

26. It is important to note that the United States voted for the draft resolution in the Special Political Committee entitled "Solidarity with the South African Political Prisoners," which called on South Africa to grant an unconditional amnesty to political prisoners, as well as for the draft resolution in the Social, Cultural and Humanitarian Committee entitled "Protection of Human Rights in Chile." See "Statement by Ambassador Daniel P. Moynihan, United States Representative to the United Nations, in Committee Three, on the U.S. proposal for a world-wide amnesty for political prisoners, November 12, 1975," United States Mission to the United Nations, Press Release USUN-144(75), November 12, 1975.

The UN publication *United Nations Action in the Field of Human Rights 1948-1973* makes dreary reading indeed. A special chapter dealing with UN resolutions invoking the Universal Declaration in regard to concrete human rights situations (pp. 14 ff.) is replete with instances of "concrete situations" in South Africa. Several General Assembly decisions thus concern South Africa's treatment of people of Indian and

Indo-Pakistan origin. None refers to the treatment meted out to this category of people in Uganda. South Africa was also called upon to end immediately repressive labor systems; no entry in the long history of these UN actions relates to the network of Gulags and slave labor camps in the Soviet Union. See pp. 5 ff. on "Origins of UN Concern with Human Rights."

27. See Professor John Humphrey's Report to the International Committee on Human Rights of the International Law Association at the Association's Fifty-Seventh Conference in Madrid (1976), p. 515.

28. *Loc. cit.*, Press Release USUN-144 (75), p. 3.

29. *Supra* p. 54 for Whitehead's thoughts on this matter.

30. See source books on American constitutional history for these related texts.

For a particularly stimulating analysis of early American thoughts about rights and liberties, see Bernard Bailyn, *The Ideological Origins of the American Revolution*, Cambridge, Mass., 1971.

For brief surveys, see James Bryce, *Modern Democracies*, 2 vols., New York, 1921, vol. II, pp. 3-165, and American Society of International Law, *Proceedings of the Annual Meeting*, 1976, Washington, D.C., pp. 88 ff. for the record of a panel discussion on "Human Rights Two Hundred Years Later."

31. Bailyn, *op. cit.*, p. 60.

32. *Ibid.*, pp. 196 ff.

33. *Ibid.*, p. 79.

34. *Ibid.*, p. 188 for this quotation; see also pp. 77, 184-89.

35. *Op. cit.*, vol. II, p. 8.

36. Cp. *supra* p. 53, Part I of this paper and see Bozeman, *The Future of Law in a Multicultural World*, pp. 34 ff.

37. See Sir Henry Maine, *Ancient Law; Its Connection with the Early History of Society, and Its Relation to Modern Ideas*, New York, 1879. See in particular ch. III "Law of Nature and Equity" and ch. IV "The Modern History of the Law of Nature."

38. For a recent analysis of the different sources upon which Jefferson drew when writing the Declaration of Independence, see Garry Wills, *Inventing America: Jefferson's Declaration of Independence*, New York, 1978. See also Paul Conkin, *Self-Evident Truths: Being A Discourse on the Origins and Development of the First Principles of American Government—Popular Sovereignty, Natural Rights, and Balance and Separation of Powers*, Bloomington, Indiana, and London, 1974.

In a speech on American independence, July 4, 1776, Samuel Adams had this to say on the subject of "happiness":

> Political rights and public happiness are different words for the same idea. They who wander into metaphysical labyrinths, or have recourse to original contracts, to determine the rights of men, either impose on themselves or mean to delude others.

For a similarly critical but modern view of "happiness," see Malcolm Muggeridge, proposition 17 in "25 Propositions on a 75th Birthday," *New York Times*, April 24, 1978:

> Another disastrous concept is the pursuit of happiness, a last-minute improvisation in the American Declaration of Independence, substituting for the defense of property. Happiness pursued cannot be caught, and if it could, it would not be happiness.

39. Carl Becker, *Heavenly City of the Eighteenth-Century Philosophers*, New Haven, 1932, p. 103. See Daniel Boorstin, *The Lost World of Thomas Jefferson*, New York, 1948, for discussions of the world views found in Jefferson's circle.

40. See Ernest Lee Tuveson, *Redeemer Nation, The Idea of America's Millennial Role*, Chicago and London, 1974.

41. See *Romans*, 10—Verse 12; *Galatians*, 3—Verse 28; and *Colossians*, 3—Verse 11.

42. Cp. in this respect Mazzini's view that nations exist to serve mankind: "Ask yourselves whenever you do an action in the sphere of your country, or your family, if what I am doing were done by all and for all, would it advantage or injure Humanity." For this quotation from *The Duties of Man and Other Essays*, p. 49, see Raymond Leslie Buell, *International Relations*, New York, 1925, p. 20.

43. See *op. cit.*, pp. 207 ff.

44. Eugene Perry Link, *Democratic-Republican Societies 1790-1800*, Octagon Books, New York, 1965, p. 105, thus notes that in the back country, where books were scarce, children sometimes learned to read and spell from the *Essay Concerning Human Understanding*.

45. See B. Mitchell and L. P. Mitchell, *A Biography of the Constitution of the United States*, Oxford University Press, 1964, especially ch. 5, "Afterthoughts," in which the different views about whether or not to include a Bill of Rights are discussed. On the same set of issues, also Samuel J. Konefsky, *John Marshall and Alexander Hamilton*, Macmillan, New York, 1964, pp. 19 ff. Jefferson who had voiced concern over the failure of the Constitutional Convention to draft a bill of rights, wrote to Madison: "A bill of rights is what the people are entitled to against every government on earth. . . ." Hamilton, by contrast, did not share this anxiety over the absence of a bill in the original Constitution. He argued (No. 84 of *The Federalist*) that the Constitution contained adequate safeguards for personal liberty, including assurance of the writ of habeas corpus, and recalled that Blackstone called the Habeas Corpus Act "the *bulwark* of the British Constitution."

46. There are references to the right to work and to education in the writings of Turgot and Robespierre, and the French Declaration of the Rights of Man and the Citizen makes references to certain rights to work.

47. See, for example, a recent biography of James Murray (Elizabeth K. M. Murray, *Caught in the Web of Words, James A. H. Murray and the Oxford English Dictionary*, Yale University Press, New Haven and London, 1977, p. 339), to the effect that Murray's life is a reminder that equality of opportunity, which the twentieth century claims as its gift to the next generation, existed in a different form in the nineteenth century in which men, however handicapped by the circumstances of birth, could educate themselves and rise high.

48. As cited in Eugene Perry Link, *Democratic-Republican Societies, 1790-1800*, p. 109.

49. *Ibid.*

50. James D. Richardson, *A Compilation of the Messages and Papers of the Presidents, 1789-1908*, publ. by the Bureau of National Literature and Art, 1909, vol. I, p. 408.

51. See Adda B. Bozeman, "International Law," Alexander DeConde, ed., *Encyclopedia of American Foreign Policy: Studies of the Principal Movements and Ideas*, 3 vols., New York, 1978, vol. II, pp. 455-472, for a discussion of the law of nations in the conduct of American foreign policy.

Felix Gilbert, *To the Farewell Address: Ideas of Early American Foreign Policy*, Princeton, 1961, for further comments on the issues here discussed.

52. Richardson, *op. cit.*, vol. II, p. 194 for the Sixth Message; pp. 217 ff. for relevant parts of the Seventh Message.

53. *Ibid.*, vol. II, p. 295. "The experiment" here alluded to refers to "our condition under a Constitution founded upon the republican principle of equal rights."

54. *Ibid.*, vol. II, p. 334.

55. *Ibid.*, vol. II, p. 554. With regard to Indians in Ohio, the message notes that "the time is not distant, it is hoped, when Ohio will be no longer embarrassed with the Indian population. However, it is noteworthy that explicit allowance is made under these policies for 'the reach of philanthropic aid and Christian instruction' in Indian communities that were to be removed, this in the hope that such assistance would

help American Indians to advance unmolested from barbarism to the habits and enjoyments of civilized life."

56. *Ibid.,* vol. VII, p. 31.

57. *Ibid.,* vol. VI, pp. 435 ff., for these parts of the First Annual Message (1893).

58. *Ibid.,* vol. IX, pp. 529 ff., for these excerpts from the Second Annual message, Dec. 3, 1894.

59. *Ibid.,* vol. VI, p. 440 (from the First Annual Message, 1893).

60. *Ibid.,* vol. IX, p. 557, for a message to the Senate, December 11, 1894, on the subject of the Armenian atrocities.

61. *Ibid.,* vol. IX, p. 531.

62. For this periodization see Richard E. Welch, Jr., "Revolution and Foreign Policy," *Encyclopedia of American Foreign Policy,* vol. III, p. 914.

63. Cp. *supra* p. 82. See Vernon Van Dyke, *Human Rights, The United States, and World Community,* New York, 1970, pp. 77 ff., and Gastil, ed., *op. cit.,* pp. 180-215, for extended discussions of "Self-Determination."

64. See Van Dyke, *op. cit.,* pp. 54 ff.

Robert E. Sherwood, *Roosevelt and Hopkins, An Intimate History,* New York, 1948, p. 231, relates some of the circumstances in which Roosevelt conceived of what were to become the "Four Freedoms." Originally they were five—two of them under the heading "Freedom of Speech." But the President had no name in mind for the Third Freedom when Richard L. Harkness of the *Philadelphia Inquirer* suggested it be called "Freedom from Want." After that conference the Freedoms were forgotten until Roosevelt suddenly recalled them to Sherwood and others on New Year's in 1941.

65. Louis J. Halle, "The Fallacy of Daemonic Enmity," *Encounter,* September 1969, pp. 60-62.

66. See *supra* pp. 66-7.

67. Clyde Eagleton, "Excesses of Self Determination," *Foreign Affairs,* vol. 31, no. 4, pp. 592-604.

68. See *supra* p. 80.

69. G. E. Von Grunebaum, *Modern Islam, The Search for Cultural Identity,* Berkeley & Los Angeles, 1962, p. 238.

70. This is not the place for a critical analysis of the American trust in détente or of the government's readiness to ratify the territorial and political status quo in Europe. See Adda B. Bozeman, "Interference or Legitimate International Concern: The Human Factor in U.S.-Soviet Relations," *Proceedings* of the National Security Affairs Conference, National Defense University, Fort McNair, Washington, D.C., 1977. This paper has been reprinted by National Strategy Information Center, Inc. under the title "How to Think about Human Rights," New York, 1978.

71. McGeorge Bundy, "The Americans and the World," *Daedalus,* Winter 1978, vol. 107, no. 1, pp. 289-303.

72. See Patricia M. Derian, Assistant Secretary for Human Rights and Humanitarian Affairs, in an address on "Human Rights: A World Perspective," Department of State, *Current Policy,* no. 42, November 1978.

73. See Jeane Kirkpatrick, "Selective Invocation of Universal Values," in Ernest W. Lefever, ed., *Morality and Foreign Policy: A Symposium on President Carter's Stance,* Georgetown University Press 1977, pp. 23 ff. for important comments.

74. See Bozeman, *loc. cit.* ("How to Think About Human Rights").

75. This and other statements by Andrew Young were collected by Carl Gershman, "The World According to Andrew Young," *Commentary,* August 1978, vol. 66, no. 2, pp. 17 ff.

76. Cp. Ernest W. Lefever, "The Trivialization of Human Rights," *Policy Review,* Winter 1978.

Comment

Alexander DeConde

I would like to comment on Professor Bozeman's paper in general terms, and then make some specific comments on the conclusions she draws. Her paper is extraordinary. The documentation is fantastic, and she ranges over a number of civilizations.

The ideas that I shall dwell upon are not necessarily in conflict with hers, but they are ideas that are different. At least, they represent my approach and perhaps that of a number of historians. I, also, look upon the rights of man as political or legal, as individual rights, or the freedom of individuals from coercion by government entities—that is, that an individual can rest assured that if he goes to bed at night, he has a reasonable chance of awakening in the morning and not being taken away or murdered.

These rights are linked, in my judgment, to guarantees by a government. Historically, they are rights that flow from governments that have been reasonably democratic ones in which the individuals have a say in the kind of government they have. I think this view probably agrees historically with some of the comments that Professor Bozeman made.

She maintained that in the age of the United Nations, self-determination is essentially a group right and that this is different from the concept of self-determination as advanced in the days of Woodrow Wilson; and that the right of self-determination as advanced by Woodrow Wilson had a great deal to do with the individual—with individuation. That may be; but I haven't quite perceived it in that way. I quite agree that the right to self-determination is a political right and that it has been a group right. I have never seen it in Woodrow Wilson's writings or his ideas referred to as a right that belonged to the individual. It is a right that went to the individual within a group. It was a political right for the individuals who belonged to some group that had historic roots.

Dr. Bozeman states further that since most members of the United Nations at the present time are authoritarian, they consider human rights for the individual as negotiable. That may be so, but I see nothing particularly alarming about that. I think that this has always been the case. Let me illustrate.

She points out that in Africa and Asia, obdurate political and cultural traditions do not favor individual liberties as she has described them and as I have delineated them. In recent years, freedom for the individual has contracted appreciably throughout the world. In effect I think that this was the message of her conclusion. The autonomous individual, if I can quote her, is being stamped out of existence. I dissent from this view. As far as I am able to ascertain, never in literate history have so many people experienced so much freedom and so much well-being as at the present time. Now, that doesn't mean that the situation is a good one; but civil liberty or human rights or individual rights or civil rights as we know them have been a rarity in the world, just as democracy and self-government have been rarities in the world. I like the analogy of one grain of sand in a bucket of sand. That's how many people in the whole history of humanity may have enjoyed freedom and individual liberty as we know it and as we talk about it. Consequently, I don't think it's alarming to look about in the world and see that individual rights and freedom of the individual are scarce things.

In Western Europe there is more democracy today than there has ever been in its entire history. More individuals are freer than ever before. Two of the countries that were remarkable for rigid totalitarian regimes in the 1930s now are reasonably successful democracies. Even in Italy, the assassination of a Prime Minister did not lead to a repressive totalitarian regime. Japan, a former enemy country, is reasonably democratic. In South America the experience is not a good one, but there are a few democratic countries such as Venezuela. Even in the Middle East we have the beginnings of the seeds of democracy in Israel, an area that has never experienced this kind of democracy or this kind of freedom for an individual. So I can't quite share the pessimism of Professor Bozeman on this score.

There are a few other observations I would like to make. Dr. Bozeman states that our nation's avowal of the rights of man is shaky and confused. I wouldn't question that, nor that they are not taken very seriously abroad and are not based on a correct estimate of moral or legal and political realities. I think, however, that the example of the United States in recent years has been an important one throughout the world. In Indonesia, for example, things have improved even though there is a military dictatorship there. At least the military dictatorship did not exterminate the opposition. They are living in exile, they can speak, and they can attend lectures by professors, which is something they couldn't do previously. Some of the old revolutionaries there told me how they were impressed, though their cultural traditions are far different from ours, with our Constitution and with the matter of civil liberties. Though they don't have them, they have been important in the world. These concepts are not confusing; they're difficult to grasp but they mean something to intelligent people. The United States has provided the example that has given human rights a concrete meaning.

Professor Bozeman commented in her paper that the foreign policy of the United States has not been influenced by human rights in any appreciable way. She comes to this conclusion by having looked through the messages of presidents; she looked at the past. Accepting this view depends upon one's perspective. Perhaps it depends also upon definition, but there have been a number of instances in which the dominating motive among the elite that made foreign policy was a concern for what we call civil liberties. In 1820, at the time of the Greek revolution against the Ottoman Empire, there were many in government who wanted to intervene on the side of the Greeks because they were fighting against a restrictive and repressive regime. Though it was not a question of civil rights in precisely the terms that we are using now, this was in the minds of a number of individuals. Again, in the Latin American revolutions against a repressive Bourbon monarchy of Spain, many North Americans thought in terms of what we call individual liberties when they considered the revolution in South America. In the European revolutions of 1848, many Americans were overwhelmed with grief because of what happened when these revolutions were defeated. A Hungarian man by the name of Lajos Kossuth came to the United States in 1850 and was greeted as a great hero. We also gave refuge to a great leader of revolution against a repressive Austrian nation—Garibaldi from Italy—and a number of others that came to this country. It's true that the civil rights and the human rights that we talk about now are not precisely the kind of rights that were talked about in the middle of the nineteenth century but nonetheless, there is a close relationship between the two.

I will conclude with just two more major points. Professor Bozeman says in her paper that today Black rights, Chicano rights and other group rights are those that really matter. She seems to deplore this, that ethnic minorities act as groups in ways that are, in a sense, almost a denial of individual rights. At another point she says the individualism and the philosophy of basic individual rights at one time met with strong support in what we would call the American intellectual establishment, that is, in academia, the media, the churches, the professions and so forth. I would dissent from some of this. First of all, I question the basic idea that in this country, the dedication of the founding fathers and others was to a universal concern for human rights. Those who ruled this country were an elite, a small group that ruled in terms that would benefit their group more than any other group. In other words, the individual rights for which they were concerned were rights that would benefit them personally. The white Anglo-Saxon Protestant minority rigged the rules of universal rights for white Anglo-Saxon Protestants. Now, it seems that is precisely what many of the ethnic minorities are attempting to achieve. What they are saying is that they want what has always been a part of American culture. They just want a chance to achieve some of the freedom, some of the rights that have been denied to them. Without this recognition of the intrinsic worth of the group, then no ethnic individual can have true individual freedom.

Comment

Ernest W. Lefever

Let me quote a statement from Irving Kristol: "The leverage of ideas is so immense that a slight change in the intellectual climate can and will, perhaps slowly but nevertheless inexorably, twist a familiar institution into an unrecognizable shape."

The theme of my comments on Professor Bozeman's singularly excellent paper is the trivialization of human rights, and a sub-theme is the debasement of the English language. These comments are made by one who is both an academic and a concerned citizen, and my remarks, therefore, are more an elaboration of her thought and some of the thinking of Barbara Jordan and Kenneth Thompson, than a critique. I am also not so much an academic as I am an observer. Many of my remarks will relate to the Third World. I have visited sixty-five countries in the Third World, many of them repeatedly over the last twenty-five years. My views do not come from the ivory walls of academia alone.

We all believe in the quest for human freedom and dignity. It is so important, so essential that it should not be trivialized by loose language and confused concepts. Hence, one has the temerity to criticize aspects of the current crusade to advance human rights in other people's countries. We are all for human rights. The question is, what agency produces human rights? I see three problems attending President Carter's posture, which tends to make the human rights stand central in foreign policy decisions. I think this is a singularly confusing guideline for responsible statecraft. This sounds pessimistic, but there is an upbeat note at the end.

The first problem is that an over-emphasis on human rights tends to subordinate, blur, or distort all other relevant considerations in foreign policy, the central ones of which are national security, territorial integrity, the protection of allies, the avoidance of nuclear war, and so on. So, as in the domestic field, when an environmental consideration is allowed to take precedence over all other considerations of cost and benefit, the policy-making process is distorted.

The second problem in the human rights crusade (not implying that the President participates in all these problems or limitations) is a profound legal, political and moral confusion between domestic and foreign policy. Legally, the principles of sovereignty, of the multi-state system, of non-interference in the domestic affairs of other states must prevail, or the system will break down. Politically, the primary purpose of foreign policy and democracy is peace and stability—a world safe for diversity. Conversely, the primary purpose of domestic policy is justice and freedom. When we imagine or pretend to imagine that we can do other people's freedom and other people's justice for them, we are deceiving ourselves. Morally, we do not have a mandate from God or from history to impose our values or institutions on other peoples. It may be possible to export revolution, as the phrase goes, but it is not possible to export justice or respect for the human person. These are things that must grow organically from the history and tradition and religion of the peoples involved.

As Professor Bozeman alluded to, there are two streams in the American experience with respect to our obligation to the external world. Barbara Jordan also reminded us of one stream and that is the great example; America is a shining example of what freedom can do to peoples. Let other people, if they will, if they have the discipline, emulate our example. There is also the messianic and crusading stream that we saw at the turn of the century, which has serious moral and political pitfalls. It is well to remember that the present occupant of the White House is a neo-Wilsonian, a guilt-ridden Southerner, and a born-again Baptist, and this says a mouthful.

The third problem with the over-emphasis on the human rights question as an instrument of foreign policy and as an instrument of reform is selective application. It leads to reform and intervention that is morally and politically unjustifiable in most cases. Some idealogues, and I do not put Carter in that category, use the human rights standard as the cloak for attacking some of our allies who are under most profound siege from communist states, notably South Korea, Taiwan and Iran. Some zealots focus on the small sins of our allies and overlook the massive sins of our adversaries. Let me give you three concrete examples of this moral confusion. Between authoritarianism and totalitarianism, there is a profound confusion, one of the most serious confusions in the Western mind. One of these examples comes from government, another from the World Council of Churches, and the third one from the mass media of communication.

First, Carter's insistence that the so-called patriotic front, a group of terrorists, trained and led by Cubans and armed by the Soviet Union, be accorded legitimacy by participation in the internal settlement of Rhodesia is a case in point. The political effect of this policy, spearheaded by Andrew Young for a mixture of reasons that are worth discussing, is support of Marxist terrorists against a group of people—black and white—who insist on a peaceful inter-racial, democratic process that will lead to a majority government in a democratic Rhodesia that guarantees rights to all minorities. This is the first and only opportunity so far in history for a democratic inter-racial government on the entire continent of Africa. Carter is torpedoing this opportunity. This destructive policy is almost beyond belief. The motives behind American policy in Rhodesia do not all fall in the "noble" category. This can be confirmed by anyone with extensive acquaintance with Rhodesia and its affairs.

The second example of moral confusion comes from the World Council of Churches. Here I speak as an ordained clergyman with two theological degrees from Yale, a person present at the founding meeting of the World Council of Churches in Amsterdam in 1948 and who served on the executive staff of the National Council of Churches for three years; an insider in the ecumenical movement who believes the church should speak to the world.

A few months back, when it was announced that the World Council of Churches gave $85,000 to the Communist guerrillas who are trying to prevent a peaceful and democratic and inter-racial settlement in Rhodesia, I telephoned Cynthia Waddell, one of the six presidents of the World Council of Churches, and asked her whether this went through the normal procedures—the Central Committee and the other procedures. Yes, it went through all the normal procedures. In fact the contribution of $85,000 was under consideration for two years. They sent people to the field, they were very sure they wanted to send it to the so-called patriotic front. I said, what was the purpose of this large gift? She said it was humanitarian, for refugees. I said, which refugees did you have in mind? She was very vague on that question. I said, there are refugees on both sides of the border and many of the refugees are caused by the very people you are supporting—kidnapped children from missionary schools, and so on. Then I mentioned the fungibility of resources; I said, if you give $85,000 for food and humanitarian relief, that releases equivalent resources for guns and so forth. She acknowledged that point. But, I said, if you are interested in humanitarian aid, why didn't you go to the International Red Cross? It is known for non-political humanitarian aid. She said the guerrillas would not have liked that; the guerrillas want us to have confidence in them and if we don't show this confidence, how could they respect us? At that point, in a friendly way, the conversation terminated. And it occurred to me before and since that the World Council of Churches, under its committee to combat racism, is not giving this aid for humanitarian reasons but for "just-war" reasons. The World Council of Churches has decided that the patriotic front is the just cause and the inter-racial, internal solution in an unjust cause. They should have the courage to say this rather than pretend that it's humanitarian.

A final example then, and I will conclude, is the media. Cambodia: I got excited about the genocide in Cambodia rather early because I don't like genocide. I think the fall of a sparrow is noted by God, and the fall of any human being is a matter of concern to me as a human being. What United States foreign policy does is a different question. Having read the book by John Barron on *Murder in a Gentle Land,* and then having gone to see John Barron and investigated his methods, listened to his tapes, checked out his data, I was convinced of his conclusion that this was the greatest genocide of the century. I wondered why the press, and particularly why network TV, did not pay much attention to it. So I examined the evening news programs on the three networks for the first twenty months of the Communist regime in Cambodia and came out with the startling fact that the Cambodian bloodbath received exactly sixty seconds of attention per month during that period, with all three networks combined. Since most people only look at one evening news program, they got twenty seconds per month on the most massive genocide of our century.

I sent my conclusions in an article to *TV Guide.* The editors returned the article and said, you are very hard on TV. I said, that's right. They said, we will consider printing your article if you say what the print media did. I went over the print media; the print media had done a little bit better and the article was printed. Now, this was eighteen months ago. Long before Jimmy Carter ever heard of Cambodia, I was reminding him and other people of the bloodbath. The real question is, why did the media ignore this? The media, part of the intellectual group in the United States, the custodians of rectitude, self-appointed custodians of rectitude, who want to tell goverments what to do and people what to think, ignored this story despite the evidence. But the *Wall Street Journal* in an editorial put the finger on the willingness of the press to ignore this story, when it said that the normal custodians of rectitude justify massive violence when it is done in the name of revolution.

There are three things the United States government and the people of the United States can do to advance the cause of human rights around the world. The first and most important thing the United States can do is to serve as an example. The second important thing the United States can do is to stick by its allies who are under siege from the totalitarians, in order to keep the shrinking islands of democracy from shrinking even further. That means we must stick by Iran, we must stick by Taiwan, we must stick by South Korea. Finally, the United States can avail itself of the traditional forms of quiet diplomacy to seek to have issues of human rights treated in a serious and effective way.

Tensions Between Human Rights and National Sovereign Rights

by Kenneth W. Thompson

The tension between human rights and national sovereign rights appears at one level to be the classic tension existent in all politics between general and particular or universal and national goals. The Universal Declaration of Human Rights proclaims the rights of mankind; the Bill of Rights declares that individual Americans under the Constitution enjoy certain inalienable rights. The observer striving to relate mankind's human rights and the rights of Americans or Russians or Nigerians may apply the concepts Crane Brinton employed when he wrote of the one and the many, the worldwide in contrast with particular local or regionally defined groups. Between the one and the many or the universal and the particular, tension almost inescapably will exist if only because full attainment of universality by definition means the undermining of what is separate, unique and particular. Philosophically, universalism and particularism are in tension in any given political order

what of the universal rights to be particular?

113

especially with reference to the exercise of sovereign authority within that order.

Reason of State

On the issue of political authority in another era, the debate over what the French call *raison d'état* or "reason of state" illustrates the tension between the general and the particular. Sir Herbert Butterfield, former Vice Chancellor of Cambridge University and founding Chairman of the British Committee on the Theory of International Relations, has discussed this concept in the first Martin Wight Memorial Lecture delivered in the University of Sussex on April 23, 1975. Using the subtitle "The Relations Between Morality and Government," Butterfield points out that the idea of reason of state has become almost a fossil or an archaism in the twentieth century. Yet in the early seventeenth century, it found its way into discussions in the market-place. Cardinal Richelieu in his *Political Testament* spoke of reason "as the rule of conduct for a state." Different writers spoke of "natural reason" or "civil reasoning" as appropriate not alone to politics and government but, as variously interpreted, the fundamental principle of governance for the state.

The concept of the state, Butterfield observes, goes back to the Latin "status," meaning in the ancient world something approaching "condition" or "standing." Professor F. M. Powicke in his presidential address appearing in "Transactions of the Royal Historical Society," 4th series, vol. XIX, p. 9, interpreted the classical Latin term as "that which gives validity to a thing." The Italian equivalent, "stato," we are told, occurs more than a hundred times in Machiavelli's *Prince* without carrying the ethical implications of the Greek *polis* or the Latin *republica*.

From 1600, the idea of the state was to expand in its meaning beyond the concept of "a power apparatus" associated with Machiavelli. Ambiguity and inconsistency surrounded the term, however, which sometimes referred only to the art of government and other times referred to the founding, maintenance and expansion of the state. At times, "reason of state" meant statecraft and at other times it appeared to be used to override ordinary reason. Certain Catholic writers distinguished between "good" reason of state but others used the idea to convey "the logic of state interests." Some publicists saw the concept as a universal one while others suggested that every one of the different kinds of states had its own version of *raison d'état*. Richelieu not only argued that this principle was the ruling force undergirding all state activity but introduced a religious view of the nature and purpose of the state.

At the end of the sixteenth century, the teachings of Machiavelli had gained a hold on statesmen and writers, and for many of them politics was associated with power politics, however offensive this idea may have been then and now. The idea of necessity was also imported into discussions of politics justifying the right and duty of the king and his associates to override positive law in the service of well-recognized common interests. For the prince or the man conspiring to be the prince, certain harsh maxims are introduced by Machiavelli not as maxims of righteous conduct but as rules to be followed by the ruler if he wished to be successful in politics.

The concept of "reason of state" achieved a more complete expression in seventeenth century France, particularly in the writings and actions of Richelieu and Louis XIV. France in 1600 suffered from the fragmentation of political authority. "Authority had been splintered into a jig-saw puzzle of local autonomies, special privileged areas, all of which were the characteristics of the *ancien régime* and had been vastly increased during recent decades of civil war. Across the entire map there was a vast thick forest of prescriptive rights—peculiar prerogatives attached now to certain individuals, now to certain towns, now to certain landed property, now to certain public offices, now to social groups, now to institutions. Confronted by this host of privileges and immunities the central government during the course of centuries would hardly be able to hold its own, until, from 1789, the remnants of them became the main target of the French Revolution." (Sir Herbert Butterfield, *Raison d'État*, University of Sussex, 1975, p. 13.)

Against this state of affairs, Richelieu argued that the subjects of the regime, including princes of the royal family who might rebel, must be made subordinate to the public power. Government officials, privileged corporations of town and countryside and even the king were subordinate to the idea of state. In foreign policy too, especially in the eighteenth century, the monarch was guided by the interests of state, the general welfare and public safety, rather than by the primacy of dynastic ambitions or family objectives. It is said that Richelieu's major purpose was state-building and Meinecke observed that without the commanding force of the idea of state, millions of overmighty subjects would have become centers of self-regarding authority. Political unification rested on the idea of the state and, with all the controversy, human suffering and threats to divine law or natural morality which most writers agreed ought not to be overridden, the main task of statesmanship was to create and preserve viable political units. The powers of the state were those that were essential in the last resort expanded to assure survival especially in emergencies but also intended to serve the general welfare and the broad interests of the body politics.

Imbedded in Richelieu's *Political Testament* were guides to the political relations among states such as the idea of continuous negotiations even when countries go to war. And although he held that the individual Christian should forgive the person who injured him, he held that failure to punish attacks on the body politic represented the most fatal kind of weakness in government. He reproached Louis XIII for failure to put down conspiracies and rebellions and quoted Christian theologians to justify the punishment of threats to and offences against the state. Governments must act while they still have the capacity to act and their actions must be prompt and decisive. Preventive imprisonment may in some cases be a more humane alternative than execution. The underlying justification for stern acts by the state depends on the idea of "reason of state" equated with the common good or public safety.

The idea of *raison d'état* has a quaint if not archaic meaning in the twentieth century and yet it remains as the historical antecedent of present day political discussions. One starting point in the discussion of the tension between universal human rights and national sovereignty is a recognition that the sovereign nation state has evolved to serve broader interests. It is fashionable to write of the obsolescence of the nation state which for the industrial or developed countries no longer is sufficient to assure either national security or the general social and economic welfare. Yet the situation in the developing countries remains not wholly dissimilar from that described in *Political Testament*. Tribal loyalties, separatist groups and local power centers threaten political unification; fragmentary loyalties and interests are more likely to be transcended by the nation than by worldwide authorities. The highest form of unity for the non-industrial world may well be national unity. Nor are the risks of political devolution confined to the developing world, as evidenced in Canada, Ireland and even the United Kingdom. The Soviet Union is opposed to expanded rights for minorities, and in particular the Jews, because the independence of any one group is viewed as a threat to the survival of the present political regime.

Viewed in the context of the totality of European history and the idea of "reason of state," human rights inescapably are seen not as universal moral principles leading to the good life but as political principles which are in tension with an evolving political order. To assert this is not to dismiss the validity of the pursuit of human rights nor to argue that the lives of millions of people around the world quite possibly would be vastly improved through institutionalizing human rights. It is rather to place in context a discussion worthy of the most dedicated thought and reflection.

However fossilized such ancient concepts as "reason of state" may appear, modern man continues to live in a world of sovereign states. The international community is half-organized and, in the words of one observer, semi-anarchic. The nation state for at least half of the world may have outlived its usefulness, but no wholly viable form of political organization has taken its place. To recognize this as a political reality for all aspects of war and peace except human rights is to do mankind a disservice and plant seeds of disillusionment and despair. For champions and critics alike of the campaign for human rights, the beginning of wisdom is a recognition that tensions exist between human rights and national sovereignty.

The Ubiquity of Moral Choice

A nation, particularly a democratic nation and most particularly the United States, tends to view its actions as taking place within a moral framework. On one hand, it sees itself as subject to certain moral limitations and judgments; on the other, it looks to national goals and historic traditions as the explanation and moral justification for its course of action. Seldom if ever is foreign policy defended by arguing solely for the maintenance or increase of national power or of national survival. Americans and most other people speak rather of standing for moral purposes beyond the state: democracy or communism, freedom or equality, order or justice and historical inevitability. Whatever cynics may say, foreign policy tends to be articulated in moral terms, even in most authoritarian regimes, whether those terms be social justice, economic equality, the overthrow of colonialism, national liberation or putting an end to an unjust status quo.

To know that men and nations espouse goals and ends that transcend national defense or survival is a first step or approach but not a solution to the moral problem. In fact, it is more a claim than an approach; it may bespeak what George F. Kennan and Hans J. Morgenthau have called moralism as distinguished from morality. Moralism is the tendency to make one moral value supreme and to apply it indiscriminately without regard to time and place; morality by comparison is the endless quest for what is right amidst the complexity of competing and sometimes conflicting, sometimes compatible moral ends. Professor Paul Freund of the Harvard Law School based his 1976 Thomas Jefferson Memorial Lecture of the National Endowment for the Humanities on Lord Acton's aphorism, "when you perceive a truth, look for a balancing truth." According to Freund, we suffer in Western civilization from the decline of the ancient art of moral reasoning, the essence of which is weighing and balancing not only good and evil but competing "goods."

Freedom and order, liberty and justice, economic growth and social equality, national interest and the well-being of mankind are all in themselves worthy moral ends. How much simpler moral choice would be if the leader could select one value as his guiding principle and look upon the rest as secondary or instrumental.

In every human community, however, the choice between right and wrong is endlessly fraught with complexity and grounded in deep moral pathos. There is an inescapably tragic character to moral choice. Within the family, men all too often may be driven to choose between family interests and professional responsibilities. Loyalty to spouse and children may conflict with caring for the needs of aging parents. Within the nation, freedom of speech and assembly may clash with the requirements of security and order. The Supreme Court has declared that freedom of speech does not involve the right to cry fire in a crowded theatre. The right to a fair trial may collide with the right to know and the freedom of the press. Freedom of scientific inquiry apparently does not justify the right of a graduate student to produce a nuclear bomb in his kitchen. Even within the most developed democracy every political and constitutional principle coexists and is related to every other principle, and each is at most a partial expression of morality; for as Reinhold Niebuhr wrote:

> Democracy cannot exist if there is no recognition of the fragmentary character of all systems of values which are allowed to exist within its frame.

Within the family and the democratic nation, however, forces are at work to protect fragmentary values and interests, to hold moral absolutism in check and to prevent men from erecting a single principle into an all-controlling moral dogma. The rights of individuals are weighed against the rights of the group. Society has long-established procedures and institutions through which claims and counter-claims are weighed and adjudicated. A vast panoply of political and constitutional rights and instruments of social legislation is invoked to prevent abuses that threaten the weakest elements of society, including minorities and the powerless, little children, the infirm and the aged. The law of love which lies beyond the reach of large collectivities (neither political parties, nor corporations, nor organized churches love one another) is at least theoretically a practical possibility within the family. Even within the family, however, some form of distributive justice may prove to be man's highest moral attainment, as even the loving husband and wife or parents and children can attest. Justice within the family involves giving each party its due and often this is as much a matter of calculating needs and interests as of unselfish love.

Within the nation, the Bill of Rights and the American Constitutional system provide a means of mediating justice for individuals and groups, minorities and majorities, the weak and the strong. As love is mediated through justice in the family, the "Higher Law" principles on which the Constitution is based support the unending quest for rights within America society. The health of democracy rests finally on the possibility of minorities becoming majorities, on some approximation of justice and on a common sense recognition that no single value or principle is a final guide to moral rectitude. In Niebuhr's words:

> The triumph of common sense is . . . primarily the wisdom of democracy itself which prevents [anyone's] strategy from being carried through to its logical conclusion. There is an element of truth in each position which becomes falsehood precisely when it is carried through too consistently.

Three Perspectives on World Politics and the Emerging Community of Nations

The moral problem as exemplified within the family and within democratic nations is more readily comprehended and understood than for the fragile and embryonic community of nations. More than one hundred fifty nations make up international society, each with its own political and economic system, institutions and practices, needs and traditions. Each has its own requirements of governance, its necessities of state and its own rights and restraints inherent in its political order. For manifold reasons, the moral problem for politics among nation states is more complex than for families and democracies. The first duty of a national statesman is preservation of the union—a requirement that both limits his actions and directs some of them along lines that are offensive to ideas of personal morality. President Lincoln pointed out in his letter to Horace Greeley that "My primary purpose is to save the Union." If this meant freeing all the slaves he would do so or none of the slaves he would do so or freeing some but not others he would do so. His choice from the standpoint of national morality was not necessarily the choice he would have made from the standpoint of personal morality. Nor could he assure national unity without paying homage to domestic political realities. Louis Halle has written:

Lincoln, in his Emancipation Proclamation, excluded the slaves in certain states because he needed the support of the congressmen from those states. This exclusion, although morally reprehensible in itself, made possible the eventual emancipation of all the slaves. I hold that the moralists who denounced him for this immoral act of expediency were wrong.

The demands of statecraft have sometimes been more severe than Lincoln's choice, prompting the words of the Italian nationalist, Cavour: "If we had done for ourselves what we did for the state, what scoundrels we would be." Or of the classical definition of the diplomat as "a man sent abroad to lie and deceive in the interests of the state," amended by the late Harold Nicolson who wrote: "Yes, but he must also return to negotiate another day." We are reminded of Niebuhr's *Moral Man and Immoral Society.*

THE TRADITIONAL DIPLOMATIC PERSPECTIVE

The crux of the matter, as viewed by most students of diplomacy, is that foreign policy is conducted by governments, as a function of their governmental responsibility; it must serve the purposes of governments generally; "its primary purpose must be to preserve the union" (Lincoln) informed by the national interest and the dictates of national security. On this point, members of a well-known group of American authorities and writers on diplomacy differ in emphasis while agreeing in their conclusions.

One champion of political realism, Hans J. Morgenthau, argues that the conduct of foreign policy is not devoid of moral significance. Political actors come under moral judgment and witness to the values of their societies. However, the contemporary environment of international politics is marked both by moral improvement and decline. There have been advances in respect for human life since the fifteenth and sixteenth centuries when, for example, the Republic of Venice carried on its rolls an official poisoner whose employment depended on his success in disposing of the leaders of adversary states. Compare this with the sweeping moral indignation of Winston S. Churchill when Stalin at Teheran proposed half mockingly but not wholly in jest that 50,000 German leaders be summarily shot to put an end to the threat of German aggression. Or contrast it with the force of public reaction in the United States to disclosures concerning possible plans for political assassinations by the CIA.

In other sectors, however, the international scene witnesses to the decline of international morality, indicating that moral restraints are weakening if not disappearing, as in distinctions in wartime between combatants and non-combatants. According to the Hague Conventions of 1899 and 1907, only soldiers ready to fight were considered combatants and objects of war, but by World II this distinction had effectively been obliterated in the saturation bombings in which both sides engaged. The international environment, therefore, was marked by a decline in international morality brought about in part by the technology of warfare and in part by a diminution of standards concerning the sanctity of human life.

Thus in war and peace the world has seen moral improvement in some spheres, but a decline in others resulting from the fact that universal moral principles which are omnipresent are filtered through circumstances of time and place and through national concepts determining their application. In peace, there remains an enormous gap between, say, the elemental American principle of respect for human life (our refusal to take human life except in extraordinary circumstances—capital punishment, abortion, euthanasia and other carefully defined and delimited exceptions) and the much less strict commitments in some other civilizations which have been far more extravagant in taking human life for political, ideological and governance purposes (Stalin and the Kulaks, Hitler and the Jews and the punishment of thieves in Saudi Arabia by cutting off their hands). The relations of universal principles to time and circumstances and to the culture and necessities of different nations and contemporary civilizations have been controlling. Particular moral imperatives are obeyed by particular nations at particular times and not by others, and this is the overarching characteristic of today's international environment.

George F. Kennan, the brilliant American diplomatist and writer goes further than Professor Morgenthau in writing:

> The governing of human beings is not a moral exercise. It is a practical function made necessary, regrettably, by the need for order in social

relationships and for a collective discipline to control the behavior of
that large majority of mankind who are too weak and selfish to control
their own behavior usefully on the basis of individual judgment and
conscience.

Ambassador Kennan declares further that "government, particularly democratic government, is an agent and not a principal." No
more than any other agent (for example, the corporation or the
church, especially since the Protestant Reformation) can it substitute
itself for the conscience of the principal. In a particularly strongly
worded statement applying this thought to the American government as agent of the American people, Mr. Kennan asserts:

> The government could undertake to express and to implement the
> moral impulses of so great a mass of people only if there were a high
> degree of consensus among them on such questions as: what is good
> and what is bad? and to what extent is it the duty of American society
> to make moral judgments on behalf of others and to improve them
> from the standpoint of those judgments? Such consensus would be
> difficult to achieve even if we were dealing with a highly homogene-
> ous population, with firm and unanimously-accepted concepts of an
> ethical nature as well as of the duties and powers of the state. In the
> case of a polyglot assemblage of people such as our own, it would be
> quite impossible. If our government should set out to pursue moral
> purposes in foreign policy, on what would it base itself? Whose
> outlooks, philosophy, religious concepts would it choose to express?
> Imbedded in our population are hundreds of different traditions,
> beliefs, assumptions and reactions in this field. Are we to assume that
> it, the government, knows that is right and wrong, has imparted this
> knowledge to the people at large, and obtained their mandate to
> proceed to bring about the triumph of what is right, on a worldwide
> scale?

THE LEGAL PERSPECTIVE

Opposed to the views of diplomatic writers is a large and respected body of thought resulting from international law writings.
The former American judge on the International Court of Justice,
Philip Jessup, has singled out five criteria as essential to "an ethical
and therefore a successful foreign policy: sincerity, loyalty, legality,
humanitarianism" and what he has called "proper objectives." By
sincerity he means the same as honesty or an absence of deceit, vital

as he sees it, especially in peacetime. A government suffers from such labels as "Perfidious Albion" which can mean for the future it is not to be trusted. Judge Jessup acknowledges there may be imperatives which lead to deceit of a government's own citizenry, but these must find justification if at all under "proper objectives." Louis Halle who belongs to the first group of diplomatic writers offers a dissenting commentary on this point, saying:

> From 1955 to 1960 . . . the United States regularly sent its U-2 spy planes over the Soviet Union at high altitudes to locate military installations and report on military activities. Presumably, such planes would have been able to detect any preparations for a surprise attack on the United States in time to give warning. . . . A Soviet system of espionage operating inside the United States was alert to detect any preparations for a surprise attack on the Soviet Union. This mutual espionage contributed to the preservation of the peace, because the observations of the spies on either side, showing that the other was not preparing a surprise attack, enabled each to remain calm and restrained. If such observations had not been available, each side might have been the victim of panic—making rumors that would have impelled it to feel that its survival depended on striking before the other was able to realize some rumored intention of doing so itself.

Halle goes on:

> However, in 1960 when an American U-2, illegally violating another country's air space, was shot down in the middle of the Soviet Union, many idealists in the West were shocked to learn that such espionage by the United States had been going on, for they regarded it as both immoral and incompatible with the advancement of the cause of peace.

> Peace is more secure today, and the prospects of arms control are better, to the extent that the Soviet Union and the United States, through their espionage (in which satellites have replaced spy planes), can each be sure of what armaments the other possesses.

There are significant differences between diplomatic analysts and international lawyers, therefore, on truth-telling. The former are more inclined to say that while there is a universal moral code of truth-telling, there are differing social contexts in which it is applied. In personal and national affairs, men operate with an integrated society where lying is seldom necessary. Mayor Daley's creed for Chicago politics was that a politician's last resource is his word and that lying is not good politics ("if you must lie, it is better not to say anything"). International affairs differ, and the difference is one between conditions of civilization and conditions of nature, where because of the half anarchic character of international society "one man is to another as a wolf." However, for the second group of writers, the international lawyers, truth-telling is an aspect of sincerity plus loyalty plus legality. Law's basic norm—*pacta sunt servanda*—is a part not only of our own moral creed but of the Koran and other religious teachings. Pragmatism and morality came together in the Hague and the Geneva Conventions on the treatment of civilians and prisoners evolving from the pragmatic test of reciprocity. Judge Jessup states:

> The principle or rule that a treaty secured by the application of force or threats to the person of the negotiator is void, is an illustration of a moral base for a legal rule. The bombing of Cambodia by the Nixon administration is an example of illegal, immoral and bad policy. The Mayaquez affair is another similar example as it was also deceitful in its alleged justification.

Judge Hardy Dillard, the current American judge on the International Court of Justice goes further. International law, for him, is not a legal straitjacket or an abstract and inflexible set of rules. It can be made to serve the security interests of the United States. Its putative advantages in specific policy choices can be measured against its costs. For him, the U-2 flight was a mistaken act because its alleged advantages were outweighed by its costs. Law has a constitutive function by ordering the bully to do what is right. It is designed not to settle but absorb disputes. Today the world is governed by a network of international treaties. Some 760 fat volumes of UN Treaties, designed to regulate international life, have been registered since World War II by the UN Secretariat. Nations are free to invoke or not this body of law, but it is a factor to be taken into account as a guide to policy decision.

It is fallacious to say law is obligatory and policy voluntary. *Pacta sunt servanda* for Judge Dillard doesn't mean that all treaties have to be observed all the time. The ultimate value of Article 2, Paragraph 4, of the UN Charter on the use or threat of force against the territorial integrity of sovereign states or of international treaties regarding human rights is that certain moral and political positions are now in place, policies have been forged into solemn agreements, and important matters are no longer solely a matter of domestic jurisdiction. To paraphrase Justice Holmes, taking law into account is not a duty but only a necessity; the end products or results of diplomacy can't be ignored. Moralistic finger shaking may prove more an irritant than a solution, but in every policy decision the good of invoking the law must be weighed against its disadvantages. All history is a tension between heritage and heresy; law and policy must mediate conflicting demands for stability and change. Taking a moral stand is different from moralizing about it.

Two Issues That Divide Spokesmen for the Diplomatic and Legal Perspectives

There are two issues between the diplomatic analysts and the international lawyers on matters of morality and foreign policy.

Workability vs. Abstract Principle

Diplomatists put the stress on workability: the objective of foreign policy should be as closely related to the reduction of human suffering and welfare as possible and not the unqualified triumph of abstract principle. Moral appeals to the generality of mankind or the mass of the people too often constitute not morality but Pharisaism.

Whatever the short-run advantages of this approach, it has floundered in the long run because an individual or a nation who claims an achieved morality that others have a duty to follow does so on an assumption of having attained perfection. Manichaeanism is a false religion which sees the world as divided between good guys and bad guys, and this disease has infected American thinking on foreign policy. Since World War I, we have divided the world into peace-loving and aggressor, freedom-loving and communist states,and based foreign policy on such a distinction. The road to Vietnam lies not in the nefarious acts of the "best and the brightest" but upon indiscriminate anti-communist thinking which ignores the test of workability. The almost inevitable result of Manichaeanism is a moral crusade, war or the threat of war, and genocide (it is worth remembering that certain Allied leaders who fought a war against Hitler who exterminated millions of Jews saw the "solution" to the German problem in the extermination, in turn, of thousands of Germans).

Workability is also the test of certain diplomatic historians, notable among them being the cold war historian, Norman Graebner. History suggests that whenever the United States has introduced towering humanitarian objectives as the guide to policy it has often added to rather than diminished human suffering, and subsequently abandoned unworkable policies. In our time, Secretary Dulles' liberation foreign policy, offered by the Republicans as a more dynamic alternative to the postwar policy of containment, inspired Hungarian freedom fighters to revolt only to discover that American national interest and the facts of geography and power precluded American intervention.

For the first thirty years of our history, the guiding principle was that the new nation by its moral and political example offered a beacon light for the rest of the world. Spokesmen for two approaches contended with one another. Benjamin Franklin exemplified one approach when he wrote: "Establishing the liberties of America will not only make the people happy, but will have some effect in diminishing the misery of those who, in other parts of the world, groan under despotism." Thereafter every major European revolution against monarchy and aristocracy evoked popular demands that the United States underwrite its cause and thereby that of humanity.

Graebner observes, however, that "never were the repeated references to the American mission in the nineteenth century the actual determinants of policy." These demands collided with an even stronger American tradition that the nation concern itself with those finite goals that served the national interest. Alexander Hamilton warned in his "Pacificus" and "Americanus" letters that the only sure guide was the national interest. George Washington resisted the popular mass movement led by Citizen Genet for intervention on the side of the French Revolution on grounds that "no nation is to be trusted further than it is bound by its interest; and no prudent statesman or politician will venture to depart from it." Even American idealists such as Thomas Jefferson, James Madison, Henry Clay, and Abraham Lincoln, especially when they were responsible for decision-making, were less concerned with American involvement in revolutions abroad than in building a good society and preserving national security.

When President James K. Polk in 1845 sought to universalize the American interest in the Western Hemisphere under the Monroe Doctrine, John C. Calhoun argued in the Senate that the ends of policy had to be calculated by the means available. It was, he maintained,

> the part of wisdom to select wise ends in a wise manner. No wise man, with a full understanding of the subject, could pledge himself, by declaration, to do that which was beyond the power of execution, and without mature reflection as to the consequences. There would be no dignity in it. True dignity consists in making no declaration which we are not prepared to maintain. If we make the declaration, we ought to be prepared to carry it into effect against all opposition.

Professor Graebner argues that a shift in the American approach to foreign policy occurred with President Woodrow Wilson, foreshadowed by President William McKinley's defense of the Spanish-American War and the acquisition of the Philippines based on sentiment rather than clearly defined national interests. "None of the nineteenth century revolutions in Europe or Asia succeeded or failed because of what the United States did or did not do. They reflected the worldwide trend toward self-determination and democratic forms of government, supported by American model, nothing more."

With Wilson, idealism and sometimes moralism replaced political realism as the cornerstone of a new world order. Maintenance of the status quo was identified with universal democracy and the Versailles peace structure; Americans linked that status quo with the abstract moral and legal principles of the League of Nations rather than a body of clearly defined interests to be defended through diplomacy and war. The goals of a universal moral order were in tension with the policies of nations who could not see their interests as served by strict observance of that order. The Japanese and the Germans turned to war in part because their leaders were able to rally their publics against the real and imagined injustice of the status quo, and in part because the principles of peaceful change did not satisfy the interests of all nations equally (the British, French, Belgian, Dutch and even American empires were left untouched by the peace settlement, but not those of Germany, Austria and Japan).

Professor Graebner writes: "In its relations with Japan the United States sought peace. But its proposals [fueled by the moral indignation of leaders such as Cordell Hull], based on the assumption that the right belonged totally to the status quo, sought not compromise but capitulation. The capitulation never came." History repeated itself in some respects following World War II. American efforts to apply the doctrine of self-determination failed to undo specific repressions which existed behind the Iron and Bamboo Curtains. Graebner concludes:

> The Wilsonian appeal . . . could not prevent the destruction of the Versailles order; the postwar appeal to the Atlantic Charter could not restore it. . . . What the American experience, in many ways unique, has demonstrated is the fact that policy goals unsupported by generally recognizable interests will not receive much credence elsewhere.

There is no dignity in goals a nation is not prepared to carry into effect measured by all possible consequences.

The international law school's response to the diplomatists' critique is to question whether words and solemn commitments do not have an effect of their own. Important ideas enshrined in the American Declaration of Independence have been written into solemn international treaties; for example, the Declaration and Covenants of Human Rights. (The diplomatists asked whether failure to ratify the Covenants gave America a strong platform from which to speak.) Words and ideas have consequences, and the evidence there is something universal about human rights and fundamental freedoms is attested in the vocabulary even of the communist and totalitarian states. (Niebuhr once wrote that "hypocrisy is the tribute that vice pays to virtue.") A nation acts by speaking out for its values and there are costs in remaining silent. (Judge Dillard introduces the qualification that in international law, protest indicates non-acquiescence, but failure to protest does *not* indicate acquiescence.)

Policy-makers ask if it is not legitimate to include in the national interest principles intended to arouse public support and interest in foreign policy. It could be argued that in recent months the rest of the world had come to believe again in the American vision, testimony to the power of words and ideas. In the days of the founding fathers, the United States was powerless to work its will; now it has become the most powerful nation in the world, its words more surely attended to. (Some see in this fact new responsibilities, whereas others warned against the corruption of power. Perhaps Niebuhr's counsel helps reconcile these differences: "Nations, as individuals, may be assailed by contradictory temptations. They may be tempted to flee the responsibilities of their power or refuse to develop their potentialities. But they may also refuse to recognize the limits of their possibilities and seek greater power than is given to mortals.")

For the international lawyer, the national interest is too narrow a concept. Enforcement is misconceived if keyed exclusively to physical enforcement. (The statement, "The Supreme Court has spoken, now let it enforce its decision," must be weighed against the success of the courts, say, in requiring President Nixon to give up the tapes despite the powers of the President as Commander in Chief.) There is only one example in the fifty-year history of the World Court of a nation refusing to abide by a judgment: Albania in the Corfu Channel case. Judge Lauterpacht wrote that the French Declaration of Human Rights was more powerful than all the battalions of Napoleon. Judge Dillard agreed on the futility of nations proposing things that can't be done effectively and raising false expectations (example, rolling back the Iron Curtain). He quoted Lord Balfour on the need for restraint in making grievances public. However, he insisted it is too narrow an approach to say nations can't do anything unless they can enforce it; there are other forms of pressures. Law may not command but it can affect what nations do in justifying their actions. If moral statements and standards are irrelevant, why do nations bother to justify themselves as measured by those standards? There are signs that even the Russians respond and are sensitive to moral appeals.

Continuity vs. Change in the International System

If the first issue between the diplomatic analysts and historians and the international lawyer is workability, the second is the nature of the international society. The diplomatic school sees the world of American foreign policy as subject to many of the same rules and constraints known at the founding of the republic. To the question posed by the historian Carl Becker at the end of World War II, *How New Will the Better World Be,* they answered it is neither wholly new nor necessarily better. Why? Because of the nature of man, of international politics and the persistence of the nation state system.

Professor Morgenthau states:

> The purpose of foreign policy is not to bring enlightment or happiness to the rest of the world but to take care of the life, liberty and happiness of the American people.

At the same time, Morenthau acknowledges that national interest in contemporary American foreign policy must be defined in terms that transcend nineteenth century concepts of national interest. In a certain sense, all nation states, large and small, are obsolete; they no longer adequately meet human needs within national boundaries. Man's protection of the environment and preservation and distribution of natural resources require the cooperative efforts of communities of sovereign states. Yet, however obsolete the present international system may be, national leaders are still held responsible for the wise conduct of their nation's foreign policy, thus maintaining the requirements of historic international politics until the day when a new international system may come into being.

International lawyers are more inclined to argue the existence of a new and better world, the birth of an embryonic world community. The Charter of the United Nations and the Declaration and some nineteen Covenants of Human Rights are said to embody core principles of human rights and fundamental freedoms foreshadowed in the American Declaration of Independence. To defend human rights abroad, therefore, is not to act in contravention of Article 2, Paragraph 7—the domestic jurisdiction clause of the United Nations. Judge Philip C. Jessup quotes Secretary of State

Elihu Root, writing in 1906 to the American Ambassador in St. Petersburg regarding a protest concerning the persecution of Jews in Russia:

> I think it may do some good, though I do not feel sure of it. I do not know how it will be received. It may merely give offense. I am sure that to go further would do harm. I am sure also that to publish here the fact that such a dispatch has been sent would do harm, and serious harm to the unfortunate people whom we desire to help. Any possible good effect must be looked for in absolutely confidential communication to the Russian Government. The publication that any communication has been made would inevitably tend to prevent the Russian Government from acting, to increase the anti-Jewish feelings and to make further massacres more probable.

But then Judge Jessup adds that the situation today may differ "since human rights have become the subject of international agreements." He concludes: "I favor the present position of President Carter."

A Theological and Cultural Perspective

Innumerable theologians who write and speak on ethics and foreign policy go back to Reinhold Niebuhr.

The Moral Marginalist Perspective: Professor Jerald Brauer observes that when Niebuhr's influence was at its height the danger was moralism, but today it may be cynicism (significantly, Niebuhr warned of them both). June Bingham reminds us that Niebuhr always stressed the tension between idealism and realism and spoke of the margins of idealism. Blue-printing in history is impossible, for both our problems and their solutions are organic, yet leaders have the choice of acting creatively at the margins. While "the field of politics is not helpfully tilled by moralists," and large groups are incapable of love for one another, President Carter on accepting the nomination of his party quoted and added to Niebuhr's words (Carter's addition being in brackets): "Love must be [aggressively] translated into [simple] justice." Niebuhr also held that "justice means giving each man his due," and the operative principles of justice are liberty and equality. Such principles are operative but not controlling.

Nevertheless, the concept of "moral margins" offers at least the rudiments of an alternative framework to those of law and diplomacy. It can help man escape from moral cynicism; it offers the possibility of transcendence. It invites studies of other cultures seeking for points of congruence.

Dr. William Bradley, having searched in vain among the world religious for common moral principles as guides to foreign policy, has introduced the concept of the model statesman. Modern Western systems tend to vest authority in institutions; some non-Western and most ancient ones vest it in their leaders. Their great secular leaders have qualities that exemplify the best in their traditions: the ability to use power without abusing it, to remain humble despite lofty status, to secure and sustain the lives of those under their authority, to practice integrity in all affairs of state, to be even-handed in the administration of justice, to have compassion for the powerless, and to have a sense of personal objectivity. Each civilization and each nation, including some Western ones, has such a model of the great ruler to hold up to those who come to power. Therefore, while we may have no concrete answers as they apply to human rights in authoritarian governments, Bradley asserts:

> Insofar as we are able in good conscience to affirm that we are attemping to live by the model of the exemplary leader which is provided by our religious tradition, we have the right to ask those who govern other nations with whom we have dealings to attempt to live by the comparable model set forth by their tradition.

Bradley concludes:

> Perhaps it is better that we should have such models rather than rule books to guide us in a world so rapidly changing as our own. Perhaps the best we can ask is that those in political authority take seriously their religious heritage and make decisions which accord with the highest standards in their tradition, weighing carefully the consequences of their actions as they intersect with the actions of the leaders of other nations.

However one searches out the "moral margins," it is an idea with its own pitfalls. All too often the moralist finds the margins in ideals that in a given historical period are seized on as simple moral solutions. Especially when the regnant idea of international morality (outlawry of war, world federalism or human rights) corresponds to our own interests and values, we forget Niebuhr's warnings: "We must never deify freedom. It is not God. It is not even an 'absolute virtue.' "

The International Political System

Most of the differences in competing perspectives of world politics result from opposing views of the international political system. Those who adopt the traditional diplomatic perspective see the world as a pluralist system. Not only do nations differ but their differences ought to be preserved. Each has sovereign rights within its territorial boundaries to fashion its own institutions. Each has a cultural tradition, political interests and objectives and its own languages, nationality and history. Even the Charter of the United Nations, the one comprehensive and universal international organization, recognizes this in Article 2, Paragraph 7, which specifies that other nations or organizations are not to intrude on a nation's domestic jurisdiction. The sovereign nation state enjoys impermeability from intervention from without or insurgency or conspiracy from within promoted by an outsie power. The nation state is more than a passing phase in the history of the international system. For all practical purposes, it will continue to be the major operational factor in international politics for the foreseeable future and its independence and autonomy must be respected. No nation nor any international organization is justified in seeking to transform or alter it, and whenever attempts are made they are expressions of moral arrogance.

Adherents to the legal approach question almost all these assumptions of the pluralist world view. They maintain that the international system is in the process of being transformed, and common or worldwide interests are supplanting national ones. The concept of the national interest is too restrictive and needs to be broadened to take account of expanding transnational activities. International treaties such as the Charter of the United Nations and the Declaration of Human Rights have granted legitimacy to worldwide endeavors and concerns. The nation state is no longer capable of fulfilling mankind's urgent demands for security, welfare and self-fulfillment. In consequence, universality not pluralism characterizes the international system and with common objectives nations will more and more move toward a monolithic world order.

According to the proponents of a theological perspective, the world order is both universal and pluralistic; universal because the great world religions all partake of some measure of universality, and pluralistic because the political order is fragmented into a multi-state system in which religion to some degree and political loyalties absolutely are shaped by the sacred and secular loyalties of the ruler and the state. Yet theologians argue that the existence of two orders makes possible living in two realms which the ancient theologians called the City of God and the city of man. When theologians speak of reaching out for policies that may be found at the moral margins, they envisage the policy-maker reaching up on a vertical plane to approximate horizontally in politics values that are found in the moral and theologian realm. When Robert Kennedy in the 1960s urged a group of theologians to continue to bring pressure to bear on the Kennedy administration to transcend the national interest, he was using a theological vocabulary and calling on his critics to press the search for policies at the moral margins.

The Interests and Objectives of States

Whatever may occasionally be possible for enlightened policy-makers, most foreign policies are based on the interests and objectives of nation states. National interest is a product of the historic objectives of states, their geographic and material position regionally and worldwide, and the cooperation of friends and allies whose interests and objectives are convergent. Spokesmen for the national interest are often the objects of criticism from those who impugn their approach as being amoral and cynical, yet crimes against humanity more often have been committed by messianic leaders who engaged in political crusades to change the world in their image. The concept of the national interest has tended to bring restraint and limitations to the conduct of foreign policy.

For example, the interests and objectives of the American republic going back to the founders were limited and well-defined. The purpose of American foreign policy so defined was to provide for the security of the "proven territories" of the republic, expanding by the mid-nineteenth century from the Atlantic to the Pacific and from north to south reaching to the borders of Mexico and Canada. National security to the south was dependent on the prevention of expansion by any major European power into the Western Hemisphere. The twin objectives for American foreign policy, therefore, were a preponderance of power in the Western Hemisphere and a balance of power elsewhere in the world. The threat, if it came, would come from a major outside power, and this meant a European power, given the preponderance of great powers within Europe and the proximity of Europe to the bulge of Brazil in the Southern Hemisphere. Outside the Western Hemisphere, the interest of the United States was to protect American citizens engaged in commercial and educational activities abroad. The calculus of foreign policy then was relatively simple and self-contained; and for the three Virginians (Jefferson, Madison and Monroe) who succeeded in formulating a rational foreign policy expressed in the Monroe Doctrine, the first rule of such a policy was to keep power and commitments in balance. If others outside the Western Hemisphere were to follow American leadership, it was by imitating the example which the United States offered to the rest of the world by the success of its efforts at home. Obscured from the public was the role of the British Navy which, through its control of the Atlantic, safeguarded American shores from imperialist adventurers.

The shift from a limitationist concept of American foreign policy began with President William McKinley, who prayed for divine guidance on the annexation of the Philippines and not unexpectedly received approval for the nation's "manifest destiny"; and President Woodrow Wilson, who combined world leadership with a moralistic crusade for universal democracy. From Wilson to the present, the most urgent task for policy-makers has been to match political rhetoric with deed. Forgotten from time to time has been the axiom that leaders ought not to make declarations they were not prepared to defend. Critics such as Walter Lippmann and Lord Keynes pointed out that European states had specific interests and territorial objectives at the Paris Peace Conference after World War I, but President Wilson spoke only the language of a towering but vague internationalism.

After World War II, the Soviets pursued definite territorial ambitions, but the United States fought the war for unconditional surrender and the creation of a new international organization which was to bring an end to the balance of power and spheres of influence. Hesitantly and belatedly, the United States fashioned a postwar response to the Soviet threat through policies leading to the Marshall Plan, NATO, an Inter-American Security System, and the Truman Doctrine. The latter, despite the pragmatic approach of its principal architect, George F. Kennan, was formulated more as a universal crusade against the spread of communism everywhere in the world and less as a rational foreign policy calculating means and ends. By the 1970s, it became clear as demonstrated in the tragedy that befell the Hungarian freedom fighters, in the Nixon Doctrine, in Baskets 1 and 2 of the Helsinki accord, and decisively in Vietnam, that even so mighty a power as the United States suffered constraints because of its worldwide interests and objectives and the limitations of its national and international power.

The Mutuality of National Interests and a Realistic Morality

If there is one object lesson that emerges from a discussion of ethics and foreign policy it is that an ethical position depends on the responsibilities a man carries and on the traditions from which he speaks. Concepts of right and wrong in international relations are overwhelmingly, though not exclusively, the result of national traditions, loyalties and interests. The nation state is both the problem-child of international relations and the highest *effective* expression of genuine moral consensus.

Morality within the nation, as even more dramatically within the family, can be manageable, convincing and attainable. The parent or child in the family brings moral concerns within an acceptable attention-span and focusses energy, devotion and resources on doing what is right for close family members. In much the same way, the moral content of the national interest tends to be more immediate, measurable and personalized while the international interest is more remote, vague and ill-defined. Moreover, the national interest at its best finds expression in various positive formulations. The interest of a nation's people in basic values and the general welfare may be an antidote to ethnic or sectional particularism and crass materialism. A citizenry that takes its history and tradition seriously assures that its reputation will not perish nor its will to survive be destroyed. The sense of membership and of partnership with ancestors who have gone before and heirs who are to follow gives moral vitality and political stamina to a nation.

In a period of crisis in British politics, Winston S. Churchill counselled his fellow Conservatives: "We are Party men, but we shall be all the stronger if in every action we show ourselves capable, even in this period of stress and provocation, of maintaining the division—where there is division—between national and Party interests." We have Alexis de Tocqueville's statement that "the principle of self-interest rightly understood appears . . . the best suited of all philosophical theories to the wants of the men of our time, and . . . as their chief remaining security against themselves." National interest so understood can guard men against reckless and moralistic crusades, and secure a more tolerable relationship between nations each of whom speaks in its national interest rather than claiming to speak for the whole world.

Thus nations, while defending the moral integrity of their traditions and interests, ought never to see them too exclusively as ends in themselves. World patterns are too complex and variegated for a single state or course of action. The periods of greatest decline in international morality have come when national purposes have been presented as pure and perfect goals for imitation and acceptance by the rest of the world. Nevertheless, there are important areas of foreign policy where national interests must be asserted confidently with courage and pride. Americans sometimes run the risk of alternately feeling shame over the fact that we are a great power with a noble tradition and shrinking back in self-abnegation and dismay when not everyone loves us. American national purposes and policies will be more honored and esteemed if we are somewhat more humble about equating them with final and absolute virtue. They can be justified as necessary and proper steps in world affairs without casting them in the form of crusades and filling the air with the most extravagant claims.

Beyond this, there is something more to foreign policy than solitary national interest. The one thing that saves the national interest from itself is its essential reciprocity. Edmund Burke declared: "Nothing is so fatal to a nation as an extreme of self-partiality, and the total want of consideration of what others will naturally hope or fear." As in all human relationships, to put oneself in another's shoes is the most difficult yet essential task of diplomacy.

It is also true that moral choices are broadly determined by where we stand within the nation and the world. It makes all the difference for men and nations, north or south, whether they are rich or poor, secure or threatened, beneficiaries or victims of the status quo, defenders or critics, ins or outs, moralists or trimmers, private or public ethicists, diplomatists or lawyers, urban or rural people, democrats or communists, absolutists or relativists, liberals or conservatives, ideologues or pragmatists, nationalists or internationalists, reformers or neo-orthodox. There is no single moral framework; and for every participant we need to examine assumptions, responsibilities, and power and their connections, coherence, and inner consistency. In the real world, ethics, politics and foreign policy intermingle and affect one another; and for every moral and political act, the consequences outweigh and override good, bad or ambiguous intentions. "By their fruits ye shall know them" is an ancient but enduring Biblical truth.

Human Rights Policies and the Three Perspectives

Of the three perspectives discussed above, each approaches the promotion of human rights with positions that reflect its assumptions about the international political system and world politics. The moral framework from which the clearest defense of human rights emerges is that of the theologians. For this group, no other policy initiative illustrates more dramatically "acting creatively at the moral margins." Professor Brauer explains that in his head he recognizes the need for prudence in pushing human rights, but in his heart he favors the government's right to act firmly and aggressively. It was necessary to do so, he maintains, for our self-understanding as a people, because concern for racism is worldwide and the risks of remaining silent outweigh those of speaking out. He prefers not to speak of specific human rights (for example, torture) and the source of our obligation to do something as a government, but casts his argument more broadly, grounding it in the universality of respect for the sanctity of human life and the rights of the individual everywhere to self-fulfillment. The risk of cynicism is greater today than that of moralism.

The international lawyers, as we have seen, are more cautious and warn openly of moral finger-shaking. At the same time, they ask (as did Judge Jessup in a minority opinion of the International Court in the South African case) whether human rights are any longer exclusively matters of domestic jurisdiction. Respect for human rights and fundamental freedoms is now written into such international treaties as the Covenants of Human Rights (the Declaration and the Helsinki agreements are not treaties). The jurists agree, however, that whether an international law principle should be invoked is a matter for policy judgment weighing "putative advantages and risks."

The third perspective, that of the diplomatists, leads inevitably to an attitude of caution and reserve on the subject of human rights. George F. Kennan speaks for this group when he writes:

> To my mind liberty is definable only in terms of the restraints which it implies and accepts. And human rights, too, operate only within a system of discipline and restraint. But if you talk about discipline and restraint you are talking about something that enters into the responsibility of government. Do we, then, in undertaking to decide what "rights" should exist in other countries, propose to tell the people and governments of those countries what restraints should also exist? And can one, then, try to tell another country what rights ought to be observed in its society without telling it what sort of government it ought to have?

Respect for domestic jurisdiction is the keystone of the questioning by the diplomatic analysts of the human rights approach. Routine interference in the essential conduct of one government (that is, its definition of rights and duties) by another is a recipe for political disaster in their relationships. There is little support historically for assuming that moral intervention changes institutions and practices elsewhere; sometimes such intervention can make the situation worse. Given national sovereignty, quiet diplomacy and individual contacts are more likely to yield results. Workability is therefore the companion principle to respect for domestic jurisdiction.

Still, diplomatists and students of international politics are not willing to see the people and government of the United States do nothing about human rights. They would have private groups and intellectual and moral leaders speak out; would have us concentrate on being a moral and political example, but not preacher, to others; would urge the government to articulate its beliefs and traditions in broad and general terms (some favored a Gettysburg address by the President as often as it promised to work positive effects); would pick targets of criticism of especially blatant and egregious violations of human rights; would seek ways of orchestrating our views on rights with other essential American goals which at a given moment may be even more important than the human rights campaign (for example, an arms agreement with the Soviet Union); and would urge that any human rights approach be seen as a long run approach toward building consensus and thereby trust for which moral steadiness and political wisdom are more important than a crash program inspired perhaps by moral revulsion to the Kissinger approach and by American domestic politics.

The question that some may ask is, does this not lead to moral cynicism? Professor Morgenthau answers by recounting an experience of President Lincoln. At the time of the Civil War, Lincoln was visited by a group of Presbyterian ministers with a petition on the emancipation of the slaves. Lincoln replied to his petitioners by saying that in every great contest each party claims to act on the will of God. Though God cannot be for *and* against the same thing, yet each believes he is following the divine will. Lincoln went on that if God had revealed his will to others, one would suppose he would have revealed it to him because of his duties and responsibilities. He was anxious to learn the will of God and to follow it but this is not the day of miracles, he said. He explained he could not do otherwise, therefore, in making moral and political choices than "to study the plain physical facts, ascertain what is possible and learn what is wise and right."

Morgenthau describes Lincoln's position as one joining cosmic humility with political realism and urged it as a guide in present circumstances. Though there may be one moral code that men seek, it is filtered through a vast array of moral particularities. The moral code is subject to historical and cultural relativism and, as our lives are precariously poised under the short time fuse of nuclear weapons, to ignore this is to court the destruction of the world.

National Sovereignty and Human Rights
in the Third World

Most human rights discussions in the United States, whether affirmative or negative, have viewed human rights in the Third World from the outside. This has made them appear narrow and ethnocentric to those who are consumers of human rights policies formulated in Washington and New York. The perspective of a leading Indonesian diplomatist and social philosopher, Soedjatmoko, therefore, is particularly helpful and worthwhile. Soedjatmoko believes that if there is one thing that characterizes the present world scene it is the absence of a single moral framework. To an Asian, what stands out as missing from present-day American debate is concern with a philosophy of history or concern for where mankind is going. Every previous historical era had this, but these world views have been shattered. Not only have the millenial views of Christianity come under question but the communist Utopia has been replaced by Soviet and Chinese authoritarianism and oppression. Man's loss of faith and his growing incapacity for deep-rooted belief have some connection with his passion to crowd as much as possible into the present. We live within shifting time frames; when one no longer can accept the hope of life after death, the time frame of justice changes.

The other symptom of ethnocentricism for Soedjatmoko is the prevailing view of violence in the world. Terrorism has changed the whole complexion of the moral problem. In many countries, no minority need any longer remain unheard; the availability of plastic bombs forces any government eventually to come to terms with a determined minority. Even American discussions of a pluralist world order lack full awareness of the ethical issues raised by violence. The present world order is seen by a large part of the world as unjust. Calls for a new international economic order are only the top of the iceberg; they are the manifestation of the inacceptability of a system where the rich become richer and poor even poorer. More violence may be around the corner and when it erupts it will be perceived by those who use it as moral.

Part of the problem is caused by differences in perception of the role and character of the nation state. To scientists, whether natural or social scientists, and the great corporations, the nation state is outmoded. The logic of the situation in the developed world requires that men transcend national loyalties. In the Third World, the problem is the direct opposite. There the nation state is a necessary instrument for the development of particular freedoms, social justice and national unity. It is also the negotiating unit toward the attainment of a better world.

Another question follows: In what kind of world order will the struggle against violence take place? Soedjatmoko sees that order as a pluralist one in which no single nation can define the moral center. The search for values will go on through negotiations, blind groping, and inarticulated adjustments. What is needed is a new morality in which young nation states can seek viability without overturning the international order. Beyond that the question is, "How, given the inevitability of political and social change, can societies reduce the cost in human suffering?" No one nation in the world can impose its authority on the international order. The American era of absolute power has been brief, not by any fault of the United States. Its decline is signaled by Vietnam, and to some this has come as a great shock. Its power and hegemony are still very great, but its capacity to shape events will depend on its adjustment to new realities.

Americans must learn to live with and help others to understand that our actions are not directed from a single GHQ and that we speak to the world with many voices not all representing our best side. All nations have their darker, subterranean side, including the United States with its Manifest Destiny, violence in the cities, loneliness and alienation. Americans need more self-honesty; scholars and intellectuals especially should not flinch from portraying our darker side and then putting it in perspective. Honesty such as this will not derogate from the world's appreciation of our moral status. It can help us in joining others in a common quest for a new morality.

Soedjatmoko maintains that neither moralism nor cynicism describes the moral position of America today. Our real problem seen from abroad is innocence. The moral hazard we face is that innocence that remains unsophisticated can link up with self-righteousness. It is true that no nation can long exist unless it seeks righteousness; when it abandons that, it crumbles. The great challenge America faces, therefore, is how to develop a proper tension between our clear approximation of righteousness and the limits and relativity of our moral base.

President Carter has restored a self-doubting and uncertain country to a sense of integrity and awareness of its national purpose. He is trying to institutionalize this mission and forge administrative mechanisms to achieve it. Soedjatmoko favors this effort and would surely not wish to see it diminished. So noble an effort leaves open the question whether an America that has discovered anew its historic moral beliefs can relate them to a rapidly changing world. Ways must yet be found to look at foreign policy as an instrument (but not the only American instrument) in the search for a new morality by the majority of the world's people. Viewed this way against the background of the striving of others, a moral foreign policy can lose much of its rigidity and compulsiveness without losing its moral content. Until now, our weakness has been our impatience. We are more inclined to speak to the world about our purposes than to listen. Mutual understanding should be the touchstone of our cultural programs.

It may also be asked: will the new international order be autocratic or democratic? Secretary Kissinger was right in saying that the highest moral value in international affairs is peace, but peace must be seen in context. A peace that is unjust or is seen as unjust can never be lasting; prior standards are not enough. A moral international order must reflect the morality of nations and of the world's peoples, requiring America to join with others to resolve their ethical dilemmas as well as our own. It is essential to understand that the foreign policies of nations are set by what their publics tacitly or openly support. An unsolved problem is how to connect up a realistic vision of a future world order with the peoples' sense of participation. No one is facing up to this problem. A number of futurologists assume an authoritarian order and in their scenarios push aside the political nature of foreign policy. Freedom for people to participate has not been a hallmark of the United Nations, but the recent world conferences on the environment, food, women and population did provide a forum for people as well as governments.

Soedjatmoko, foreshadowing his comments on human rights, carries this proposition further. There are risks in the involvement of people in all their innocence and naivety; they can be led up the garden path by jingoists, populists or demogogues. Moreover, their participation may introduce an additional element of uncertainty into foreign policy, but their voices carry force. We need government-to-government relations but also relations of people-to-people and political parties-to-parties. The great risk in leaving public declarations to chief executives is that you exhaust prematurely the court of last resort. Furthermore, there is danger in a great power talking big and doing nothing. (President Theodore Roosevelt spoke of "talking softly and carrying a big stick.") In Western countries why can't parliaments, political parties and civic and religious organizations carry some responsibility for speaking out? Any president will have to reserve some of the hectoring and rhetoric for spokesmen of non-governmental relations in much the same way USIA must leave cultural relations to the broad international scholarly and cultural community.

The acceptance of a pluralist and democratic international order, which Soedjatmoko favors, is more than the intellectual acceptance of otherness; it requires trust in those who are members of different cultures and political systems. Within all systems there are bound to be those who share common values. Soedjatmoko finds in the present outlook of some Western countries an almost desperate thrust to get other political systems to accept a common code. A more hopeful task would be to help recognizable peoples in different systems to embrace common values. Who are such people? The dissidents to be sure, but they are no more than the tip of the iceberg (it is tempting to make the search for dissidents the beginning and the end of human rights). In the long history of man going back to biological origins, man's innate belligerency has always required that there be an enemy. We may now be at a juncture in history where man has to learn to develop moral positions without directing them at a single identifiable enemy. The root question is whether we are capable of trusting the essential humaneness of other people even when the man at the top is a gangster. Once we are capable of doing this, we will find those who share our ideals. It would be sad if we were incapable of transcending an earlier, more primitive state of nature.

Soedjatmoko believes that the problems of social change and violence in the world can never be resolved apart from religion and the philosophy of history. The new head of the Lutheran World Federation is a black African militant. Does this make him moral? Soedjatmoko began as a pacifist, believing that Indonesia could gain its independence because its cause was just. He dropped pacifism during the national struggle. In any struggle it is easy to become a total moral relativist and justify the unlimited use of force. If mankind develops a shared sense of the direction in which it is going, then it is possible to keep violence within bounds.

When speaking of a philosophy of history, Soedjatmoko makes plain he is not speaking of Hegelian or Marxist concepts under which only certain social groups are designated as history's chosen instruments. A closed system always perpetuates injustice. He finds little that is appealing in a rigidly coherent political philosophy or a system of ends that seeks by its claim of inevitability to justify the use of any means. He is talking rather about a general and evolving scheme of values. At any given moment, societies may give different emphasis to, say, freedom and justice. In the long view of history, however, it may not matter where societies start. It is true that countries that begin with only concern for justice end up with the loss of freedom. However, out of Soviet terror, a different system may emerge. It is moral arrogance to imagine that all mankind would limit its political choices to a single system; the present world order is a pluralistic and multiple-value universe. Khrushchev and Brezhnev have prided themselves that Russia has chosen justice over freedom, but other nations choose freedom over justice. The argument over priorities is endless, but in the final analysis nations must find their own acceptable modes; history and circumstances limit every nation.

If there is a way out of relativism it is to be found not in politics but in religion. The search for meaning in the international order must not be dissociated from mankind's search for meaning. Americans who are a pragmatic and a positivist people are embarrassed by talk of the need for a new religious faith. It may also be asked what can anyone do about man's struggle to discover or rediscover an ultimate faith. Soedjatmoko's answer is "probably nothing except to recognize the need to link up the search for religion with what we see as the secular problems of the world." Our secular problems cannot be solved apart from a religious dimension. There is no discipline within the present range of man's scientific and intellectual arsenal that can give the answers to meaning. Someone should be making the case for religion but theologians shy away from it. The new religious groups tend to be authoritarian and fail to match faith with tolerance; for the first time in history, survival depends on combining the two. A legend from Japanese mystical religion may help:

> God is at the top of the mountain. One man lives east, another west, another north and another south of the mountain. No other path is open than for each man to reach the top by his own road. Each seeks the top but each must find his own way.

This legend, Soedjatmoko suggests, casts light on how to match faith with tolerance.

It may be significant that it was an Asian who proposed that men could best find their way through all the tangled complexities of morality by the capacity to relate faith and the ultimate value of man to an essentially secular and historical framework.

The Third World Appeal for Broadening Human Rights

If Soedjatmoko's thoughts challenge some prevailing American assumptions, he is fundamentally sympathetic and committed to the United States. Many Third World leaders are less favorably disposed. It would be the height of folly, therefore, for the American leadership group, and in particular officials of the Carter administration, to continue to ignore his wise counsel. Soedjatmoko as a Third World leader affirms his total commitment to a human rights outlook, but taken in isolation it distorts the real problems. The present human rights effort must be sustained but become more broad-gauged. Many societies give almost no emphasis to rights but rather to a structure of obligations and duties. Too narrow a human rights perspective may shut the door to a broader understanding of other cultures and polities. A more pressing need than rights in some parts of the world is to discover a new balance between individualism and collectivism, the same issue that preoccupied the United States in the 1930s and 1940s. Human survival requires this, for if the capacity of local systems to meet urgent problems breaks down, violence on a far larger scale will follow and more grievous violations of human rights.

There is also need to make our human rights campaign more sophisticated and grounded in realism. Examples arise as in present day Argentina, where a new military President is struggling to regain control over both the irrational acts of wanton violence of urban guerrillas and the equally irrational acts of secret intelligence services operating beyond the authority of government. What happens when the strongest political figure a system can throw up is threatened by an American human rights campaign? How can we help people or groups in a political system where order has broken down? Soedjatmoko is not saying the United States should do nothing or call off human rights, but cautioning regarding the consequences if outside intervention destroys the limited capability of somewhat responsible leaders to work effectively within their own system.

Looking at foreign peoples it is easy to forget the essential disjunction between power and morality, a disjunction never wholly resolved in any country, which leads to the religious concept of the tragic dimension of life. Pragmatism on the American scene prompts us to forget the tragic element in life, especially without the reminders of a Niebuhr. Lincoln understood that the essential irreconcilability of power and morality forces any leader to bow in humility and to throw himself on the mercy of Providence. As we look abroad, are we able and willing to recognize this same capacity for evil in man and find ways not of eliminating but containing it?

Despite such limitations omnipresent in the human drama, there are many positive actions that can be taken in behalf of human rights. We should look, first, for new instrumentalities capable of advancing human rights without endangering other worthy ends. Perhaps we might take a leaf from the communist book where

Pravda and the worldwide apparatus of communist parties speak out when the Premier may prefer not to be engaged. We should look for new ways of reducing nationalistic reactions against intervention and new international rules for pushing back the barriers of domestic jurisdiction without counter-productive effects. There are, of course, instruments associated with the United Nations; the Covenants should be taken seriously and should be ratified not primarily because of their legality but their consciousness-raising potentials. Everything points to the importance of raising our human rights effort to a cooperative international level. Once the United States has ratified the Covenants, its leadership position in the U.N. will be stronger.

Through another new instrumentality, perhaps a National Endowment for Human Rights, we need to understand more deeply the reasons for inhumanity in certain cultures. Why do certain systems moving through states of political and economic development transform themselves while others do not? An agency created by government or the foundations should finance studies of the social, moral, and economic preconditions that allow a society to deal with its problems in a more humane fashion. New instrumentalities could be found for meeting specific human rights violations. The problem of getting international agreements on the control and restriction of torture and long detention without trial can be solved. Seeing to it that torture is not used is a manageable possibility.

Seen from the Third World, there is yet another problem concerning human rights about which the United States should be aware. Every time the United States becomes outspokenly moral, its foreign assistance drops. It is hard to explain to people in the developing world that there is no connection between these two phenomena. Such people ask whether human rights is simply a means of putting a good face on the unwillingness of the American people to provide foreign aid. A developing country deprived of essential assistance while it is trying to make the turn from economic growth to social justice may become far more vulnerable to violence and other abuses of human rights.

Another serious problem for the developing countries stems from the insistence on linking foreign aid to help for the majority poor.

While Soedjatmoko applauds the attack on poverty everywhere, which in a sense advances another human right, Americans ought to remember that projects directed to an attack on poverty require far more national than foreign financing and changes in national as well as international structures. He poses the question, "Is it right for another country, the United States, to insist that a developing country spend a certain percent of its GNP or its national budget on poverty or social development, thus foregoing economic growth?" The poverty emphasis, which has meant lowering the level of more general aid, can make a developing country incapable of continuing other long-run projects that have no immediate bearing on poverty but may in the future affect its capacity both for growth and social justice. Here is a key ethical and political dilemma which is not adequately recognized in current American discussion and policy.

Yet another Third World dilemma which could portend the most serious future consequences is what happens to countries that have addressed themselves single-mindedly to poverty. It seems to some Third World leaders there is a taint of hypocrisy in the poverty emphasis. What has happened to China, Cuba, India, Allende's Chile, Jamaica an Tanzania, the countries that have attacked poverty directly? The United States has either not shown any interest or has actually tried to destabilize such regimes. Not only are some Third World countries unable to devote the proportion of their resources to poverty programs required, but in many countries the question is being raised, what will happen if they make the extraordinary effort and Japan and the United States shift their policies or, to take the extreme case, become tomorrow's enemy? If this seems far-fetched to Americans, Soedjatmoko replies that other peoples read American history as suggesting that rhetoric and proclamations have not been good guides to future foreign policies.

Then too, as with other human rights, it is wrong to isolate poverty from the total needs of a country. The American experience with blacks should have taught us that a direct attack on the poverty of black areas is only one (and sometimes the least successful) means of assistant the disadvantaged. Instead, in a manner that has not gone unnoticed, we have sought to widen social and educational opportunities, have opened up business and the professions, and have enabled blacks to move to other neighborhoods.

Soedjatmoko also has thought about America's style and its attitudes in any human rights endeavor. When the United States speaks out through private or public instrumentalities, it should ask whether its statements about human rights are being made to make Americans feel good or are gauged to be helpful to people and forces in other natons who support human rights. There are those abroad who see the present human rights campaign as a jag of moral self-indulgence. They ask about our moral consistency. We glamorize the dissidents, but when they emigrate they can't find work in the United States. Immigration laws weaken the force of our moral example, and we have done very little to look for new mechanisms of employment. The dissidents are not only intellectuals but working men and artists. One can ask, what are we doing to help them as well? The mounting problem of refugees also needs attention.

If the United States is serious about human rights, it must take the lead internationally; it should not go it alone. It must confront with others a whole panoply of human rights problems. These problems will only increase and are compounded by the incapacity of the weaker states to do anything about them.

Fundamental to all the rest, however, is the need to build new constructs of theory and practice for the achievement of development with freedom. Almost every development theory leads away from freedom. Japan and Germany gained development by limiting freedom and became totalitarian monsters; only military defeat made it possible for liberal forces to emerge. Outsiders who would help must face up to the fateful clash between freedom and growth in the developing world. The United States, while preaching freedom, has trained thousands of economists, scientists and military leaders who return to their countries with a narrow and elitist technocratic view of development. Against these groups, there are in the Third World countless people who yearn for development but remain respectful of freedom. When they look at most of the universities in the West, however, they find among both liberal and socialist thinkers an acceptance of the notion that development requires the subordination of freedom.

Who is doing anything to help with the search for alternative development models? It is not civil rights leaders or theologians but Western scholars who are training the economists of the world. It is a "moral cop-out" for the West, therefore, to seize on the easy and legitimate issues of human rights when the essential and hard question is, can we shape a viable democratic development theory? The area remains an intellectual desert. Western intellectuals do little; hard-pressed national leaders are too embattled to think straight. Latin American "dependencia theories" help explain certain weaknesses and give vent to nationalist anger but do not constitute a guideline for development. Traditionally, Latin American nations have been shaped by literary, legal, and historical thinkers. Today's social realities have become too complex for them.

Social scientists trained largely in the United States have stepped in to fill a void, but when they have returned from their technical, quantitative studies, they become either narrow government technocrats who are morally crippled; or opposition leaders no less crippled but also politically polarized and full of nationalistic hatred; or members of respectable research institutes doing useful but limited research not directed to broad social problems. Add to this that much of American foreign policy in the developing countries is shaped not by the State Department or USIA but by military-to-military relations, and the problem is complete. The military in Latin American governments (and to some extent the United States) is narrowly anti-communist, largely defense-minded, and therefore unable to accept the need and desirability of social and economic change. There is no intervening civilian mechanism or perspective. If the United States wants to gain stature as a bulwark of global human rights, it cannot continue to ignore this problem.

Concluding Thoughts

From the discussion of human rights and the different perspectives on the problem of promoting them around the world, certain conclusions appear to emerge. Noteworthy is the fact that human rights as a dominant theme of American foreign policy is a fairly recent development. Oftentimes human rights are discussed as though they were coextensive with morality and foreign policy, but the best interpreters suggest the latter is far more inclusive. Some proposals for advancing human rights have been offered as if their attainment were an exclusive objective of foreign policy and need not be weighed in relation to other objectives. Actually, it has not been primarily the more experienced foreign policy officials but rather activist leaders in minority and civil rights campaigns within the United States who have most aggressively pursued international human rights. It is premature to judge the ultimate effects of the public campaign.

Friends in the Third World feel compelled to remind Americans that human rights policies should be designed not to make us feel good at home but to advance realistically the cause of true defenders of liberty and justice abroad. By implication they suggest that liberty must never be conceived of in isolation from justice, anymore than world peace can be achieved without justice. They also warn of national self-righteousness and lack of humility in formulating and applying human rights policies, and the need for a broader vision of human rights more attuned to the urgent needs of Third World countries. If there is a common theme to all the questioning of the current American human rights approach, it is the need for greater realism especially with regard to the differences in conditions within individual nations and the persistent requirements of national sovereignty.

Alongside the doubts expressed and issues raised by critics, a balanced appraisal of human rights must take into account factors that protagonists have stressed. It is not accidental that the emphasis on human rights has come in the late 1970s. Collectivism, viewed as the hope of mankind in the 1930s and 1940s, is now seen as posing contradictions and conflicts. Neither National Socialism nor Stalinism has brought the millenium. Tyranny has accompanied authoritarian approaches to social justice, and even the moral liberal experiments in social planning have created as many problems as they have solved. Collectivist political orders have stifled individual initiatives and trampled individual rights in the dust.

James Reston has written: "A generation or so ago it was the Western nations and their institutions that were defending the status quo while the Communist nations were demanding change. But now all this is quite different." The West, he points out, has taken the initiative diplomatically and ideologically, and while it has not yet found a way to harness together its two offensives in some more coherent grand design, it has begun to throw off the shackles of self-doubt and intellectual and spiritual malaise. Proponents of internationalism and the national interest have hardly reconciled their differences or even begun to listen to one another's valid points, and no-one in any of the leading Western governments has grappled convincingly with the tensions between human rights and national sovereignty. Diplomatists and lawyers pass one another in their arguments at every intellectual and policy crossroad, yet the beginnings of a valid exchange can be found in some of their more perceptive statements. The sense of longing for a different future world is evident in the selection of a new Polish pope, the first non-Italian elected in more than 400 years. Symbolically, the new pope appeals to the world because he is both a foe of communist authoritarianism and a social liberal on questions of justice. Reston concludes:

> It is not Moscow or Peking but Washington that is trying to bring about a reconciliation between the Arabs and the Israelis in the Middle East or between the blacks and whites in sub-Sahara Africa. It is not Moscow or Peking but Washington, London, Paris, Bonn and the other Western capitals that are worrying about the control of population, nuclear weapons and nuclear wastes, industrial pollution and international anarchy in the airways of the world.

Perhaps significantly, Mr. Reston in his column entitled "The West Is Ready to Embrace Change" made no mention of human rights, but the significance may result not from his rejecting the issue of human rights but in placing it in the broader context of national and international politics. Human rights, it would appear, is too important and too many-sided to be left exclusively to the protagonists of civil rights. Human rights is one facet of worldwide change but not the totality.

President Carter as a candidate, having raised the issue late in the Presidential campaign of 1976, first rather tentatively in a Democratic issues forum in Louisville in late 1975, then in a speech the following March in Chicago, and finally in a more general statement in October 1976 at the University of Notre Dame, pressed his views aggressively in the second debate with President Ford. The issue, according to his pollster Patrick Caddell, was "a very strong issue across the board," appealing to the followers of Senator Henry Jackson, to Jews concerned with the Soviet treatment of Jews, and to liberals concerned with Korea and Chile.

The politics of campaigning are often far removed from the politics of governance, and once in office the task confronting the administration was to fashion viable human rights policies. In the words of the brilliant Washington journalist, Elizabeth Drew: "Having arrived, through a variety of circumstances, at a policy idea, the Administration's next problems were to define it, to find methods of implementing it, and to reconcile it with various conflicting goals." ("Human Rights," *The New Yorker*, July 18, 1977, p. 41.) The issue had moved from the realm of ends to one of means.

The sequence of early administration effort is well known: the letter to President Carter from Andrei Sakharov, the Soviet nuclear physicist and dissident leader, on January 28, 1977; President Carter's personal reply made public by Sakharov on February 17; the State Department's charge against Czechoslovakia for arresting and harassing signees of Charter 77 (a petition to the Czech government for protection of rights outlined in the Helsinki agreement); and President Carter's messages in February to Brezhnev and Ambassador Dobrynin, as well as several public statements making his intention clear to speak out when human rights were threatened. In March the President declared in a speech at the United Nations: "No member of the United Nations can claim that mistreatment of its citizens is solely its own business."

Not long thereafter, following the breakdown of talks on arms control in Moscow, Secretary Vance on April 30, 1977, in a speech at the University of Georgia Law School sought to define more precisely the main elements of American policy. The Secretary distinguished among governmental violations of the integrity of person (torture, arbitrary arrest, denial of a fair trial); fulfillment of vital human needs such as food, shelter, health care and education; and the right to civil and political liberties such as freedom of speech, press, religion, assembly, movement and participation in government.

Developmental loan assistance by multi-national organizations—the World Bank, for example—through which the United

States channels about one-third of its aid to developing countries, presented a special problem. So did linkage of human rights with SALT talks between the Americans and the Soviets, and efforts to control nuclear proliferation in countries like Brazil and Korea. There, American policy-makers found it necessary to make trade-offs on conventional arms assistance along with economic incentives, such as status within the International Monetary Fund and like agencies.

Human rights became a part of the overall policy-planning process called Presidential Review Memoranda (PRM) under the chairmanship of Undersecretary of State Warren Christopher. Private groups were enlisted. (One, made up of international lawyers, diplomatists, theologians, Third World authorities and diplomatic historians, met with high-ranking State Department officials from June 14-16, 1977, at the University of Virginia. The summary discussion of their views provides the basis for much of this essay and is used with the permission of the State Department.)

It should be obvious that a struggle has gone on within and outside the government between spokesmen of contending viewpoints on human rights policies. References to human rights by President Carter and other administration officials have continued to be made but, following the urgings of Secretary Vance and others, with less stridency. Human rights continues to be one of the cornerstones of American policy, but not an exclusive focus for policy isolated from other concerns and objectives.

The administration has been criticized alternately for doing too much or too little. Such criticism would appear to reflect more the difficult task of policy formulation then the abandonment of human rights. If universalizing human rights exceeded the limits of American foreign policy, a selective response brought charges of hypocrisy. The administration has trimmed its sails on human rights in South Korea and the Philippines because of common security interests in Southeast and Northeast Asia. Criticisms of repression in Iran have been muted because of Iranian oil and investments and Iran's strategic role in relationship to the Middle East and the Soviet Union. In February 1977, Secretary Vance had reminded the Senate Foreign Operations Committee: "In each case we must balance a political concern for human rights against economic and security goals." Earlier statements of key administration leaders suggested a line of policy in which prudence replaced idealism. Marshall Shulman had warned in 1974 in testimony before a Senate Committee that any United States effort to improve human rights in the USSR would "pose conditions which the present Soviet regime cannot but regard as terms of surrender and of self-liquidation." Even National Security Advisor, Zbigniew Brezinski had admitted that "a limited democratization of the Soviet society . . . would threaten the present political leadership."

When Secretary Arthur Goldberg represented the administration in the autumn of 1977 at the Belgrade Conference, which sought to review compliance with the Helsinki Accord and its human rights provisions for Eastern Europe, he found little enthusiasm for a human rights campaign on the part of Common Market states. Furthermore, the American delegation directed attention to human rights violations in the Soviet Union, Czechoslovakia and East Germany but not Poland, Hungary and Rumania with whom it had more favorable relations.

At the time of the Shcharansky trial, President Carter announced, "We have a deep commitment to human rights"and then added, "I have not embarked on a vendetta against the Soviet Union. We cannot interfere in their internal affairs."

The historian Norman Graebner has written:

> What the Carter leadership achieved for human rights defied accurate measurement. . . . But they could point to a new worldwide interest in human rights; to the heavier price which governments paid for their repressions; to the changing image of the United States; and to the decisions of some countries to release political prisoners and grant permission to international agencies, such as the International Red Cross and Amnesty International, to conduct investigations within their borders. (Unpublished paper presented to the Human Rights Study Group of the Council on Religion and International Affairs.)

Then Graebner concluded:

> In the administration's failure to achieve more there is nothing strange. Whatever its power or self-assigned obligation, no nation has ever succeeded in serving more than its own interests. . . . The country's power to create a utopia on either side of the Iron Curtain

was always limited. . . . Because no government, in its foreign policies, is compelled to do what it cannot do, the United States might
more profitably and legitimately seek the fulfillment of its ideals at
home. Human rights, wherever they exist, thrive best under conditions of international relaxation. Thus the country could have no
higher purpose abroad than to maximize world stability by protecting
its friends, to the extent of its capabilities, against aggressive war. It
was the American contribution to victory in the two world wars of this
century . . . that gave this nation its reputation as the defender of
freedom. *(Ibid.)*

It is well for both leaders and the public to recall these words as we
proceed in the continuing and exacting task of seeking to balance
foreign policy objectives and human rights.

Comment

Ross N. Berkes

Professor Kenneth Thompson's presentation is a brilliant exposi-
tion of subjects precisely of concern in a conference on the international dimensions of rights and responsibilities.

Over the years Professor Thompson has made the scholarly community well aware of his unfailingly intelligent and humane discussions of vital topics through the impressive parade of papers, books,
and scholarly productions that have found their way into print. Dr.
Thompson tackles complex subjects in international relations with
the cautious respect that they deserve and, predictably, he comes
out with some rather complex answers.

In September of 1966, Professor Thompson was at the University
of Southern California to participate in the dedication of the Von
KleinSmid Center for International and Public Affairs. His paper
then was entitled "Individualism, Nationalism and International
Morality." A review of that paper discloses a vein of thought similar
to one running through the present paper. In the earlier paper he
warned his readers, just as he seems to be doing in the later paper,
that "there are layers of ethics in politics and international affairs.

They deserve study, especially when the stronger voices are crusaders and cynics." And, he went on, "The ethical dimension is comprised of shades that are not black and white but predominantly gray." Then, as now, Kenneth Thompson advised that "frequently distributive justice is the highest attainment of states."

During the twelve years that have passed since Dr. Thompson made the remarks just quoted, many things have changed. Judging from the paper under discussion, he may now be willing to settle for Aristotle's less ambitious commutative justice.

In this paper, Professor Thompson sees human rights partly in terms of the threat—threat not in a pejorative sense, but nevertheless threat—that such a concept represents to the more firmly institutionalized concept of state sovereignty. He has not said so directly, but one wonders if the more serious, far-reaching challenge to what has been inherited as an international system comes not just from the threat of a nuclear holocaust. There is a suggestion in this paper that there is a threat to the system from the beach-heads of penetration into the so-called sovereign state by the evergrowing assaults of such projects as human rights. That does not place Professor Thompson as a defender of state sovereignty or as an opponent of human rights, but it may put him in the position of at least hinting that too eager or successful a campaign for human rights might result, not in the establishment of an effective system of human rights throughout the world, but rather a bitter struggle for the reassertion of an anachronism, state sovereignty.

In Dr. Thompson's paper there is the suggestion of a position which has the potential of being represented in a way that he did not intend, but which needs to be brought forward for inspection. Careful reading of the paper discloses the notion that human rights has a highly explosive potential, one that must be treated very carefully by those in positions of international responsibility. This might have led to the statement (maybe he would have been quoting someone else) that human rights is too important and too many-sided to be left exclusively to the protagonists of civil rights.

The paper presents an interesting rivalry between the lawyers and the diplomatists in their approaches to human rights. Professor Thompson offers a third approach, and a third perspective as well, that of the theologian.

The language in which Dr. Thompson's paper is couched would lead one to believe that his preference is for the approach of the diplomatist. Actually, he is at heart a theologian who is willing to let the diplomatists win the game. This willingness seems to rest on the issue that all policy alternatives should be screened through the sieve of national interest; but that is the diplomatist's argument. This argument is put forward at length and rather refreshingly, not because anyone can be sincerely pleased with the concept of national interest, but because this is the first time in many years that the argument has been boldly and effectively defended. Professor Thompson asks for a restoration and return to an older meaning for the term "national interest." Essentially, he asks for a review of all the consequential fallout of each vigorous pursuit of human rights.

If that is an appropriate path, one could predict a rather uncomfortable uneasiness about the times and situations with which the conduct of international relations are now faced. One suspects that it is this conclusion that led Professor Thompson to suggest that perhaps the United States should run most of its human rights drive through international machinery and not try to act unilaterally. Use of international machinery would, presumably, lessen the strain on the international system.

Kenneth Thompson notes that the lawyer's approach to things projects national interest as too narrow a concept. It is the lawyers who are really trying (and trying very hard) to establish a new international system. Ironically, however, their new system depends on the main actors of the old system—the national states—to carry out this revolutionary task.

In fact, it is not only the lawyers who are busily proclaiming that world-wide interests must now and indefinitely supplant national ones. The legalistic formulation of a new world order is receiving support from many groups of scholars and thinkers who until very recently would not have been found in the legalistic-moralistic camp. For a growing number of persons, to pursue the national interest these days is to back away from the chief problems on the world agenda. One shares the diplomatist's view—perhaps it is also Kenneth Thompson's view—that the lawyers and academicians would be wise to accept the painful truth, patently apparent to the diplomat, that it is a pluralistic world.

One of the best parts of Professor Thompson's paper is his observation that while the developed world is beginning to look scornfully at the national state, and willingly sowing seeds of its destruction through human rights and other assaults on national sovereignty, the Third World looks, ironically, to the national state as its greatest protection. Going beyond that observation, Professor Thompson is quite right in expressing distress over the moral abdication of the West. He says, "We seize on the easy and legitimate issues of human rights, when the essential and hard question is finally shaping viable, democratic development theory."

In these acute observations Kenneth Thompson has continued his lifetime habit of keeping a complex subject complex. One can be grateful, however, for a paper about human rights that ends on a cautious theme of prudence.

Comment

Andrzej Korbonski

Let me begin by saying that I very much enjoyed reading Professor Thompson's paper. I liked it very much, in fact, and I agree with all his major thesis conclusions, and therefore it is hard for me to be critical. It is a well-argued paper, one that lays out in great detail the complexities surrounding the concept of human rights and national sovereignty. I particularly liked his discussion of the three approaches to the problem, the theological, the diplomatic and the legal, and his examination of the differences among these approaches. I must confess to one minor disappointment, namely lack of a basic conclusion. On the one hand, the absence of a firm conclusion is not surprising because of the nature of the concept of human rights. This has been indicated in much of the fuzzy conceptual thinking that has taken place over the years. The concept is, after all, very difficult to come to grips with. In any event, I have been tempted to ask at the end of the paper, so what? what is the bottom line? where do we go from here?

I would like to make a few comments on the problem of human rights in more concrete terms, particularly in the context of United States relations with the East, primarily with the Soviet Union. I have been interested in that problem for the last couple of years, partly because I have had the good fortune (or misfortune) of having been appointed as the so-called public member of our delegation to the Belgrade Conference. I had, therefore, to read up a little bit and think about the problem of human rights and United States foreign policy.

This issue we are talking about is the emphasis on human rights as one of the major objectives of United States foreign policy in the past three years or so. The Helsinki Conference culminated in the so-called "final act," in August of 1975, containing ten principles known as the Decalogue. Among those ten principles, two (Principles 6 and 7) illustrate very well the dilemma so well discussed by Professor Thompson. On the one hand Principle 6 emphasizes non-intervention in the internal affairs of other countries. Principle 7 on the other hand emphasizes respect for human rights and fundamentals freedoms, including freedom of thought, religion, conscience, and so on. In a sense, making the perfection of human rights an international concern raises a conflict inherent in the ideas enunciated in Principles 6 and 7. The conflict has very much affected our own policy toward the East, especially toward the Soviet Union, which the Carter Administration has been emphasizing. It has also stressed the significance of detente, calling for all sorts of major treaties between us and the Soviet Union, denying the so-called linkage principle characteristic of previous administrations, which tied questions in one area with those in others. I would like to deal with this dilemma and also in a sense with a question of U.S. concern for human rights and the concern of our allies, particularly in Western Europe.

The emphasis on human rights has been reflected so far, or at least in the initial stages, mostly in rhetoric, in speeches, in addresses. There were some attempts to link, for example, the question of human rights with foreign and military aid. We tended to be, as well, ideological in some of our pronouncements. This new emphasis on human rights caused considerable bewilderment among our allies, particularly within NATO. Also, this emphasis met with considerable criticism in the United States, particularly by the diplomatic school mentioned by Professor Thompson, including persons like Mr. Kennan, Mr. Shulman, principal advisor to Secretary Vance, and a number of others. This concern was valid because as much as we can admire and praise the new concern for human rights, we must be aware of one major point, that this concern is neither a policy, nor a guide to policy.

The major difficulty for the present administration is, how does one translate the concern for human rights into policy? Would it be effective, would it raise false hopes without changing anything? How far will the present policy be hindered or helped by pushing the human rights issue? These are very important problems. Let us take the whole area of East/West relations. What are our objectives toward the East? Just to mention a few for example: the maintenance of strategic deterence and adequate military strength in Europe that involves the protection of Western Europe; the prevention of nuclear war; the reduction of tension; bringing the Soviet Union closer into what may be called the compatible international system; encouraging the Soviet Union and Eastern Europe to cooperate to solve many global problems; gradual enlargement of a degree of independence for these East European countries.

Now, how does the human rights campaign affect all these objectives? I think it cuts across nearly all of them. It certainly affects the question of detente with the Soviet Union and East/West relations in general. It really impinges on the future of Eastern Europe and on the evolution of Soviet domestic and foreign policy. While the moral imperative is there, what we say depends very much on the configuration or the balance of the factors enumerated above. There are countless examples that illustrate the linkage problem and the conflict between these policy objectives and the human rights stand. One that strikes me as mirroring or reflecting our dilemma is our policy toward Eastern Europe, and how we deal with the various governments there. Three of our presidents have visited Poland, Yugoslavia and Rumania. We consider these governments to be independent of Moscow; at least we encourage independence. At the same time, we also have supported dissident movements in these countries, movements which tend to undermine the governments we try to strengthen. The question arises: what are our priorities?

Let me pose some questions concerning our priorities—again emphasizing the dilemmas. Would our relations with Western Europe be damaged because of our insistence on human rights? There is a school of thought in Washington that became quite prominent during the Belgrade Conference which says that indeed the West Europeans are not at all interested in the human rights issue, that our NATO allies just couldn't care less. Therefore, it would be wrong for the United States at Belgrade or elsewhere to push this public issue. I do not agree with this point of view. I was in Belgrade and Prague and in many ways I saw smaller NATO allies (Belgium, Holland, Britain, Canada) being much more aggressive than the United States in the human rights area. In a sense it is a myth that we are the champion of human rights and the Western Europeans don't care. Also, and this is a matter of record, the so-called "basketry" at Helsinki resulted not from our insistence but from that of Western Europe. Yet, as I said, the myth persists in Washington that we mustn't push too hard because of our relationship to the NATO countries.

The second question: Will the communist systems in Eastern Europe and the Soviet Union be liberalized or tightened or made more repressive because of America's support for dissidents? So far, open advocacy of human rights has not really liberalized these systems. We saw that this summer at the Moscow trials. Despite our rhetoric, our verbal threats, we witnessed, I think, a return to Stalinism in the way the trials of Shcharansky and Ginzburg were conducted. This happened in spite of the fact that the Soviets knew that was a matter of major concern to the Carter Administration. Our human rights statements seem not to have had any effect.

Nevertheless, clearly we should support the human rights campaign. Here I speak from my own experience, from talking to people in the communist countries in Europe. The emphasis on human rights has regained a good deal of respect for the United

States, particularly following the Vietnam war. We are again seen as a moral leader of the free world. Still we ought to be cautious. I liked Professor Thompson's paper because he did not advocate any major sort of policy but he really emphasized the tremendous complexities of the issue.

It is much too early to say, but it seems that the Carter Administration policy has served to increase rather than decrease the tension between East and West and it did, unnecessarily, raise false hopes in Eastern Europe. It did very much undermine East/West detente, which is still seen, and rightly so, by many as the supreme objective, as the greatest good. The West should really not go beyond offering moral support but should maintain a low profile with regard, for example, to dissidents and opposition in the East. Again, we should not take any action that might be seen as intervening in internal affairs of other countries.

Yet, here one must agree with Professor Thompson and others that each time we assume a highly moral position in international relations, we have tended to hurt rather than to help people or countries or societies we wanted to support. Therefore, while on one hand I am proud of this country and find that we did again, after years of silence, assume a kind of leadership by emphasizing human rights, on the other hand I think we have to be very cautious not to overdo it. One should be thankful to see that after the outburst of '76-'77, at least in its recently published statements the Carter Administration has tended to be much more cautious and much more realistic.

Human Rights, Foreign Policy, and the Social Sciences

by Irving Louis Horowitz

At first glance it might well appear that human rights and social science are perfectly isomorphic terms; the conduct of organized reason called science should issue into an expansion of human rights; and conversely, the unfettered exercise of human rights should allow for the expansion of social scientific research. While there is an obvious moral sentiment that leads us to wish for such a combination of human rights and social sciences, any sort of careful reflection makes clear that the two are quite distinct; occupying discrete realms of reality no less than ideology. Tragically perhaps, the connection between human rights and social science is less one of aesthetic balance than of creative tension.

Specifically, social science must examine the issue of human rights with the same critical dispassion and reserved cutting edge that it would any other political slogan or social myth. To do less than this is to substitute aspirations for experience: a fatal confusion that may itself issue more into human misery than human rights, by using up, exhausting meaning to words. The social scientists too have a bill of particulars: the first human right is that of criticism, the second human right is that of analysis, and the third human right is that of construction. Let me take up the subject of human rights precisely in terms of these three notions: criticism, analysis and construction.

I shall first criticize the human rights movement, insofar as it has political coherence, for its conceptual failure to take into account human obligations. I shall then analyze how rights are frequently in competition with each other, hence still require the exercise of social science for rendering analytic judgment. Finally, I shall indicate those mechanisms by which the human rights question can be monitored and evaluated to determine its centrality in social and political practice. This is admittedly a tall order for a short paper, but one which at least should be broached if we are to get beyond the present state of political opportunism followed too frequently by moral bluster.

The Dialectic of Rights and Obligations:
The Critical Dimension

The widespread disregard, even disdain, for a concept of human obligation paralleling that of human rights, has generated the sort of one-sided, interest group politics that has tended to sacrifice the whole for the parts, all but destroyed a notion of international or national community in favor of regional, local, even entirely personalistic "issues." Single interest politics, and its attendant special issue lobbying efforts, have made the political process a jungle of impenetrable hazards. Any sort of political statement on matters ranging from taxation to education to defense policy becomes part of a concerted effort either to depose or impose the public official. A government of laws runs the risk of being reduced to one of lawyers, the force of institutional affiliations is eroded and transformed into a baser force of personalities and influentials. To have an obligation to more than the bottom line, or to perceive of obligations as anything beyond a pay-off matrix, becomes absurd in this perfect world of an exchange system in which one hand continually washes the other.

When purusit of human rights becomes a demand for sameness, a hedonist calculus of statistical claims, in which the least reward differential within a society becomes a *cause célèbre,* and a reason for creating a public outcry, then social science and human rights must obviously part company. For at such a point, the question of human rights becomes one of private avarice. Demands for statistical parity also raise serious questions whether a national structure can exist, or whether creative powers can be acknowledged, or whether incentive and reward can be recognized. This transvaluation of the value of human rights into one of perfect egalitarianism holds open the spectre of Robespierrism: an ideology and a system in which democracy is secured through a totalitarian mechanism; such an approach to rights becomes all-absorbing and hence quickly dispenses with democracy, in favor of massification.

With human rights, as with other public concerns, political events often dictate public discourse. Since the beginning of the United Nations in the mid-1940s, the question of human rights has remained in the province of UNESCO conferences; in the late 1970s it emerged, suddenly, as a central issue. Certainly, this new sense of concern cannot be explained on the basis of an intellectual breakthrough in the past thirty years. Rather, human rights have become a major instrument of American foreign policy. It should be evident that the passion for human rights, however genuine, is a measured response to the interests of this (or any other) nation.

Yet one should not be cynical about the subject of human rights simply because the sense of concern appears so clearly related to national interests and mandarin policies. Intellectuals, and social scientists in particular, have long inhabited a world where desultory issues locked away in library archives, become dramatic events of considerable public consequences. The War on Poverty was a political invention long after the emergence of a literature on poverty; and even though that particular rhetorical war has passed into oblivion, the realities of poverty remain. No matter how the major collective issues of the century are placed on the agenda of public discourse, the best efforts of social scientists must be put forward, however cynical one might be with respect to the national origins or even the frivolous nature of such commitments.

Politics is a game of vulnerabilities, and the human rights issue is clearly one in which the "socialist" world has proven most vulnerable, just as the economic rights issue is where the "capitalist" world is most open to criticism. The very interplay of forces, the competition of world historic systems and empires, thus provide an opportunity for individuals and smaller collectivities to register marginal advantages over the systems they inhabit. Because of the practical potential of concerns for human rights, rather than because of an effort to capitalize on a policy quirk of this specific moment in time, social science can provide a useful, albeit limited, role. The various social science disciplines have pioneered in transforming the question of human rights from a series of indecisive philosophic propositions to a precise sense of measurable statistics and theorems.

The debate on human rights can be conceptualized at its most general level as a struggle between eighteenth century libertarian persuasions and nineteenth century egalitarian beliefs—that is, from a vision of human rights having to do with the right of individual justice before the law to a recognition of the rights of individuals to social security and equitable conditions of work and standards of living. Whether human rights are essentially a political or economic concern is not a secondary issue. However, the social sciences need not choose between politics and economics. They have enough on their hands in demanding an accountability system of monitoring and evaluating both.

The social sciences have introduced precisely an element of accountability not only into their disciplines, but also into the policy systems and networks that social scientists find themselves in. As a result, the quantification or measurement of human rights has become the monumental contribution of social science. Big words are rightfully suspect, but concepts doubly so. It therefore becomes a central act of faith to translate the abstract into the concrete. This is largely what has been accomplished by economists, sociologists, psychologists, political scientists, and anthropologists through the use of social indicators.

The right to justice, or formal education, are concepts easy enough to absorb within the framework of almost any social system. But when rights become carefully stipulated in terms of costs, when freedom of beliefs becomes translated into freedom to impart information and ideas without harassment, when social security is translated into old age insurance, when rights to privacy are viewed as the right of every individual to communicate in secrecy, when rights to work involve protection of actual workers, when social rights are translated into the rights of mothers and children to special care and protection, when rights to work involve the right to form and join trade unions and the right to strike, when rights to personal security involve measures to protect the safety of conscientious objectors, when rights to fair trials include protection against arbitrary arrest or detention—then the entire panoply of rights assumes an exact meaning that lifts them from the realm of sermon to one of seriousness.

The habitual interest in human rights in part reflects the absence of these rights. There is a great deal of concern on matters of cruel, inhuman, or degrading treatment because there is so much cruelty, inhumanity, and degradation present in world affairs. There is concern about the rights of self-determination because there are so many violations of those rights in the name of national integration. International law calls for the punishment of genocide because the twentieth century has seen the alarming development of mass homicide practiced for statist ends.

There is a colossal dichotomy between practices and principles. This split between reality and rhetoric gives the human rights issue its volatility. Yet the one enormous breakthrough that has evolved over the century is the sense of right and wrong. A common legacy of democratic and socialist politics, of marketing and planning systems, of libertarian and egalitarian ideologies, is the assumption that there is such a goal as human rights. When one recollects that it was only one hundred years ago that slavery and serfdom were vital forces in human affairs and that wars were fought to protect chattel slavery as states' rights, then the extent and velocity—at least conceptually—of how far we have come become evident.

The central characteristic of the twentieth century, what so profoundly demarcates it conceptually from previous centuries, is that a world in which obligations were taken for granted has been transformed to one in which rights are presumed to be inalienable. Our institutions were largely concerned with theories of human obligation: what individuals and collectivities owe to their societies and to their states—an automatic presumption that one has an obligation to fight in wars whatever the purpose of the war, or the notion that economic failure is a mark of individual shortcoming rather than societal breakdown. The hallmark of the twentieth century and the achievements of the social sciences, is to have made the question of human rights the central focus, and at the same time, to place the question of obligations on the shoulders of institutions rather than individuals.

There are risks in this transvaluation. One might well argue that the tilt has turned into a rout; that issues of the duties of individuals to the community, or the limitations of human rights to ensure national survival, have not received proper attention; that social research has so emphasized the minutiae of imbalances of every sort that even homicides are now blamed on violence on television. But such transvaluations of values carry within themselves potential for hyperbole and exaggeration; and there is little point in discarding the baby with the bathwater. The literature of the past was written in terms of dynasties, nations, and empires. As long as that was the case, the matter of human rights hardly counted. Only now, when these larger-than-life institutions—these dynasties, nations, and empires—are dissolving, can it be seen that the individual is the centerpiece of all human rights and that the expression of these rights must always remain the province of the free conscience of a free individual. In this very special sense, ours is the century in which individualism has emerged beyond the wildest imaginings of previous centuries. Paradoxically, it is also the century of the most barbaric collectivisms, which put into sharp and painful relief the subject of human rights by assuming the right of States to terminate individual life for political reasons. If the momentary strategy of the political system is such that the subject of human rights now is central, the principles of social research must convert those strategies into durable gains. How is this to be accomplished?

Choosing Between Rights and Selecting Among Goals: The Analytic Dimension

The most serious presumption about social science involvement in the human rights issue is the uncritical identification of one with the other; that is to say, an unstated commitment to the idea that clear human rights policies can and should emanate from social science information. One suspects that social science interest in human rights is not unlike past such involvements: the mandarin-like features of the social scientists perceiving their interests to flow from political messages to the point where true meanings in social science are inextricably linked to political guidelines and attractive slogans. In the past, social scientists did not so much lead as follow political guidelines. Whether it be a presumed War on Poverty or a revolt against taxation, the social science community has had a strong proclivity to follow public officials rather than provide self-motivated leadership.

The human rights issue has sadly tended to follow a similar "natural history" of a political ideology. This is not to deny the reality of the human rights cause. Clearly, whatever operational guidelines are employed toward maximizing human equality and fairness among citizens and governments is worthy of support; so too are motherhood and apple pie. However, the presupposition that social scientists have the capacity to extract new meanings from the human rights cause, or manufacture innovative politics, pre-sumes that the social science community is privy to a normative structure not granted to ordinary mortals. This is clearly not the case.

At the mundane level of national policy, human rights, like the New Deal, the Fair Deal, and the Great Society, represent a histori-cal tendency on the part of the American executive government to give distinction and individual character to each of their administra-tions. This seems especially true for the Democratic party which has traditionally seen the need of each administration to delineate itself in contrast to previous administrations. In part, this trend is a consequence of a breakdown of party loyalty as such in America, and the substitution of political formulas based on mass communi-cation in their stead. Under such circumstances, it is understandable that the political system does not await the social science community to establish national guidelines. Rather, the large political system expects support from the relatively small social science community, and is willing to underwrite handsomely such support in the form of ongoing research grants and contracts.

What is interesting about the human rights issue, in contrast to previous executive political rallying cries, is its international dimension. In the past, most major slogans were confined to the national political system. Human rights is located in the international arena. Quite beyond the disintegration of party organization in America is the obvious fact that the United States, like every other major power, places its best moral foot forward whenever possible.

In the 1950s, the key was modernization, a term easily enough defined as the maximization of consumer goods and human resources. In fact, in operational terms modernization was strongly equated to transportation and communication, or those areas in which the United States was a world leader. In the 1960s, with the growing apprehension that material abundance, or modernization, may actually be counterproductive to national goals because it leaves intact the uneven distribution and class characteristics of such consummatory impulses, the key phrase became egalitarianism; or the drive toward the relative equal distribution of world resources and goods. But by the end of the 1960s, a new dilemma soon became apparent: as we were urging upon others egalitarianism as an international ideology, the virtual monopoly by the United States of material conditions of abundance in the West, converted the drive for equality to a domestic rhetoric. The actual costs of international egalitarianism were not voluntarily born by the richest nation on earth. There were other problems in driving the equity stick too hard: lower innovation, higher taxation, and the huge shift in moral specifications. Above all, egalitarianism came to mean that growth itself had a higher price than many environmentalists and social ecologists were willing to pay. When the growth curve leveled off, and even began moving downward as a result of energy shortfalls and oil boycotts, the slogans of the 1960s became increasingly dubious.

The key to the 1970s, at least in explaining the turn towards human rights, has been an American policy presentation that found it more amenable to convert equity demands into liberty demands. It was the long and strong suit of the West in an era of declining American hegemony and corresponding growth in Soviet power. The human rights issue, covertly for the most part, celebrated the fact of high political and social freedom in the West—just as modernization in the 1950s celebrated the fact that America was a consumer society, and egalitarianism in the 1960s celebrated the fact that there were large numbers of people sharing in this largesse. The long and short of it is that the human rights issue like those political formulas of previous decades, provides a sharp contrast to the socialist sector with its prima facie constraints on human rights: from exacting high punishment for low crimes, to refusal to grant travel visas for immigration purposes. Thus, human rights, whether measured by press standards, due process of law, freedom of worship, voluntary associations, multiple parties, etc., become the strong suit of the West in the 1970s. Such issues both offer a contrast to Soviet power and provide an illustration of a certain inability of slogans of a previous decade to become transformed into reality.

THE PROBLEM OF BIG POWER PRIORITIES

If one takes a newspaper on any given day, it becomes apparent that human rights, however potent as a normative instrument of foreign policy, is constantly tempered and even temporized by ongoing realities. Let me draw attention to one day in the life of the *Financial Times of London* (August 11, 1978) to illustrate this point: The United States, which had urged sanctions against the Soviet Union for its persecution and imprisonment of dissidents and human rights policies, generally relented on the sale of drill bit equipment and technology vital for the Soviet oil industry. Such equipment represented a considerable financial windfall for the United States, and it also meant that the Soviet Union was spared from generating new forms of research in a complex field. On the other hand, when the United States confronted a far weaker nation, such as Argentina, it held up the financial packaging to help in the sale of Boeing jet liners to Argentina because of its alleged human rights violations. As a result, on the same day that the United States sold equipment vital to the Soviet oil industry—with a pained admission that this violated human rights considerations—it denied a jet package to Argentina on precisely the same human rights grounds.

THE PROBLEM OF POLITICAL-ECONOMIC RIVALRY

When one thinks of the human rights question in the context of international economic realities, it become apparent that there are limits to the implementation of any policy, especially by a weakened United States at this point in time. Vacuums are filled; economic vacuums are filled rapidly. Thus, while the United States denied certain loans to Brazil, again on the basis of presumed human rights violations, the Japanese and Italians were more than willing to fill this gap, providing for a $700 million arrangement whereby Japanese and Italian capital will help in the long-term financing of new steel projects in Brazil. In addition, three companies, Sidebras, Kawaski, and Finsider of Italy, have provided terms that assist in Brazilian capital needs on more favorable terms than United States loans in the past.

THE PROBLEM OF INDIFFERENCE TO HUMAN RIGHTS

There are countries helping each other for whom human rights is not a particularly important constraint. For example, Pakistan, one of the more overt violators of human rights for its masses, has developed close links to the Muslim countries and to Iran, with the Iranians underwriting everything in Pakistan from highway construction to wheat importation. In this situation, not only has Iran been helping Pakistan, but the orchestration of this pact was done through the Eurodollars provided by none other than the American Citibank Corporation, which also helped set the rate of interest to be charged to Pakistan by Iran. These technicalities are replicated every day of the year. As a result, it is impossible to speak of the implementation of a human rights policy as if it were a geometric axiom. It might well be that the politics of boycott is the ultimate expression of a policy of human rights. But this presupposes a monopoly of goods and services, which the United States does not now possess.

THE PROBLEM OF INDIRECT SUPPORT
FOR HUMAN RIGHTS VIOLATORS

One serious dilemma which constantly arises is the need for diplomatic, political and military assistance pacts between big powers, which in turn filter such aid to other nations. For example, the United States may, on strictly military grounds, be compelled to enter hardware sales to say, Egypt and Israel, and find that some of such weapons ultimately come to be employed in supporting despotic powers such as Libya. This may work in reverse of course. Egypt may decide to sell advanced Soviet MIG-23 fighters to China, the very nation that the Soviet Union would be least inclined to see such aircraft go to. What this suggests is the multilateral nature of human rights considerations, and not just a presumed bilateral character. Aid and trade can be contained only in unusual circumstances, i.e., when a threat to cancel future agreements of an urgent sort are involved. Hence, unless a nation is prepared to monitor the circuitous routing of its entire foreign sales and aid effort, it must accept as a fact the relatively secondary status of human rights as a central foreign policy plank.

The Problem of Which Humans, What Rights

A special dilemma that plagues politicians interested in the centrality of human rights is a choice of persons to be preserved and rights to be guarded. In a situation such as the Cambodian dispute with Vietnam, one in which an alleged two million Cambodians have been subject to genocidal liquidation and another one million Vietnamese are languishing in concentration camps, a choice between evils is often faced by appeals to larger political considerations. For example, new diplomatic recognition of the People's Republic of China by the United States not only dampens criticism of China's internal human rights violations, but also leads to playing down the grotesque violations of human rights in Cambodia, a China proxy-state. It may also lead to heightened consciousness of human rights violations in Vietnam, as a mechanism for dealing with the Soviet Union. In short, decisions are required in the treatment of nations that have little in common, other than the harsh treatment of citizens by states.

It is appropriate that the West, and the United States in particular, pay stricter attention to the primary and secondary forms of constraints and contradictions. The simple moralism that would deny aid to both Nicaragua and Brazil because of human rights violations, fails to account for the differential importance of the two nations in the maintenance of United States foreign policy. As a result, even if there is a basic human rights policy, implementation tends to be differentiated if it is to make any sense, or if it is not simply to be ignored as a political spoof or bluff. In this sense, a central task of social science is to make clear situational realities and contradictory tendencies within a policy network. Social scientists must not simply lend moral weight to these efforts without regard to empirical realities and world situations, but must also lend their practical weight to appropriate decision-making.

Making Rights Operational: The Constructive Dimension

The discussion concerning human rights, at least on a global perspective, has been linked to choices between political deprivation, presumably characteristic of the East (Second World), and economic exploitation, presumably characteristic of the West (First World). Aside from the reification and polarization involved, the problem is that the human rights issue is thrown back upon ideological grounds. One senses a growing apathy with human rights questions because that rhetoric has not expanded beyond the Cold War or Iron Curtain countries.

A fitting and proper role of social science in the human rights issue is to move beyond such broad abstractions and seek out concrete expressions of both the exercise and abridgement of human rights. In this regard, the human rights issue can be joined to a framework larger than itself and more politically significant. It can be fused to questions about social systems, political regimes and economic frameworks.

One contribution that social science can make at this level is the expansion of social indicators; that is, the breakout and disaggregation of the human rights question. Therefore, instead of talking abstractly about the right to work, social scientists can talk concretely about conditions of work, protection of migrant workers, occupational work and safety measures, and social services for employees. Instead of talking about the right to life and liberty, social scientists can talk specifically about protection under the law, a right to a fair and open trial, security of a person who is incarcerated, rights of individuals to deviate from official standards of behavior. If we are talking about political rights, questions should be raised about conditions of voting, levels of participation, numbers of parties permitted to contend, electoral expenses, and the role of local vis-à-vis national government. Instead of talking about citizen rights, social scientists can raise issues of the conditions of migration outside a nation, freedom of movement within a nation, rights of asylum, protection against deportation, and the character of national and ethnic affiliations. These are the sorts of distinctions that are increasingly being made by Amnesty International and by select, specialized agencies of the United Nations.

There are national varieties in presenting the issue of human rights, and these cannot easily be eliminated. But at least the social scientist, through a sophisticated series of social indicators, can provide some flesh and not just flab to the human rights issue. For example, the Yugoslavs have carried questions of the right to work to include free choice of employment, conditions of employment, protection against unemployment, equal pay for equal work, the right to favorable remuneration, and even the right to form trade unions. On the other hand, the Yugoslav program does not include the right to strike. So at this point in time, the need of the social science community is to achieve a stage beyond the aggregated national data of the United Nations, and develop firm internationally recognized characteristics to which all nations in the civilized world adhere, at least in terms of ideals to reach.

There will doubtless still be strong ideological components based on whether a society has an "open" or "mixed" or a "central" economic system, or whether it has a multi-party, single-party, or no-party political system. There will also be differences in terms of the character of punishment and restraint characteristic of a region or nation. But these items can themselves become an area of comparative investigation. That is to say, what nations under what circumstances are in violation of human rights when the same practices in other nations may be characterized as fully observant of such rights becomes a problematic rather than a paradigmatic.

Another facet beyond that of social indicators is the study of social norms. What are the norms that are expected from a nation in the field of human rights? Here certain items can be addressed: *First,* that there be annual country reports on social questions, just as there are annual country reports on economic questions, and in that way focus attention on specific patterns of human rights violations or observances. *Second,* the encouragement of independent, non-governmental organizations which can both monitor and pressure official reports in order to gain creditability and reliability. *Third,* social science is uniquely equipped to monitor unusual conditions or emergency situations, such as famine, floods, and earthquakes, and generally victims in chronic misery and distress. In this way human rights reporting will not become mechanistic and ignore flash dangers. *Fourth,* an area that can be examined at this normative level is whether violation of human rights is being conducted officially or unofficially by governments, or whether governments use conduits to engage in human rights violations: this distinction too will prevent the monitoring of governments from becoming mechanical, ignoring the utilization of agencies perpetuating human rights violations. *Fifth,* insofar as possible, human rights reporting should be made uniform and should be monitored by the social scientific community so that agencies like the International Sociological Association, or the International Political Science Association, do more than meet every four years to exchange nationalistic platitudes and develop standing committees for monitoring, evaluating and estimating human rights gains in any period of time.

Admittedly, these are complex as well as ambitious tasks. But at least they provide a central role for the social scientific community beyond servicing the state as mandarins. The social science community is responsible for both the construction of a better future, and the criticism of present realities. It cannot subvert one for the other in the name of national unity; it cannot become a permanent positivist arm of state power, nor a perpetual destructive critique of such power. In the dialectic of construction and criticism inheres the great strength of social science. The utilization of social science by each nation in the international community of nations, will itself provide a bona fide measure of human rights. But this entails a serious recognition that the tasks of policy-makers and social scientists, although intertwined, are by no means identical either in principle or in practice. Such an awareness of the durability of differences between social sectors and intellectual forces is itself a clear representation of the status of human rights in any given society.

Comment

Carl Q. Christol

I would like to divide my remarks into two parts: one, a comment or criticism as to the things that Professor Horowitz has indicated; and, second, some remarks on what might have been said. First of all I do not think the social sciences should be allowed a monopoly on or special preoccupation with human rights. In assessing human rights issues, the emphasis should be on the gathering of the facts. I believe we can glean some important insights from areas beyond the social sciences, going into the natural sciences and elsewhere. This is point one.

Point Two: I do not think that human rights is a "Johnny-come-lately advance in the history of humanity." It should be considered in the context of political slogans, as Professor Horowitz has indicated, or in the context of the assumed philosophies of political figures that we are able to derive from their recitation of human rights expectations.

Third, I think a red herring was introduced insofar as emphasis was placed on the assertion of rights with the assumption that obligations or duties somehow are not a part of a single whole, the so-called right-duty relationship. In some ways we are talking about the right to hold opinions, to express them and to do so in an honest and responsible fashion. Another of the Universal Declaration of Human Rights is the right to work. I suppose if there is a right to work, there is a duty to perform that work in a responsible and meaningful way. I do not see that one can talk about rights and obligations as being separate and distinct. They are correlatives and they are associated one with the other.

I was intrigued by the proposition that the pursuance of human rights would produce a lower denominator of human fulfillment within the reaches of egalitarianism, within the reaches of sameness.

The history of the British law, as Barbara Jordan reminded us, was a transformation from status to contract. In status, the relationship was of the master and the serf, the elite and the subordinate. The British experience developed the notion of contract whereby the individual was allowed into a special relation with others and thereby to avoid and to separate himself or herself from the oneness of the conditions of status. As we look at that proposition at the present time, it may be that we have got to add on the further thought that we have gone from status to contract and maybe back to status again. This is the egalitarian status that was referred to in the presentation, the condition of sameness. In Barbara Jordan's consideration of the problem, she didn't say in effect, there has been governmental intervention in order to achieve this new status; rather this new status is in effect a floor. Thus the opportunities for the fulfillment of a creative person can be based upon this flooring and prevent what is in effect a quicksand of mediocrity that is a product of a new condition of status. In other words, we may have a status degree, but within that framework there are great opportunities for people of intelligence, ability and good luck to move forward into higher degrees of fulfillment—a new status, a quite different kind of status from the one of the past.

I am concerned that human rights could be identified from the national, or domestic, and international perspectives. I suppose it was simply for the purpose of making a point that Professor Horowitz suggests that human rights are domestic. It is probably an artificial way of looking at the problem of human rights to say that they are national or domestic and to exclude the thought they are international. I would suppose that the language that was used in a recent article on foreign affairs might be of some utility here. Phyllis Manning suggests that nowadays the world has moved into a new kind of community in which the problems cannot be said to be wholly domestic or wholly international but really a combination of the two: intermestic. I think that this intermestic conceptualization should be taken into account in assessment of twentieth century human rights.

I was troubled by Dr. Horowitz's argument that the United States human rights policy should be applied with a high degree of consistency. Cannot a case, in fact, be made that some unworthy beneficiaries of American largesse are more likely to be moved toward an acceptable human rights stance over time than others? Recently I was in Washington and heard a statement that intrigued me very much. The idea was presented that in this world community in which we live nowadays we are the product of a high technology. The idea was that technology produces better forms of communication, that we are in closer contact with the people around the world, and as a result of this we are going to have more contacts.

Finally, on the specific points that Professor Horowitz made, I would agree with him that the application of social science methodology is fine and ought to be used to mark adherence to human rights concepts. But I have some problems with the application of the social science methodology to the "laundry list" that he gave to us. Admittedly they are all sound propositions; I would not be critical of them as such. But I think maybe we ought to elevate our sights a little higher, as the saying goes, and try to have a vision of human rights that we could turn to the attention of the public policy people in the field of social sciences.

I will state a quick "laundry list" of my own, a vision for the concept of human rights. A concern for human rights will allow humanity to elevate its sights above the pressing and passing problems of the day. Second, this vision of human rights signals our own nation's commitment to the inherent worth of the individual. I think that's really part of the totality of the American way of life. I don't think that Mr. Carter's current involvement in human rights is anything new. I think he's simply going back to the basic premises upon which this nation was founded. It is calling them to our attention in a very important way at the present time. Third, this vision of the concept of human rights would provide a rallying point for all Americans as we come to consider in a few years from now the Bicentennial of our own Constitution and the constitutional way of life. Fourth, a vision of human rights is that it has "that something" that can restore and bring new life to a sense of harmony that now seems to be so sadly missing both at home and in many parts of the world, a new sense of purpose founded on the notion of human rights.

The next item on my "laundry list" is a vision of the perfection of institutions that can come to grips with the specific violations of human rights and the specific problems of human rights that Professor Horowitz very properly identified. And I would include within these institutions a possibility of an adjudicatory process. Those who have followed the negotiations of many of the important international conferences at the present time can see that adjudicatory processes are being worked into regimes and institutions.

Finally, there should be a vision that assures all humanity that the words in the song, "Love Is in the Air", are not merely an identification of pleasant emotion but also inspiration for the flowering of an inalienable sense of freedom and liberty.

Comment

Alan Gilbert

Professor Horowitz made the point that social science often follows politics. It is an important point and a good place to begin in a discussion of this paper.

A few years ago Robert McNamara wrote a book about poverty and the need for international redistribution of wealth. It depicted in mournful terms the situaion in India where, it said, some 200 million people live on less than $40 a year per capita. This is one example of many concerning world poverty. The plea that Robert McNamara made then was taken up by many and there ensued what is called the development decade.

The development decade failed and there has occurred an actual worsening of the distribution of income shares, including in many of the countries with which the United States is most heavily involved. International income redistribution is no longer at the top of the priority list, nor is it often said that the United States can play a big role in creating economic conditions in which rights may flourish.

Viewed against this backdrop, Dr. Horowitz is quite correct to state that the rhetoric of human rights is largely a manifestation of a decline. In other words, the United States no longer is seen to be as powerful and all-accomplishing as it once was. One has the sense that in presenting and defending human rights, particularly vis-à-vis some of the nastiness and viciousness that goes on in the Soviet Union, one is trying to preserve the credibility of the American system.

The theme of individual human rights is nothing to be particularly sanguine about in itself. The rhetoric of the human rights debate says nothing about what the United States actually is going to do about such matters in other countries, particularly in those countries that are her allies. One hears increasingly more about how state sovereignty limits the ability of the United States not only to help the least economically advantaged countries, but also to defend liberties elsewhere in the world. Social science explanation follows political reality.

It is very well to criticize ineffective or even harmful preaching about individual rights and responsibilities. But the issue does not end there. It is not merely a question of what is *preached* by a nation or a government. There is also the question of what actually is *done*. The cold fact of the matter is that many oppressive and totalitarian regimes are armed by American corporations and are the recipients of corporate investment. These are not rhetorical matters; they are actions and should be looked at as such.

A further comment deserves to be made about the issue of decline. In international studies the question of war and peace is not genuinely discussed. If one asks the question, do we live in an era of peace or an era of war, one is very likely not to get an answer. One feature of the current situation is the rising influence of the Soviet Union. This influence has an imperial and, if widely exploited, oppressive character. A recent issue of *Fortune Magazine* carried an article by Fred Iklé entitled "No. 2." The United States is no longer No. 1, it is No. 2, Iklé contended, and it is a very different thing to be No. 2 rather than No. 1. He demonstrated that United States influence is on the wane in a variety of ways.

Both social scientists and those interested in moral philosophy should explore the situation of human rights in the world, particularly when one speaks as an American. One has an obligation to look very hard at what both moral prescription and social analysis put forward, and to try to think out as clearly as possible the likely consequences of any recommendations put up by social scientists.

Given the character of its interests in many places, the fact is that the United States is in a very difficult position to defeat the Soviet challenge. It is in that position because it has aligned itself with unpopular forces that produce opposition. The Soviet Union does not have the heritage of interest in these areas that the United States does, and in fact can appeal to some forces that have perhaps more genuine popular claims.

To return to one of his themes, Professor Horowitz is concerned about the necessity for actions. Suppose that he is right in his remark that human rights is "a dead dog." Perhaps it is, perhaps it is not; the evidence is not fully gathered to support the conclusion. Even if human rights is "a dead dog," after human rights, what? One needs merely to observe the trends to note that these are very dangerous times. Pressures to go to war are increasing rather than diminishing. And these pressures are to go to war on behalf of regimes which, on the basis of any reasonable criterion of justice, would be very hard to defend.

This matter relates to another important point in Dr. Horowitz's paper. He speaks quite eloquently of the excesses of egalitarianism. These excesses create "demands" that have no reason to be met but are there nonetheless. Social scientists need to deal with this matter on a philosophical level which incorporates considerations of what are "just" demands and what are "unjust" demands. This must be done at two sub-levels. One level involves a social theory explaining how things work so that there can be some understanding of what demands mean in their own context. The other level involves much more difficult and complex questions of moral or philosophical theory.

In his book on genocide, Professor Horowitz offers a theory of genocidal regimes. It is an important subject, relating quite directly to matters involving social science applications to human rights issues. Dr. Horowitz's views are somewhat confusing, and these confusions relate to difficulties one might have in coping with the arguments he has put forward in the present paper.

In the book, Dr. Horowitz states that genocide is the systematic extermination or limitation of the life possibilities of a national minority in whole or in part. It is clear that this definition refers to a restrictive and overtly racist regime, one that pursues certain political policies. He then says that, in fact, it is a government that engages in a systematic slaughter of innocent individuals. On the one hand sociology owes an explanation of how a political policy of genocide becomes a part of a social structure. On the other hand he says the nature of genocide is to transcend any political or economic structure. Thus genocide is both a concrete thing and has an existence apart from the concrete. This makes genocide as a policy of a regime a question of choice and its adoption must therefore be a deliberate and conscious act.

In this century there are and have been societies that have predispositions to oppress or to eliminate national minorities. Indeed, some societies have selected large segments of their majority populations for oppression. One does not wish to confuse in any way the United States with the Nazi regime of Germany, and yet there is a sizeable eugenics movement in the United States. It was once a movement that got immigration laws and various implementing legislation passed on the basis of preferring a so-called pure racial stock. Today, there is much hostile feeling about minority groups in the United States. Proposition 13 in California demonstrates the feeling that there is too much government spending, especially for people on whom it is not worthwhile to spend.

With the trend toward Proposition 13 mentalities, issues surrounding questions like reverse discrimination, and the like, social scientists very properly talk about quantifying human rights in an effort to try to discover where are all the indicators that will help to predict events or help to control them. It is not only minorities but majorities whose human rights are affected by repressive policies and attitudes. The international setting in which the United States must act cannot help but be affected by internal developments. Americans particularly have advanced very broad claims on the basis of very little social science and sociology. It is time to have a look at what is happening at home and in the conduct of foreign policy before advancing rhetorical claims and statements that do not congrue with American behavior.

Comment

E. Raymond Platig

These remarks must be prefaced by the statement that they are made in a personal rather than official capacity.

Professor Horowitz is a learned and considerable authority on a wide variety of subjects. He has been involved in a number of important controversies concerning vital issues that command the attention of serious and thoughtful persons. He is well-known for his ability to defend vigorously and effectively his points of view, and there is little doubt that he can defend his views as put forward in his paper, "Human Rights, Foreign Policy, and the Social Sciences."

This paper has not fully met the expectations its readers had for it; it does not seem to address the topic which it was predicted to cover. The issue was to be new approaches to human rights, images of the future. Dr. Horowitz's paper deals primarily with certain special claims social science may have in addressing questions of human rights.

These comments will not deal directly with the substance of Dr. Horowitz's paper. Professor Christol and Professor Gilbert have done that with considerable skill. Rather, these comments will try to suggest some images of human rights for the future. These images do not necessarily represent new approaches to human rights. It is hoped, however, that each image will be seen as related to one or another of the approaches to the question of human rights that have been presented by other writers contributing to this work. It will not be an exhaustive list for there may be other approaches with which the reader is already familiar or which will be found in subsequent pages. It is mainly an attempt to order some thoughts about these matters and to bear an implicit comment on the paper given by Dr. Horowitz.

Image One of the future is a world that marches forward to a global culture in which human rights, in all their dimensions—political, social, economic—are increasingly realized in practice in all the communities of mankind. It is a global culture in which the rhetoric of international human rights becomes universal reality.

This image seems to be what is buried in Professor Horowitz's approach to the subject of human rights. He does indeed take the rhetoric of human rights very seriously and assigns to the social sciences the task of social construction, of social criticism, of social monitoring. These are the tasks that will force the governors of human communities to translate the rhetoric into practice.

This is a vision of the future in which a homogenized culture emerges. It is a culture that looks suspiciously like the world of reason and science, like the world of liberty and equality, like the world of peace and plenty, like the world of technology and progress. All these goals and values are ones toward which certain strands of Western liberalism and socialism have long been leading and which are the chief intellectual equipment of a large number of Western thinkers. It is, however, a typically, if not merely parochial, Western view or image of the future.

Presumably, in this image of the future, it is the United States that will lead the world into the promised land which these goals and values undergird. Professor Horowitz seems to suggest that the West may already have begun this transformation. Nevertheless, he states that the United States has tragically and unnecessarily retreated suddenly from its leadership role. Not everyone shares this view. This is a sketch of one possible image of the future.

Image Two is of a world in which cultural diversity persists and finds expression in a multiplicity of political cultures and systems that continue to defy the effort to find a universal conception of human rights having any reference in the real world of political practice. Indeed, it is conceivable that as the age of Western colonialism recedes even further into history, there will be a resurgence of traditional political cultures in which the concept of rights as vested in the individual will be totally alien and increasingly rejected even in the rhetoric. It is certainly conceivable that this could happen. If a trend toward this kind of future begins, it will be accelerated as the "silver plating" of Westernization that has been applied to some of the non-Western cultures wears off and the true metal of indigenous culture begins to shine through.

This second image of the future is one conjured up by the approach to world affairs and human rights taken by Professor Adda Bozeman. In her very important work she has done a devastating job of pointing out the pretentiousness of many modern Western assumptions concerning the universality, not of such obviously political concepts as human rights, but of some of the very fundamental concepts that shape our whole perception of the world.

Professor Bozeman has demonstrated that there is no universal conception of time and that a conception of time has something to say about how history and the future are understood. There is no universal conception of nature understood in all cultures in the same way. A conception of nature has something to do with how man is understood. Rationality is not found in the Western sense in all cultures and, therefore, the sense of what is efficacious action in not necessarily universal. Science is clearly a Western invention. Other cultures have other ways of knowing what law is. There is no universal conception of law and that has something to say about differing ideas concerning authority. The conception of community varies tremendously from culture to culture and that has something to say about what is called nation-building. The list of differences could be lengthened.

If Image Two, a world of plurality, is a description of what the future will be, then there must be developed an approach to the future that matches what is likely to be. Professor Horowitz's approach to the future seems rather inadequate for moving into a future of pluralistic societies. One would have to recur to Professor Bozeman's suggestion that there be introduced a considerable note of modesty into discussions and actions about human rights in other countries and cultures.

A corollary to this note of modesty is a re-examination of Western conceptions of rights. If the West is to locate itself in a future increasingly dominated by diversity, then it is highly important to insure that internal notions of rights and responsibilities be sufficiently cognizant of differing attitudes to make a comfortable spot in the world possible. A further necessity, if the ideas imbedded in Image Two are correct, is the need to move very quickly to become much better conversant with some of the world's non-Western cultures and to do it with as few predispositions as possible. That is certainly a difficult thing to do. Everyone carries his own heritage with him, and immersion in another culture is not easy to achieve. Even if one can immerse himself in it, learning anything from the immersion can be very strenuous. It does seem, however, that the world of the future is bound to be pluralistic. The thrust to introduce Americans of all ages and levels, in all occupations, to the complexity of a multi-cultural world, is something that should begin to accelerate very quickly.

Image Three is not a pleasant one to contemplate and most avoid thinking about it. It is an image of a world in which all political systems spin out of control or collapse under the burden of population growth, resource depletion, environmental degradation. It is an image of the future that has been proposed by many persons. In such a world, human rights would be irrelevant. It would be a world in which each man may indeed appear to each other man as a wolf, and in which life would be nasty, brutish, and short. This is a future all would wish to avoid.

The wish to avoid this future raises a fundamental question. Does the approach taken to individual rights and responsibilities have anything to do with the degree of success needed to avoid moving into this third image? Are the ideas that individuals carry around in their heads and on which they act concerning human rights and responsibilities important elements in shaping a policy that avoids creating a world according to this third image? More specifically, would policies designed to create Image One, the homogenized culture, or policies designed to recognize Image Two, the multi-cultural world, be more likely to avoid Image Three, complete collapse?

It is one thing to speculate about alternative images of the future, and there is certainly a tremendous need for trying to determine alternative models. Most practical people, however, will soon tire of these exercises and will want to know something about a course of action to be undertaken with the objective of achieving some sort of goal. The United States government has official spokesmen who talk about human rights to Americans and to the world at large. But those statements that are made as representing official policy pronouncements may or may not coincide with the ideas that individual citizens may have about how these matters ought to be treated.

A profoundly important exercise for every citizen to undertake, then, is to attempt to determine for himself ways in which to achieve the desired future. One of the important things to remember in this exercise is that the United States, contrary to what many are saying, continues to carry the major burden of leadership in these matters in the world, and that the utterances of the President of the United States indeed carry important and considerable weight. They need to be attended to and influenced by as many as are able.

Tenets of
Official Policy
on Human Rights

by Mark L. Schneider

It is a pleasure to address this symposium and to offer a view from within the Carter Administration on our human rights policy.

This forum is reaffirmation of the special nature of foreign policy in a democratic society. Through these interchanges between scholars, citizens and officials, greater public awareness of American foreign policy can be matched by greater government awareness of public concerns. Without that mutual awareness, government in a democracy will find it first difficult and then impossible to maintain its policies.

The Carter Administration came to office with a determination to raise the priority accorded to human rights concerns in American foreign policy. It was a determination born of our experience over recent years when the Congress and public opinion clearly pressed for greater reflection of our domestic values in our foreign policies.

I believe few can challenge the flat assertion that the original determination has yielded both a new rhetoric and a new reality.

Human rights issues have a far higher priority in the design and implementation of American foreign policy than before.

Critics can have legitimate grounds to challenge particular decisions, the tactics chosen in a specific country or the balance accorded to other U.S. interests in a policy review.

But no one can fail to recognize fundamental differences in the visibility of human rights concerns in American foreign policy today.

— Instead of funneling more and more support to a regime in Chile which had drawn consistent international criticism for its human rights abuses, we have a clear record of pressing for a return to democratic values in that country. I believe the American people support that change.

— Instead of remaining on the margins of the process of change in Southern Africa, today we are a central player in the drama seeking to promote racial and political justice in that region. I believe the American people support that change.

— Instead of silently observing the lack of fulfillment of the human rights provisions of the Helsinki Final Act, we have spoken out clearly in support of the rights of Soviet dissidents guaranteed within that document. And I believe the American people support that change as well.

Policy Objectives

Across the globe today, in too many countries, men and women face prison and even death for daring to exercise rights guaranteed by all the nations of the world thirty years ago. Yet the words of the Universal Declaration of Human Rights still are unkept promises for hundreds of millions of human beings.

The impact of those unkept promises is understood fully only when you talk to the victims—the woman whose two sons and daughter were abducted from their homes by security forces and never heard from again; the community organizer who told of being hooded and tortured with electric shocks; the exiled wife of a political prisoner who can only pray that she will see her husband again.

These are individuals whose futures have become living tragedies because governments still fail to keep the promises set forth in the Universal Declaration.

This Administration has tried to speak for those victims far more frequently than in the past.

That message has been heard by countless governments. To them, it expresses deep concern. It has been heard by the dissidents in countless countries as well. To them, it expresses hope. Governments would like it to be muted. Dissidents would like its cadence to be even louder.

The overall objective of our policy is to be effective in encouraging greater respect for human rights around the world.

The rights we promote are not parochial United States values that we are foisting on others. They are standards first laid down in the Universal Declaration of Human Rights, whose thirtieth anniversary we commemorate this year. They are standards reiterated by the membership of the United Nations a dozen years ago in the crafting of the covenants on civil and political rights and economic, social and cultural rights. They are standards that speak to the basic dignity of human beings.

Thus, the standards we use were forged in the cauldron of international consensus over the past three decades.

First, the right to be free from governmental violation of the integrity of the person: gross abuses such as summary execution; torture and cruel, inhuman or degrading treatment or punishment; arbitrary arrest or imprisonment; denial of fair public trial and invasion of the home.

Second, the right to fulfillment of such vital needs as food, shelter, health care, and education.

Third, the right to enjoy civil and political liberties: freedom of thought, religion, assembly, speech and the press; freedom of movement; and freedom to take part in government.

We view each set as important and reject the notion of trading one against the other.

Some have argued that economic development must be the first priority. They assert that political repression is an unfortunate but acceptable pre-condition. President Carter has given our response in his address to the Parliament of India, a nation that has accepted the challenge of both development and democracy.

The President said, "There are those who say that democracy is a kind of rich man's plaything and that the poor are too preoccupied with survival to care about the luxury of freedom and the right to choose their own government. This argument is repeated all over the world—mostly, I have noticed, by persons whose own bellies are full and who speak from positions of privilege and power in their own societies."

All too frequently governments that deny their citizens basic political freedoms blithely undertake economic policies whose benefits are aimed at the few. As John Dewey once wrote, "without exception, dictatorial governments deny to their citizens freedom of thought and expression, because they rightly fear the consequences of such freedom." Citizens with freedom to speak tend to challenge inequity in economic systems as rapidly as they do injustice in legal systems.

There are other governments that justify their own abuses by citing the unconscionable acts of terrorism within their society. The threat of terrorism is real; but as Secretary of State Cyrus Vance stated to the Organization of American States, "The surest way to defeat terrorism is to promote justice in our societies—legal, economic, and social justice. Justice that is summary undermines the future it seeks to promote. It produces only more violence, more victims, and more terrorism."

Those who question the standards we apply rarely are interested in a change of definition. What they really want is for the U.S. to stop asking questions about torture and arbitrary imprisonment and denial of freedom. What they want is for the international human rights covenants to remain on library shelves and not on the desks of State department decision makers.

We are not going to yield to those demands. We are going to continue to pursue human rights as a fundamental aspect of foreign policy. Where there is progress, we are going to try to respond with more cooperative relations. Where there is failure to progress, we are going to continue to demonstrate that there will be costs in our bilateral relations.

Others assert that we cannot implement a human rights policy in our foreign affairs until we have resolved the flaws in our domestic performance. We acknowledge those gaps between the promise of our own laws and Constitution and reality; but we are seeking to close those gaps.

Yet we cannot deny our own role in the international community while we improve our performance at home. The only question is how we act in the international arena and with what objectives. We believe that we should seek ways to support human rights and democratic principles.

We do so because we have international obligations that demand it of us. We do so because it is in the interest of the United States. And we do so because it is right.

Policy Implementation

To understand the way we have implemented the human rights policy, I would argue that there have been three underlying principles.

First, the policy is global, not aimed at a particular country or directed with an ideological motive, but aimed at advancing human rights for all peoples. Second, the policy will not be implemented in rigid lock-step, bound by automatic formulae. The assessment of short-term and long-term objectives and the choice of tactics must reflect the political, social, and cultural reality of each country. Third, human rights objectives in U.S. foreign policy are flanked by other fundamental interests as well, some such as the avoidance of nuclear war, that go to the very core of our security and the security of all peoples. However, the fundamental change in our analysis is that human rights concerns no longer are at the margins of discussion; instead they have moved to the center of debate.

INTERNAL ORGANIZATION

From the inside, one can see the following shifts in structure and behavior that reflect a new reality.

Internally, there now is an independent Bureau of Human Rights and Humanitarian Affairs in the State Department. Given the nature of the bureaucratic system, this means we enter as equal combatants in the struggle to design policy. The National Security Council also has accorded special responsibility for human rights to individuals on its staff. And we have established inter-agency mechanisms to review the full range of U.S. bilateral and multilateral assistance programs.

"QUIET" DIPLOMACY

In our bilateral relations, we are talking about human rights issues with presidents and prime ministers, not with second secretaries. By raising the level of diplomatic discussion, other governments inevitably re-examine their own practices and calculate anew the costs and benefits, knowing that continued repression will impose penalities in the character of bilateral dealings with this government.

Our approach has not been limited to quiet diplomacy. We have practiced vigorous diplomacy in which all of the instruments of diplomacy are applied but in a graduated and sequential order.

That process may involve symbolic affirmations of our concern through our meeting with opposition political figures or exiled victims of human rights abuses. When Administration officials visit a country, as President Carter did in Brazil, as Vice-President Mondale did in the Philippines and as Secretary Vance did in Argentina, we have insured that there would be visible evidence of our human rights concerns. These officials did not meet only with government officials; they met as well with political opposition leaders and with those who have dared to champion human rights causes in those countries.

ECONOMIC ASSISTANCE RELATIONSHIPS

Where there is no response to our human rights concerns, both our laws and our policy demand that we examine our assistance relationships. As Deputy Secretary of State Warren Christopher declared, "When countries we assist consistently curtail human rights, and where our preferred diplomatic efforts have been unavailing, we must consider restrictions on the flow of our aid, both overall levels and individual loans and grants."

Increasingly, our bilateral economic assistance programs will channel larger shares of aid to countries that are improving their human rights records.

We also have opposed more than thirty loans in the international financial institutions to countries that engage in serious and persistent violations of human rights, and told other countries that if they brought the loans to a vote we would oppose them. A half-dozen

. loans have been withdrawn from consideration as a result. We have advised the Export-Import Bank and OPIC on our views about the human rights conditions in other countries and made those countries aware that all aspects of our relationship can be affected by continuing violations of human rights.

SECURITY ASSISTANCE RELATIONSHIPS

In security assistance programs as well, we have incorporated human rights concerns.

During the course of recent months, we have reduced or declined to increase our military aid to a number of countries and refused to sign certain military assistance agreements or to issue export licenses for commercial arms sales because of human rights concerns.

We have denied crowd control equipment and radar surveillance devices, radio emission locating equipment, armored cars and personnel carriers, infrared and other night vision devices. We have denied handguns, machine guns, automatic rifles and ammunition to national police agencies in countries engaged in human rights violations.

All of these decisions are sprinkled with difficulty. They are made infinitely more complicated by the necessity to be aware of other fundamental interests of the United States. The diversity of history and culture and the different stages of development of individual countries also make the choice of the best approach ever more complex. Yet, we cannot be paralyzed by these problems. Individual rights are abused. People are tortured. People disappear. We cannot ask the victims to wait for us to elaborate the last detail of our policy instructions. We will reach judgments, we will act. The victims cannot wait.

INTERNATIONAL ADVOCACY

I have sought to describe a calibrated approach we have used in the bilateral arena to press our human rights concerns. However, the policy also has been characterized by a sharp rise in human rights advocacy within international organizations as well.

This year, in the UN Human Rights Commission, action was

taken on Uganda, Cambodia and Equatorial Guinea. For the first time, there was consensus that the 1503 procedures of that body should yield action by the international community rather than have its reports disappear into the dust of bureaucratic oblivion.

UNESCO also put into operation a new complaint procedure in which individuals can denounce directly violations of their economic and social rights. Governments are called on to respond.

We are seeking in the UN General Assembly this year to establish a registry of human rights experts that the Secretary General can draw on to assist in his own efforts to use his good offices to promote greater respect for human rights.

We are working to incorporate legal procedures to buttress the 1975 Declaration Against Torture, moving us closer to the time when torture is alien to our experience.

President Carter, on signing the international human rights covenants a year ago and submitting them to the Senate for ratification, has emphasized the ultimate goal of an international system of legal standards and enforcement mechanisms to monitor and protect human rights. We intend to press for full public education on the importance of these documents as part of our commemoration of the thirtieth anniversary of the adoption of the Universal Declaration of Human Rights.

Hopefully, we will start the next Congress with the ratification of the Genocide Convention, to place us alongside the eighty-two other nations which have joined in condemning the massive destruction of human life that occurred in the Holocaust.

Policy Effectiveness

In any assessment of strategy a key question is what have been the results. Our goal has always been to be effective, to ease the suffering of individuals and open the political process.

Last December the International League for Human Rights issued a year-end report and made the following statement:

First, within the past year, human rights has for the first time become a subject of national policy debate in many countries. Second, human rights concerns have also been the focus of greater discussion in international organizations such as the United Nations, the Organization of American States and the Belgrade Conference. Third, the world media has focused on international human rights issues to a greater extent than ever before. Fourth, consciousness of human rights among the peoples of the world has increased significantly. Fifth, there has been an easing of repression in a substantial number of cases.

The League then went on to state: "A most significant factor has been President Jimmy Carter's affirmation and advocacy of the United States' commitment to the international protection of human rights and United States encouragement of other states to undertake a similar commitment." They then listed improvements in some twenty-nine countries.

The Deputy Secretary of State cited in a recent speech to the American Bar Association in New Orleans some of the changes we have seen during the past year. Those changes affected countries on every continent—prisoners released, political liberalization, a lifting of censorship, even return to democracy. He noted that we would neither take credit for them nor accept them as evidence that repression had ceased. Nevertheless, in some cases individual human beings were no longer behind bars and, in others, some move toward the rule of law had been made.

Yet, the sobering realization remains that repression continues unchecked in numerous countries. Men and women remain behind bars because they will not be silent and because they aspire to be free. Governments use torture and brutally violate virtually every right contained within the Universal Declaration on Human Rights.

In all too many countries, fundamental legal protections for the individual against the overwhelming power of the state either do not exist or are so fragile as to be meaningless. Albert Einstein once wrote, "A large part of history is therefore replete with the struggle for those human rights, an external struggle in which a final victory can never be won. But to tire in that struggle would mean the ruin of society."

The struggle goes on. And we are part of it.

Comment

David H. Bayley

I want first to say something about the theme of the conference. A point has been in my mind and it simply has to do with the relation between rights and responsibilities. There is a logical relationship between those concepts—one that has enormous political signifi-cance that I would like to elaborate upon briefly. A right is a claim for validation by an individual upon the group in which he lives. In other words, it makes no sense to say that I have a right to free speech if, when my free speech is violated, I can't appeal to some-body in order to defend that right, in order to restore the right that had been infringed. If this is the case—and I think this is a view of rights that agrees with legal theory and with most definitions of rights—this suggests that as the ambit of rights in any society in-creases, so do the obligations of that society, as the validating group of people, to the individual.

This is a point that needs some lingering on for just a moment. I am suggesting that as the scope of rights that people can claim grows, the power and influence of the state must also grow in order effectively to meet those I.O.U.'s, which is another way of describ-ing what a right really is. One of the paradoxes between rights and responsibilities, at least in the Western world, is that as we act out of concern to vivify a larger group of rights, we inevitably augment the power of the state. It is a mistake in Western political theory that we often pretend that rights are to be asserted *against* the state. What I am suggesting is that in the assertion of rights, there must be a group that makes them real. In the Western world, that is the state. Curi-ously enough, then, one of the engines that pushes the growth in the capacity of the state is the desire itself for rights.

Now, this is not to say that the power and influence of the state grows only in a relationship to demands for rights. That would be nonsense. There is a host of other mechanisms or motivations and political phenomena that also cause the power of the state to grow. But one of them is the demand for rights. This can lead to a very significant legitimacy problem. That is, when large groups of people ask for rights of a certain sort and the state is unable to validate them, the state is then called into question. It seems clear that in the United States now to some extent, as well as other places in the world, the demand for rights has highlighted the fact that the state must do something on their behalf. This requirement that the state act effectively, imposes new reponsibilities and new demands on the citizenry—and in some cases, the citizenry is saying no. It is the case that there are demands for rights which then require demands by the state on the citizens to give something—often money, or time or talent. The result is, in effect, a legitimacy crisis because one group of people is asking for rights and the logical conclusion is that other groups of people in society must provide the wherewithal whereby those I.O.U.'s may be cashed.

I said that as the ambit of rights grows, so must the capacity of the state. The interesting question is, at least logically, is there a symmetry in this relationship? In other words, wouldn't it be satisfying if, as the responsibilities and capacity of the state grew, so also grew the rights of individuals? Unfortunately, that is not the case. The relationship between rights and responsibilities as I've outlined them very quickly is asymmetrical. The expansion of rights, I believe, does lead to the expansion of the capacity of the state, but the converse is not true. There are certainly many cases in which the capacity of the state has grown enormously, but it would be foolish to pretend that this has created on the part of the state obligations toward the individual that are always validated. When state power grows, and therefore citizen responsibilities, and this happens without a corresponding growth of rights, the result is tyranny by definition. On the other hand, when state power grows and citizen responsibilities can be exercised and expanded with respect to rights, you have democracy. Both systems may have legitimacy problems. That is, the state may make promises it cannot keep because the responsibility—the obligations, therefore—of the citizens toward the state are rejected by the citizens themselves.

As I have thought about this, it has become clear to me that tyranny and democracy, and rights and responsibilities, are integrally related in a way that requires considerable thought. This scheme seems to me very neat. In fact, it is so neat that it may have something wrong with it.

Mr. Schneider's defense of what is loosely referred to as the Carter policy of human rights in foreign policy has been very well done indeed. I have been appalled at the level of discussion of this so-called policy in the United States. I do not think it makes any sense at all to be either for or against a human rights policy in the abstract. Others have said that what is needed in human rights policy is balance. I submit that it is meaningless to talk about balance unless you get down to specifics with respect to three features of human rights policy: Which rights are you talking about? What means for achieving those rights are you talking about? And which countries are you targeting for your activities? To talk about being for or against Mr. Carter's policy does not make intellectual sense unless you begin to get down to cases. You have to specify the nature of rights, the nature of means, and the target of countries. This seems to me absolutely elementary.

But I do not hear people in the media going into such refinements of the topic. They are either approving or disapproving in the abstract. For example, if Carter went to the Court of St. James's in London and simply referred to the fact that American government is based on the Declaration of Independence, that's a foreign policy action. Is it exceptionable? Of course it isn't. On the other hand, if the United States were to take a suggestion out of some of Senator McGovern's recent comments and invade Cambodia in order to prevent genocide, the cost would be very large. Each of these activities represents foreign policy having to do with human rights. Almost no one would disagree with the one action. The other would probably get people in the streets again. If both of these actions qualify as being part of a human rights policy, how is it sensible then to say that you're either for the policy, or against it, or that you like a balance in it? One person's balance is another person's tyranny, or another person's indifference. One really must talk about cases.

In his paper, Mr. Schneider says that there will be no trade-offs among various human rights. I don't believe that will work. When you are making policy, surely you are going to have to decide in the case of some countries that violation of a particular right is worthy of action, even if the country has done well on other dimensions. In other words, in the practical world, there will be some countries that do well and others that do not. India, for example, certainly is not doing well in vivifying the right of economic and social well-being. Indeed, I am not sure the Indian government could ever meet claims of rights in those particular areas. The fact is, however, that at the moment we are applauding India on the dimension of political and civil liberties. We are choosing, and again rightly, to be quiet about India with respect to the problem of economic development. Other cases could be found where the reverse is true, where in fact the country may at the moment be doing very well mobilizing resources for economic development. But it may not be doing so well on political and civil rights. We might choose, for reasons that many might accept, to be quiet for the moment. In a practical world, there will be some trade-offs; at least there will be some priorities.

On the second point, which is the means of making these rights real, Mr. Schneider did indicate that the Administration is very discriminating in the choice of means it chooses, all the way from advocacy of meetings with dissidents, to letters to dissidents, to economic leverage, to boycott, to the restriction on arms sales, and so forth. And it's here that the expertise of the diplomat really comes into play.

It is the third point, or dimension, that is especially interesting. It has to do with features in a specific foreign country that might affect a decision to press either some right or some other right in some particular way. Adda Bozeman perhaps provided an insight on this problem when she suggested that it might be possible to divide the countries of the world into a couple of batches: those that understand radical individualism in the West and are capable then of understanding intellectually a posture or a policy that presses for human rights, and those countries which do not, by virtue of culture. There is a subcategory that includes those countries that understand basic human rights, but decide not to allow their people to enjoy them. Then there is the group of countries that both understand and allow their people to enjoy these rights. It seems that there might be different policies toward countries, depending into which category they fall. There are other characteristics of countries, useful for categorizing them, that would be important, such as their strategic relationship with the United States, their historical friendships, the alliance structure and so on.

What is suggested here is a cost-benefit analysis that would involve an analysis of the human rights policy according to these three dimensions. It should be possible to work out some kind of cybernetic model that could assist in determining what kinds of rights to press for, and how, in specific countries. There would be different costs depending upon the means used. This kind of analysis would probably get very complex very fast. It is, however, the kind of analysis that intelligent policy makers are required to do.

The dimensions suggested here are only three, and there probably are a hundred others that could cascade from a fertile mind. But these are the three I have chosen and they lead to some very simple principles. For example, a prudent foreign policy probably presses hardest those countries that understand human rights, but don't allow even elementary rights and which have very little strategic cost to the United States. Which countries might fit into that batch? Chile, for example, is a case in point. It could be pressed because Chileans do understand Western individualism and they have denied certain elementary rights of the civil and political character. It is unlikely that Chile has great strategic value, although honest people may differ about this evaluation. The only real question would be, what are the costs of alternative measures of leverage?

A second point would be that with countries that understand what it means to have human rights and have made real a great number of them, those countries are pressed much less hard than countries such as Chile. Here Britain and France serve as examples. Let us take, for example, Britain, which may from time to time infringe certain rights. One certainly withholds leverage from that particular country as opposed to the Soviet Union where the number of rights, at least of a political and civil sort, are much less real than in Great Britain. One could play this game for a long time, but the point is that this game is essential if any discussion of human rights is to be real.

There is one final point to be made. There is in all of this one huge normative problem that should be underscored. There is a real conflict in the minds of many thoughtful people between an alleged right of self-determination and individual rights. In other words, self-determination is the right that belongs to groups; individual rights by definition belong to members of groups. The resulting clash between these notions is the dilemma one sees abroad and the dilemma one sees for groups in the United States. If the United States government, either at home or abroad, presses to make individual rights real within certain groups, either foreign countries or ethnic groups in the United States, it may destroy the cultural cohesion of those particular groups. Can the United States government then justifiably be accused of abridging the right of self-determination of those particular groups?

This is a charge that native American Indians, for example, have talked about a great deal. They have said that the intrusion of the dominant legal system into the reservations has been a force for the destruction of the coherence of certain kinds of cultural values in those areas. The same may be true in the pursuit of human rights policies with respect to foreign countries. The question is, do people have a cultural right not to be treated according to the tenets of radical individualism? If it is essential, in making an American policy of human rights intelligent, that the kind of analysis I have sketched very briefly be undertaken, is it important that the alternative trade-offs, be exposed publicly? Should the people of the United States be taken into the confidence of the government with respect to these kinds of trade-offs?

Comment

Timothy Fuller

I would like to begin by echoing David Bayley's remarks about Mr. Schneider's paper. It was a strong and eloquent defense of the Administration's commitment to human rights. I would single out two points that he makes in the course of his paper that seem to me worthy of note. The first is that there is no point in being detained by the fact that our country is flawed in the pursuit of a commitment to the values that represent our tradition at its highest.

Second, in regard to the relationship between economic deprivation and the value of liberty, I would say that he also makes a good point. His point is that it is not necessary for economic deprivation to be eliminated completely before liberty becomes a value. To link them in that way seems to me to represent two mistakes. First, while it is obvious that there is a certain level of deprivation at which human beings cease to be engaged in the pursuit of the higher things of human life, that level is undoubtedly much lower than is supposed by many of the people who offer this theory. And second, as we ought to understand in our own society, and as has been pointed out to us on numerous occasions during this conference, those who believe that the prerequisite of valuing liberty is to be economically well-off, end up postponing their commitment to liberty for the infinite aggrandizement of their own material condition.

So far then, I have a positive response to Mr. Schneider's paper. At this point, though, I must say that my reservation about it is not so much for what it is in itself, but because in a certain sense it does not reach to the heart of the theme of this conference. If there is a central theme in all of these discussions, it is a question of who we are and what we stand for. Thus, I will try to comment on the question of human rights with respect to the way in which it reveals our self-understanding or lack thereof, and try to suggest what I think to be the central theoretical question that is posed in our attempt to understand ourselves.

The current debate over human rights must be seen in part as the renewal of a long-term quest for American self-understanding. I don't mean by saying this that the issue has no significance for the rest of the world because it is undoubtedly true that the settled or unsettled condition of American self-understanding is an important factor in the fortunes of the rest of the world. As one recent writer has put it in a very well-known article in *Commentary Magazine*, the human rights issue presents an immense challenge to the Administration. Having made it a cornerstone of his effort to restore the authority of American foreign policy, President Carter may stand or fall with his performance in this field. If it is mishandled, carried out without judgment or discrimination, or based on a false symmetry, a global campaign for human rights can lead to the further isolation of the United States and a further lowering of its prestige. Firmly and prudently pursued it could give an enormous impetus to the cause of freedom all over the world and enhance American stature and influence. Excuses for inaction may be made by small countries whose capacity to influence the course of world politics is by necessity limited; but a great nation, hesitant or afraid to speak up and to act on its beliefs and values at a critical juncture of world history, is forfeiting its international standing and embarking on a course of moral and political decline.

It would be hard to put the case for this policy in a more dramatic way. The suggestion is, and I think it is echoed also in Mr. Schneider's paper, that not only the fortunes of people around the world are at stake but also the historic destiny of America herself. And I think the significance of this cannot be fully understood if we do not see that this issue is the complement to the issue of Vietnam, because Vietnam also is taken to be a great watershed in American history.

According to many commentators, Vietnam taught us that the pursuit of the American purpose in the world might inevitably require the use of methods contradictory to that purpose, particularly intervention in the life of other states. Would we not then be restricted to relations with those states encompassed by external interaction, contrary to Professor Bayley's suggestion? And would this not mean that the centrality of the American experience in the world under these restrictions would be in the hands of fate? Would we be able to believe that our historic experience was any longer relevant to ourselves? Should we to whatever degree possible turn away from the world? Is that the only course left for a society that has experienced the climactic self-contradiction when men must struggle against the consequences of actions they themselves have initiated?

It is no doubt in light of questions raised by Vietnam, like these, that there is considerable uncertainty and doubt as to the prospects for an explicit commitment to the cause of human rights. Beyond that, there is a deeper uncertainty as to what the commitment to human rights can mean for us. Is it to be taken as uniting ourselves to an abstract universal humanity, a kind of relevance without cost?

Or is it to be taken as evidence of the re-establishment in the world of a presence that believes itself to represent a substantial and fundamental moral good? The difficulty is recognized in Mr. Schneider's paper and not resolved there, nor would I expect it to be resolved. The point is clearly made in his paper, where he on the one hand commits himself to global implementation of the policy of human rights, and on the other hand acknowledges that the meaning of the policy will vary with the infinite diversity and variety of peoples that compose the international society. That is the tribute that this policy must pay to that virtue of statecraft which, so far as I am aware, is still the hallmark of successful statecraft, namely improvements.

The traditional instruments of statecraft cannot be dispensed with. And it is only a mask of that fact when we begin to understand the formation of our policies in abstraction. That is, instead of beginning from the historic practices and commitments that inform our self-understanding, we begin with an abstract statement of those principles and then hope to find a way to reinsert them in a world which is resistant to them and which does not have the historic practices and commitments that give them concrete meaning.

To cite only one example, it is a commonplace now, among many commentators on foreign policy who advocate a policy of human rights, to talk about a convergence of value in the world community. We have heard a good deal of talk of that sort during this conference, and we were reminded by Professor Horowitz that technical instruments are about to be provided to us which will give us the illusion that we have accomplished that. But the question is whether there is a comparability between one state and another that would be necessary to provide any demonstration that a convergence of values is available to us now or has been at any time in the past. There seems to be a refusal to recognize the ambiguity a doctrine of convergent values contains.

The historic experience of America is based on a certain commitment to rights; there is no doubt about that. The commitment to rights that Americans have is based on a long-standing tradition of thought and action, embedded in specific attempts to create freedoms for people to enjoy under specific circumstances. The long course of struggle to achieve those freedoms in various ways, and the continuing struggle to improve upon them, have evolved a theoretical conception of what the significance of that historical struggle must have meant. But it is not sufficient, under the current circumstances, for us to believe that there can be a form of universality which can now realize itself in concrete circumstances all over the world. The lesson in Vietnam was, of course, that this is doubtful, if at all possible. And a commitment to human rights is to some extent mitigated in that it becomes a vehicle for avoiding the lesson that commitment and its failure represented.

There are two kinds of universality in moral thought, and unfortunately they are both not adequately understood by most people who discuss them. One form is the universality that is achieved at the price of abstract statements of principles. Its more concrete form at the present time is the argument of the convergence of value or the universal aspiration of freedom which informs the behavior of all human beings whatsoever. No questions are raised in these discussions as to whether the symbolization of that meaning in a specific constitutional order or historic practice is possible or shareable. Consequently, in a world that is admittedly hostile to our interests and in which we have recently suffered a major defeat in our commitments, it becomes a question for us whether we can be satisfied with a universality that comes with the belief that there is a moral right in the historic practice which we enjoy.

The other kind of universality, in short, is not an abstract statement of principles, stated in such a way that they can have universality because they can apply everywhere and nowhere. It is a kind of universality that exists from being a presence in the world, and which recognizes itself to be a fundamental positive value to the world, without having the hope of a concrete actualization everywhere. We must consider whether this means that all concrete moral practices are barriers to moral universality, or whether the more genuine task is, as it has always been, to discern as clearly as possible what are preferable among the concrete actual moral practices of mankind.

If the values we consider to be of the highest order are those which, however imperfectly have been historically enshrined in a particular tradition, our own, we shall have to accept the fact that in the natural course of things, what is universally significant is not self-evidently so and can never be, because it must arise in particular times and places, and in particular institutions and practices.

This is an embarrassment only if those who have been fortunate enough to be the bearers of this manifestation fear the responsibility, never easy to bear, thus thrust upon them; or if they make the prideful mistake of confounding their self-indulgent desires with the carrying out of that responsibility. In this there could be a true act of moral transcendance but it is not the transcendance of the moral practice in question; rather it is the overcoming of the temptation to believe that human unity is to be sought by affirming only what all affirm and rejecting what all will not accept. Either we have lived under the guidance of the true insight into the nature of man and his situation, or we have not. We must decide that for ourselves. And if our decision is to reaffirm what we have historically believed, it is incumbent upon us, as quietly as may be possible, to refuse to compromise our knowledge of who we are.

We must ask ourselves whether universal significance lies in defending a form of moral knowledge both accessible and familiar in a concrete practice or in the form of a moral obscurity, an abstract. The current debate over morality and foreign policy will be of little value if these questions are not clarified. Accordingly, if we are to discuss in a serious way the question of the rights and responsibilities of individuals, we must return to the perennial task of understanding ourselves in our historic commitments and practices.

Comment

Vernon Van Dyke

In connection with American policy on human rights, an area where we face extremely difficult problems in Southern Africa—Rhodesia, South Africa, Southwest Africa. There the central slogan advanced is majority rule. A majority rule is to be the solution to the problems there, and I simply want to address myself to this fact and raise the question whether majority rule is a good and sensible guide. I consider it a superficially appealing kind of slogan. One does not often find people opposing majority rule and yet it seems to me that it's an inadequate slogan, a misleading slogan and one that we should, if not reject, at least discourage. We should not accept it as a useful guide in politics to pursue.

I had better say at the outset that I am making an assumption here that the notion of majority rule at least suggests the idea of universal suffrage with the majority free to work its will. Given that concept of majority rule, the first proposition is that we do not have it in the United States. I doubt whether any country has it. We do not have majority rule or majoritarianism in this sense. Let me indicate how we limit at least the concept of majority rule.

In the first place, our elections occur not on a majority basis but on a plurality basis and that is true in most of the Western world. In the second place, though we do pretty well in this country in insisting that votes have equal weight (and that is one part of the general idea of majority rule), many other countries do not. And even we do not, in connection with the Senatorial election; a vote for a Senator in one state has a good deal more weight in this country than a vote for the Senate in another state.

Even if we neglected these considerations and assumed that elections are usually won by a majority, even this does not mean that the majority is then free to work its will. We impose limitations in a number of ways on what the majority can do. In the first place, we have a constitutional system that imposes limitation after limitation on what can be done. Some countries are limited in what they can do not only by constitutions but also by treaties and international obligations. In this country we pride ourselves on a system of separation of powers, and checks and balances, and these principles are limitations on what the majority can do. For certain purposes in the Congress, we require special majorities—an ordinary majority will not suffice. When offices are appointive rather than elective, and when tenure of office is prolonged, particularly as in the case of American judges, any notion of majority rule is at least seriously qualified.

When we decentralize government, as we do, into states, cities and counties, we are at least saying that the majority of the country as a whole is not to work its will just anywhere it wants. As an Iowan, I don't vote on issues that are distinctive to California and Los Angeles, and those who live in Los Angeles do not vote on issues that are distinctive to Iowa and Iowa City. What we do when we decentralize, is in a way to ask within what kind of unit, within what kind of population or territorial unit is it sensible to have things run by voting of the people. When we make local affairs subject to the decision of a local electorate, we do not assume that just any conceivable aggregation of people is a suitable unit within which to have a majority rule.

Further, when we decentralize, not only in the United States but in many other countries, it is often—not always but often—on a basis other than the strictly territorial. We may take ethnic characteristics of the population into account and assume that perhaps there is something about majority rule that should not ignore ethnic differences. In this country the main evidence of this is the treatment of the American Indians. I was glad to hear David Bayley refer to them. They are in a separate category: they have all the powers of sovereignty except those that Congress has taken away. India has established linguistic states. Canada happens to have a linguistic state—Quebec.

So far I have really been describing factual situations. Now what I would like to do is ask whether it would be desirable to have a system in which there is universal adult suffrage and the majority free to work its will. My answer to this is negative. It would not be desirable. I think it is a good exercise to use one's imagination a little bit and to imagine all humankind to be one electorate, a global electorate with adult suffrage all over the world. Then examine the proposition that majority rule should be the principle followed. As I see it, it does not take very much thought to come to the conclusion that this is impractical and that in fact it would be unacceptable to a high proportion of the people of the world. A very high proportion of the people of the world would be in such small minorities that they would have extremely limited influence on the decisions of a global government. Even the United States would have an extremely limited influence. We are a fairly large country but our population is about five percent of the population of the world.

Would the American people want to go into a political system in which their total vote was five percent of the grand total and in which there might be four or five Chinese votes and two or three from the continent of India, for every American vote that was cast? I think this would be unacceptable to the people of the United States. I grant that some individual person will say, why not? In general, this would be unacceptable to the people of the United States, and I believe it should be.

The differences that exist among the peoples of the world, differences of language, differences of religion, differences of tradition, differences in value, differences in social custom, would make it unworkable to throw all humankind into one electorate and to say that the majority should rule. If you follow that, if you agree, you ought to think about the implications that flow from such an agreement. If you agree with what has been said, you accept the principle that majority rule does not work everywhere. You accept the principle that one needs to be concerned about the population unit within which majority rule is prescribed. If you reject majority rule in an electorate consisting of all humankind, then in principle you might reject majority rule in connection with any number of other aggregations of people. And I, of course, think you should. I think majority rule is not the universal nostrum that it's sometimes assumed to be.

Practically all countries in the world are multi-ethnic. We sometimes talk about a world of nation-states. I have been fighting against this expression for years. I think it is terribly misleading. It suggests that the population of each state is a kind of homogeneous nation, whereas in fact such a state is a very rare exception. We ought to assume that the populations of the states of the world are multi-national and multi-ethnic, and if you reject majority rule for the world as a whole because of the diversities in the population of the globe, then in principle, you might also reject majority rule because of ethnic and other diversities that are found within various states.

Actually, a number of the states that exist in the world now came into being not because of affinity among the people involved; not because of common traditions, common language, common religion or anything like that; a great many of them came into existence because imperial powers from Europe went out and found political units of various sorts in a given territory and created one state out of what had never been one state before. When independence from the imperial power came, the independence was to the artificial entity created by the imperial power. What we now call Sri Lanka was never a united country until Britain came in and made it a united country. Later there was an assumption that there is a unity called Sri Lanka that should get independence. What occurred was the artificial putting together of very diverse people who would never have been put together in one political system had reason prevailed, had serious consideration of establishing workable political systems been the order of the day.

I reject majority rule because I don't think it will work in many of these diverse countries. The question is, then what alternative do I have in mind? Here I am in a very weak position because I have no alternative in which I have any great amount of confidence. Usually, the alternative is expressed in terms of a supplement to the slogan of majority rule, and that is, you couple majority rule with minority rights and then somehow you have solved the problem. This is a minimum essential. If you do go along with the notion of majority rule, you at the very least must attach to it the condition that minority rights be provided for. But this is not really adequate. The thrust of that proposition, majority rule with minority rights, is still in the direction of the majority. It is still the notion that, in general, the majority should prevail. I would rather take the position that the general conference of UNESCO has explicitly asserted—that peoples, not individuals, have the right to preserve their cultural identity. In general I am inclined to accept that proposition, and I apply it not only to minority peoples but also to majority peoples. I would like to get rid of this division of minority and majority and try to identify peoples and let each people have a right to preserve its culture, its identity. How to arrange that?

Let us try for an analogy here with the international political system. Internationally, we have long ago become accustomed to the notion, not of one person-one vote and majority rule, but rather, internationally we go on the principle of one state-one vote, regardless of disparities in population. China has one vote in the General Assembly of the United Nations and so do the Maldive Islands. We couple this one state-one vote principle with the proposition that, in general, each state is free to veto any change in its own legal rights. We have operated under that system internationally since the Western states system developed. Here is a curious contrast: for domestic politics you have the proposition so widely endorsed—universal suffrage and majority rule; for international politics you have almost the polar opposite—the individual person doesn't count, rather it's the state that counts, and each state has one vote, regardless of the population involved.

I suggest we are in a position of great inconsistency in terms of the political principles that we are applying at the two levels. I think, further, that we need to look for a way to combine the two ideas or make adjustments in each of them so that we can have a more nearly coherent and consistent system. In particular where there are sharp social cleavages within the population of a country, we ought to be recognizing the different peoples comprising the population of the state as different political units analogous to states in the international sphere. Then, somehow votes are allocated to the peoples within the state but not necessarily to individuals.

It is interesting to see this principle being accepted in connection with the development of a European parliament. The system developing is not one state-one vote, nor is it strictly representation proportional to population. Rather, there's a quota allocation of votes to the different members of the European Parliament. It is this kind of system that I think we ought to consider very seriously.

Western European Perspectives Concerning the United States' International Posture on "Human Rights"

by Henry Koeppler

I have been asked to talk about the perception of Europeans concerning the human rights posture of the United States, and perhaps I should warn you that I think I am very likely to disappoint quite a few of you. I will try to be fair to the point of view which I suspect you are expecting of me because one ought to see both sides of the question; what I have to say is something that seems to me to go beyond the issues of the image of the United States amongst its allies. Perhaps the best way to start is simply to ask for a moment, what exactly do we mean by "human rights?"

It is often proclaimed, not only by public opinion or what goes for it in the East, but also in the West, that human rights are many faceted; and while the West has stressed facts like freedom for personality, freedom of speech, all the things we associate with the American Constitution, the East provides freedom from hunger and want, and provides freedom to serve the community.

I believe this claim to be profoundly false. While the Soviet

Union—and the peoples who are voluntarily or involuntarily following it—cannot, in truth, claim the intellectual, emotional, and personal aspects of human rights, I do believe that the West's record
even in the matters of basic human needs of shelter, work, and
health is considerably better than the East's. We don't have to be
ashamed of saying that our combined human rights record—not
only the political individualistic one—is very much better than that
of the other side. It is necessary, particularly in the United States, to
be quite clear what it is that has changed within the field of human
rights.

With regard to Soviet satellites, I read too often—and mostly
coming from this side of the Atlantic—that one of our tasks in the
pursuit of human rights is to *re*-establish democracy in countries like
Poland or Hungary, or something similar. I think this is profoundly
unhistorical, and it is a political mistake. Some believe that all nice
and decent people have, or have had, a constitutional environment
with guarantees for human rights which we accept as basic. This is
not the case, has not been the case (with the sole exception of
Czechoslovakia) in the whole area now satellite to the Soviet Union.
One might well talk about helping them to establish their own
structure of human rights; but it is a profound historical and, to my
mind, political mistake to believe that these basic freedoms fundamental to pluralistic democracy did exist in these areas before World
War II. (I am using the term "mistake" advisedly and seriously;
remember Fouchet said of one of Napoleon's actions that it was
more than a crime—it was a mistake.)

Even within the opposition inside the Soviet Union—and I yield
to no one in my admiration for the heroic courage of the resisters, of
Solzhenitsyn for example—even within this resistance there are
deep differences on the meaning of and priorities for what we call
"human rights." Academician Sakharov and his friends are people
who share our belief in the basic needs of a pluralistic society; but
Solzhenitsyn (and let me repeat that I find it difficult to say this of a
man who has suffered as he has) represents a constitutional position
that was expressed in pre-Hitlerite Europe by the governments of
Poland and Hungary: there were all the human rights you
wanted—for those who supported and profited from the authoritar-

ian regime in power. Solzhenitsyn is opposed, and rightly, to Soviet tyranny; but from his utterances in the West I have to draw the unavoidable conclusion that the sort of human rights structure he would like to see is the one Czarist Russia had in the late nineteenth century; a pluralist society is a form of decadence. What men need is a single hierarchical structure—which is fine for those who are on the right side of the fence.

Public Opinion—Guardian of Domestic Human Rights

Let me, therefore, having tried to show a certain amount of differentiation in what man has meant by "human rights," discuss pragmatically and not at all philosophically a proposition that has always given the Americans the right to their own freedoms and to their own human rights; and that proposition is "the pursuit of happiness." I believe that if you want a definition that is all embracing for our policies on human rights, it is to establish ways of life in society in which the pursuit of happiness is possible.

From this definition follows my most important point for this discussion. I am not unaware of many different views. These views have in common an unease just below the surface of public opinion, both for human rights in the various stages in which you might find them in Europe, but also in the European attitudes to the public posture in foreign policy of the United States. Let me here add to the admirable and profound paper delivered by Professor Thompson, who very rightly included theologians, philosophers, diplomatists, lawyers—important people who are concerned with human rights. Let me, as a simple citizen, say that is why these groups have to do the thinking. But let us as happy members of a pluralist society never forget that ultimately the safety of human rights is guaranteed by public opinion. In the discussion of what theologians, what diplomatists, what industrialists, what lawyers have to say and to contribute, let us be quite clear that if we want to preserve our pluralist society, it must be anchored, the understanding of human rights must be anchored, in public opinion.

Therefore, the main thesis of these remarks is that the impact of the renewed preoccupation with human rights is essentially for the benefit of the internal policies of the "free world," a term that I am not afraid to use. I know "free" does not mean 100 percent free; it does not mean 100 percent just; it does not mean that our societies are paradise; it does mean, as language goes, we are proudly and rightly entitled to claim that we are living in a free society.

I shall try to say a little later something about the pursuit of human rights as an instrument of foreign policy. Let me stress here, it is the advocacy of human rights essentially as an internal matter, whatever its purpose, which makes me support the posture of President Carter on this issue. For we are in danger of taking all the ideals we stand for too much for granted.

We have lived, most of us, through a period when these ideals were tested, perhaps more consciously and bitterly in Britain between 1936 and 1939 than in any other country or period of which I am conscious. It became clear and has been clear ever since that democracy is sustained by certain assumptions which we are sometimes too shy to express because we do not want to appear too pompous or we do not want to appear too flag-waving. However, the firm belief in human rights, as I tried to present it in that definition, is one of the vital motives that make people ready to undergo sacrifices. If there is one good thing to be said about Mr. Chamberlain's policy—and there is very little to be said for it—it is this: postponing the war for a year-and-a-half, he made it the universally accepted truth in Britain that the things which were being attacked by the Third Reich were worth fighting for and dying for, whatever the odds. Now let us remember that foreign policy, however brilliant, however much supported by the latest armaments or by the best political warfare—which I am certainly not inclined to underestimate—cannot in a free society do its job if it is bereft of a firm belief in human rights. If this motor of belief in human rights does not work, the vital inspiration fails. You only have to remember France in 1939-40 to see what I mean.

France was by no means the only country, but it is the most obvious example of people getting separated from the principles of the French Revolution to an extent that they no longer provided a gut reaction in their individual lives. Therefore, whatever the foreign policy implications, let me say that the main purpose of the renewed discussion in human rights is to give a new spring of conscious awareness of what we have, of what makes society worthwhile. Cromwell was cited earlier in this conference, and I think he was as good a pragmatic political philosopher as he was a general. He said about his soldiers: "They know what they fight for and they love what they know." A passionate discussion in the free world on the essence of human rights is the sort of thing Cromwell would have approved of. We are not only defending our material prosperity.

In the Federal Republic of Germany, there is a small minority which says "better red than dead." This small minority feels that Germans are doing very well, but that if political freedom were to be tested again, they would not wish to face such a test, and therefore, prefer to be "red" rather than dead. I believe that what is necessary for the health of our Western society and for the true enjoyment of our professional and family advantages, which we need not despise, is an awareness of what we stand for and why we stand for it. This is indispensible for coping with crisis. It is not indispensible when there is no crisis, but, fortunately for journalists and professors of international relations, there is never a shortage of crises. We must in those initial periods be able to count on our fellow citizens, not only on our leaders of thought—the theologians and lawyers— but on our common citizens to have this gut reaction: human rights do matter.

Diplomacy vs. Human Rights in Foreign Policy

Now I said that I would try to be fair and understand the diplomat's view with which Professor Thompson dealt. I have been privileged to have been associated with the British Foreign Office for almost forty years. I greatly admire its staff. I ought to make it clear that I never was a professional member of the diplomatic service; I was what the people who do heraldic studies call a "Bar Sinister" person.

Having studied the mind of British diplomats, and having found amongst them some of the finest people amongst my contemporaries and older people, I am struck, but not altogether surprised, by the fact that diplomats are not free from the "professional" syndrome. I recommend to you one of the best studies of current

British foreign policy in which the issue of human rights is discussed. It was written by Lord Trevelyan, a very great British diplomat, and came out last year in April in the Chatham House publication, *International Affairs*.

In analyzing British foreign policy, he shows a professional lack of understanding that diplomacy is only one facet of policy— particularly in a pluralist society. Time and again, when discussing issues of foreign policy he says: If only Parliament had not meddled, or if only the press had not interfered, we could have settled that issue perfectly satisfactorily. That seems to me a profound professional mistake which is made not only by diplomats; it is made by lawyers; it is made by academics and perhaps even by theologians—I am not quite sure, but I think it might well be. It means that you hold, quite rightly, your specialization as of vital importance; but then, quite wrongly, you fail to allow for what you have to allow for in a pluralist society, namely the interaction of other factors, both foreign and domestic.

Many diplomats feel that President Carter is rather unnecessarily interfering with the fine chess game of diplomacy by stressing human rights. They say it will cause irritation among the Russians, and thereby it will prevent progress in SALT and in balanced mutual force reductions. I do not accept that for one moment. If the Russians want SALT, and if the Russians want to have mutual force reductions, they will be quite capable of controlling their irritation. However, their threat of irritation clearly is a useful tool of Russian propaganda, because it affects diplomats in the free world. Many veteran diplomats also stress the ineffectiveness of any action on human rights, and certainly nothing world-shattering has happened in this field yet.

However, let me remind you—quite apart from what may happen as a result of the election of the first Polish pope—the phenomenon of Euro-Communism would not be explicable if the issue of human rights had not featured prominently on the world agenda. Italy is a good example. We must make bigger efforts than we have done to evaluate the philosophy and politics of the Italian Communist Party, while certainly not taking their present words for future actions. The Russians, from their point of view rightly, are much concerned with the evolution of the Italian sister party. So, to say nothing has been achieved, or can be achieved, by a proclamation of our belief in human rights may well be counter-productive.

Furthermore, in adopting this negative attitude we are throwing away all the advantages of the Helsinki Agreement. We gave the Russians something they had got already de facto, but which they like on paper: namely, recognition of present frontiers in Europe. We got from them "Basket 3." This means we got from them a commitment to human rights. This by itself is a justification for all the resistance you find in the Soviet empire now. For what are the resisters saying? They are saying, we are not against the state, we are only helping our beloved government to carry out its obligations under the Helsinki Agreement. And, while I would certainly not overestimate the importance of that, I think it is not right and not even good policy to belittle its achievements. Finally, the Helsinki Agreement has had a beneficial influence on our trade with the Eastern bloc, and it is influencing the chances for supplies of energy. Here again, I do not for one moment believe that Russian policy towards the Middle East and Iran, or Russian policy towards acquiring technological know-how from the West will be negatively influenced by our stressing human rights. The Russians have their priorities. If they feel that they need electronic marvels from the West, they will put up with our *sincere* claims for human rights.

Let me just stress this word: of course, these claims must be sincere. We must in the struggle between Sakharov and Solzhenitsyn be on the side of Sakharov. If we want to be credible, we must acknowledge that our lay government is based on public opinion. I apologize for telling the assembled descendants of rebels against monarchical absolutism about the basic value of public opinion. Our politics must appear to this sober public opinion to be honest and fair. What I call the Solzhenitsyn doctrine, which is being preached very often in all of our countries by people who like to call themselves hawks, is to stress the lack of human rights in the Soviet Union—quite right—but to go slow on the lack of human rights either in our own society or in other societies who are convincingly anticommunist but equally dictatorial and interfere with human rights. I think this a pre-committance, where you have to watch against the temptation: anybody who speaks out for human rights at home and abroad should not automatically be labelled a cold warrior. We must be just as shocked—and I think many of us are—by revelations in Chile as we are by revelations about Mr. Dubczeck in Czechoslovakia. We should be shocked by South African apartheid, but also by the cruel tyrannies in new black countries, where often the ruling tribe treats other tribes worse than they were ever treated by the colonial powers.

A Foundation for Pluralistic Democracy

I was delighted to hear in one of the discussions emphasis on an issue which I believe we must be much more aware of than we are, and without which human rights and their limitations cannot properly be assessed. That issue concerns the framework in which to exercise human rights.

Human rights are seen as an instrument of foreign policy. I have said, whatever it does for foreign policy, it is an essential part for giving a firm foundation to our pluralistic democracy. I believe that human rights, like many other topics I mentioned, are profoundly affected, and will remain so affected, by the change in the unit of government, the unit of action, through which we are clearly passing. So often when specialists get to work, there is an unnecessary confrontation in the discussion on "whither the nation-state." There are people who say the nation-state is gone; we already have a United Europe, we may soon have a federal union; we may have world government. And there are people who say the nation-state is the only historic framework in which civilization has developed and can develop; all our political loyalties are concentrated on the nation-state. I want to stress, so that my conclusions are not misunderstood, that, certainly for the rest of the century, the main operating unit of government will continue to be the nation-state. That will be where taxes are collected; that will be where social benefits are effectively transferred; that will be where all the familiar contacts between an individual and his government will be undertaken. Anybody who says the nation-state has withered is wide of the mark.

Let me give you two examples where the nation-state is clearly involved in human rights. I believe in international discussions one had better start with one's own country if one wants to give examples of something bad. Now the great human rights issue for the United Kingdom is, of course, Ulster. Ulster, Northern Ireland, is not a simple case of Protestant British oppression of Irish Catholics. I think that most Irish-Americans now understand this. This problem is involved and complicated. It has more in common with what I saw in Pittsburgh some years ago when hard-hatted, skilled construction workers went to smash the Town Hall because the mayor had decided he would like to recruit some less skilled black workers in order to ease unemployment. That is the framework, the practical economic framework, of the situation in Ulster, with the Catholic minority in Ulster in the role of the blacks in Pittsburgh.

Here we must accept that we do not live in tidy national or racial units. This point, Woodrow Wilson—great and good man that he was—never got clear in his mind. It is very easy to overlook this point in the United States where you have your 49th parallel with Canada. What Wilson did not accept, or did not accept enough, has been a fact of Central and East European history, which is reflected in Ulster—that is why I mention it. You do not have nice, neat packages of Czechs, Serbs, Germans, Poles, and Russians in clearly-defined, separate compartments. For very good historical reasons, you find national intermingling such as you will not find in the United States. This mixture becomes highly explosive when a group that is a minority state-wide, locally is the majority. Sudeten Germans in Czechoslovakia were one of the many examples. You will find the same explosive mixture in Ulster. So here is an issue defying for historic and political reasons a quick solution, but it is an issue that has made the British people conscious of what human rights might and should involve.

The other example comes from the Federal Republic of Germany. I am always a little irritated that, while we do show a great deal of understanding for the political difficulties of our other allies, everybody—whether the *New York Times* or the *Times* of London—always feels entitled to preach a sermon to the German government. Now, the political development in the Federal Republic of Germany has been miraculously better than any study of previous German history could have led one to believe. The origins of that miracle may be found in post-war Soviet policy and in the help given to the Federal Republic by the United States and other allies. But the miracle also reflects internal German development. From the eighteenth century on, what we now call Western liberal values were not unknown in the intellectual, even in the political life of the Germanies. The fatal flaw, the decisive difference between German political development and that of the United States, of the United Kingdom, of France, the Netherlands, and the Scandinavian countries, consists in the fact that these democratic, liberal, and pluralistic concepts never managed to become dominant in the German Reich, never played the fundamental role in the political evolution of society which they have played in the countries just mentioned.

You know how in all our countries there has been great concern about what would appear to be a purely German problem of human rights, viz., the legislation undertaken to find out whether a man is politically qualified to be a judge, to be a teacher, to be a soldier, or even to be an engine driver on the railroad. Now my point here again is that this appears to be a problem that is clearly within the framework of one nation-state. Germany is a very recent democratic Western state. She must have the right, indeed she has the duty to protect this young, tender plant of democratic government against attacks from within. Our concern should not be with these protective steps as such. But we have a legimate concern—shared by many Germans—that these loyalty tests are administered only by people whose past and present behavior qualifies them as authentic protectors of democratic institutions; overzealous, politically unqualified "protectors" rightly raise doubts in our minds as to the value attached to human rights in West Germany. What appears to be an issue of human rights well-contained within a nation-state, does in fact, and with justice, concern a wider grouping.

A Bond in Alliance Management

Having stressed that for practical purposes we still have to base all our political actions within the framework of the nation-state, let me end by saying that I believe the tendency to bigger units is irresistible. Well-established systems have a way of surviving long after they are justified. Therefore, when I speak of tendencies, I do want you to understand that this is something I do not expect to see in the very near future, but which to my mind is irresistible. We are moving out of the age of the nation-state as the highest form of constructive politics, towards alliance management of how the former independent units, the nation-states, can rearrange their affairs jointly because these affairs have burst the borders of the nation-state.

Let me give you the most obvious example, and in a way the most far-reaching and deepest, and that is defense. In all definitions of the nation-state, one characteristic attribute of such a state is its ability to defend its citizens. A collection of people who have a common defense—that makes a nation. With the exception of Britain, all the warring nations in Europe during the Second World War saw their nation-states smashed completely, whether it was the French, or the Germans, or the Italians. Yet the nation-state was supposed to be entitled to your loyalty—and to your taxes—because it claimed to be able to protect life, liberty, and property, because it claimed to be able to let you pursue happiness.

So there is no longer that reverence for the nation-state that survives in the United States and survives in Britain because in those two countries the nation-state has not failed. Americans and British will be slower to accept the inevitable tendencies to alliance management and away from purely national politics. We need alliance management not only in defense, we need it in the delicate balance between industrial cooperation within the European or the Atlantic framework. We see these tendencies in all the questions of advanced technology, which go well beyond the capability of the individual nation-state. We see it, if I may mention such a touchy subject, we see it in the 500 billion of Euro-dollars which the mightiest state in the West (namely the United States) no longer controls. Whatever the Federal Reserve Bank can do, it cannot control Euro-dollars. It cannot control 500 billion which are floating about impervious—not indeed to market forces—but impervious to direct government intervention. There are many other examples I could mention but have not the time for.

I conclude by saying, yes, I do believe that President Carter's position on human rights, although it has aroused criticism, although it has been misunderstood, is a positive action. First of all, because in all the free societies, it brought us back to basics, to the inspiration and to the reason why we are free and enjoying our freedom. Second, because if—albeit very slowly and with great hesitation—we are moving out of an era in which the nation-state was the operative unit into something that I call alliance management, then human rights can be one of its vital assets and a firm bond among the members of the alliance.

Rights and Responsibilities of the Newsman

by Anthony Lewis

Martin Chuzzlewit, the hero of Dickens' novel of that name, arrives in the United States on a packet boat. As the boat reaches New York harbor, it is boarded by a gang of newsboys who shout out the latest in their papers—the New York Stabber, the Plunderer, the Peeper, the Family Spy and so on. "Here's the Sewer!" cries one of them, "The New York Sewer. . . . A full account of the Ball at Mrs. White's last night . . . with the Sewer's own particulars of the private lives of all the ladies that was there! . . . Here's the Sewer's exposure of the Wall Street Gang, and the Sewer's exposure of the Washington gang, and the Sewer's exclusive account of a flagrant act of dishonesty committed by the Secretary of State when he was eight years old, now communicated, at a great expense, by his own nurse."

Well, Dickens could be extravagant, and in *Martin Chuzzlewit* he vented some extremely unhappy feelings about the United States. But just a few years earlier, in 1835, a most judicious foreign observer who deeply admired this country indicated similar doubts about the uninhibited character of the American press. Alexis de Tocqueville, in *Democracy in America,* quoted a rancid newspaper attack on President Jackson as, among other things, corrupt, ambitious, intriguing and shameless. De Tocqueville said:

"I admit that I do not feel toward freedom of the press the complete and instantaneous love which one affords to things by their nature supremely good. I love it more from considering the evils it prevents than on account of the good it does."

Nowadays the American press feels unloved—especially by judges. Cases decided in the last year have left many editors and reporters and publishers with an acute sense of living under threat from the law. Two cases in particular have aroused that concern. In the first, the Supreme Court last May upheld the right of the police to search the offices of a newspaper, the *Stanford Daily,* for evidence of a crime in the same way that they would search other premises. In the second, the courts of New Jersey sent Myron Farber of the *New York Times* to jail when he refused to produce his notes for possible use by the defendant in a murder trial. Looking at those cases, a *Wall Street Journal* reporter wrote:

"The judiciary—certainly not all of it, but enough of it to lay down the law—has for all practical purposes declared war against the press."

Strong words. Can they be true? Have our courts forgotten the First Amendment? Is freedom of the press in jeopardy? Or why is there this feeling of embattlement, of hostility between the law and the press? Those are the questions that I shall try to explore.

Court Protection of Rights of the Press

American courts cannot fairly be charged with any general insensitivity to freedom of expression. Over the last two decades judges, especially those on the Supreme Court of the United States, have interpreted the First Amendment generously, even imaginatively, to protect freedom of speech and press. They have given editors what I think is beyond the widest measure of legally-enforceable independence that exists in any country, perhaps that ever has existed.

Consider libel as an example. Before 1964 there were no constitutional limits of any kind on libel actions. That is, no award of damages for a defamatory publication—however large, however outlandish—was then thought to infringe on the freedom to publish under the First Amendment. If a statement critical of someone turned out to be false, he could recover even though the person who published the comment did not know it was false and had no reason to know. Then came *New York Times v. Sullivan*. In that case, in 1964, the Supreme Court said that the First Amendment did put limits on libel. A public official who was defamed could collect damages only if a false statement about him had been published with knowledge that it was false or in reckless disregard of the truth. In a series of other libel cases over the last fourteen years, the Supreme Court has applied the Constitution to suits by public figures as well as officials, and in a looser way to private citizens. It has transformed the American law of libel. There are still serious burdens in its application, notably the cost of defending lawsuits. But compared with, say, Britain, the threat of libel actions to freedom of expression is minimal.

In other areas, too, the press has acquired significant new legal protections in recent years. The Supreme Court decided, in the Pentagon Papers case, that a newspaper could not under existing law be restrained from publishing Top Secret documents that the government insisted might compromise the national security. The Court has similarly said no to what the press calls "gag orders"— injunctions prohibiting publication of a defendant's confession and other such material before or during the trial of a criminal case. It has held that the press cannot be punished for printing information, such as the name of a rape victim, that appears in court records but is designated to be kept confidential. And it has held unconstitutional a state law requiring newspapers to print replies from political candidates whom they have attacked; editors, the Court said, cannot under the First Amendment be made to "publish that which 'reason' tells them should not be published."

Those are among many recent legal victories for the press. Why, then, the feeling of anxiety, almost of persecution by judges? It stems primarily, I believe, from a single concern: the protection of confidential sources. The fear that the names of sources may be discovered in unannounced police searches of newspaper offices explains the very critical reaction to the Supreme Court's decision in the *Stanford Daily* case. And the need to protect the identity of sources was the main legal argument made by Myron Farber and his employer in resisting the demand for his notes.

Freedom to Gather News—The Farber Case

The argument is straightforward. Information about wrongdoing in our society can often come only from people who fear retaliation if their names become known. So the reporter may have to promise confidentiality if he is to get the story—and his effectiveness in future depends on keeping the promise. The Constitution must protect this essential aspect of journalism.

Most editors and reporters believe that strongly. How strongly is indicated in a statement made during the Farber case by the Executive Editor of the *New York Times*, A. M. Rosenthal. He said:

"Mr. Farber and the *Times* have been fighting this case because they feel it goes to the heart of the constitutional free press guarantees of the First Amendment.

"It has always been believed that the First Amendment guarantees the right not only to print the news freely but to gather it freely. It is quite plain that without the right to gather information, the right to print it means little.

"We believe the right to gather information will eventually be destroyed if any branch of government, including the judiciary, has the right to seize and make public a reporter's notes, confidential information and raw material."

But the argument, however strongly believed, is not the law in this country. I know of no case in which the Supreme Court has enforced a constitutional right to gather news. The specific claim of a right not to disclose the sources of news was considered by the Supreme Court in 1972, and rejected. By a vote of 5 to 4, the Court said that reporters who had witnessed crimes after promising their sources confidentiality had to testify before grand juries investigating those crimes.

In that 1972 case, *Branzburg v. Hayes*, the majority said that the asserted reasons for a journalist's privilege not to testify were outweighed by the needs of law enforcement. The opinion, by Justice White, emphasized the ancient right of the grand jury to "every man's evidence." But what if the party seeking the journalist's evidence is not the prosecution but the defense? That is the Farber case, and it has to be described in some detail.

Mr. Farber is an investigative reporter on the *Times*. In 1975 he was told about thirteen suspicious deaths in a New Jersey hospital a decade earlier. He looked into them, talking to many people, some on a confidential basis. In 1976 he published stories suggesting that a "Doctor X" might have killed those patients with the poison, curare. By then the local prosecutor was looking into the matter. Five bodies were exhumed. And a grand jury charged Dr. Mario Jascalevich with five murders.

When Dr. Jascalevich was tried, his lawyer subpoenaed all the notes that Mr. Farber had made during his reporting of the story in 1975 and 1976. Mr. Farber and the *Times* refused to produce them. As a legal ground they relied, first, on a broad new journalists' Shield Law enacted by the New Jersey legislature, which says that reporters may "refuse to disclose" information they have gathered "to any court." They argued, second, that the First Amendment protected journalists from such a generalized and indiscriminate demand for evidence; at a minimum, they said, Dr. Jascalevich's counsel should have to point to particular material in the notes that might be relevant and material to the case—and unobtainable otherwise. And, finally, the *Times* and Mr. Farber said they were entitled to a hearing on these arguments before being compelled to respond to the subpoena.

The trial judge would not hold a hearing. Instead he ordered the notes delivered to him so that he could study them *in camera*—in private—and decide whether they could be subpoenaed under the state Shield Law and should be. The *Times* and Mr. Farber said that he should require a particular showing of need, and hold a hearing, *before* any such *in camera* inspection. The judge disagreed and, when they would not produce the notes, held them in contempt.

The New Jersey Supreme Court, reviewing the case, agreed with some of the main arguments made on behalf of the *Times* and Mr. Farber. But that turned out not to do them much good. The Court said that the language of the new Shield Law did indeed cover Mr.

Farber—but it held the law unconstitutional. It agreed that even before *in camera* examination by a judge of a journalist's notes, the party that had subpoenaed them should have to show that they would probably be relevant, material and essential—but it had looked over the facts of this case, the Court said, and they were so obvious that no hearing was necessary. The contempt findings were affirmed. The end result for Mr. Farber was forty days in jail and fines of $2,000; for the *Times* a total of $285,000 in fines.

Now it seems to me quite unfair that a citizen can be imprisoned for having mistakenly relied on a statute whose plain words, the Court concedes, protect him. Again, if a court says a party must make a showing of need before he subpoenas a reporter's notes, that should apply in all cases—not in every case but the one being decided.

Along the way in Mr. Farber's case there was a red herring about his book contract. A federal judge said that the reporter had already disclosed all the confidential material in question to his book publishers and literary agent—a statement that was the opposite of the truth, since the book manuscript contained nothing confidential. More than one judge in the case also suggested that Mr. Farber had somehow lost his journalistic status in the case by cooperating with the prosecutor—a view that shows total ignorance of journalism. In fact, Mr. Farber had given nothing of significance to the prosecutor. But it is commonplace, and entirely proper, for journalists to trade information with officials in the course of reporting. The judges even seemed to think that there was something wrong with a writer being paid for his work; the federal judge, apropos of the book contract, spoke of Mr. Farber "standing on an altar of greed." Well, I suspect that writers will do their work for nothing, as a charitable contribution, as soon as judges are ready to do the same.

So there is much to criticize in the judicial handling of the Farber case. But there is also much, I fear, that does not reflect favorably on the good sense of the press.

In Camera Inspection of Journalists' Notes

One question I would raise is whether *in camera* inspection of press material should have been resisted so strongly in the Farber case. To be sure, counsel for Mr. Farber and the *Times* argued only that the defense should have to make a showing before the judge looked at the notes—an entirely reasonable and moderate argument. But there was never any undertaking that, if the courts required such a showing and the defendant actually made it, Mr. Farber would produce his notes. And the language of some of the public comments from the press side indicated antagonism to the whole idea of judges looking at press material to decide a claim of privilege. Courts are just another arm of the state, it was suggested.

But in this country, courts are *not* an arm of the state. They often stand up against the state, even its highest officers. It should not be necessary to say that after the case of *United States v. Nixon.*

Mr. Nixon said that his White House tapes included highly sensitive material, and no-one can really dispute that. He said he had a privilege against having to disclose them, and the Supreme Court agreed that in general there was such a privilege: one based on the Constitution. But the Court said the privilege could be overriden by the needs of law enforcement. It stood against the President in a judgment that led to his resignation.

The procedure followed in the Nixon case is also relevant to the press argument in the Farber case. The Supreme Court directed the Nixon trial judge, John Sirica, to listen to the subpoenaed tapes and winnow out any matter not required by the grand jury. Judge Sirica did so, and I do not know of complaints from any quarter that he failed in that delicate responsibility.

Submission of highly sensitive material to judges for their private scrutiny is in fact standard procedure in this country. Trade secrets, national security matters, embarrassing family records—all these are seen by judges as a matter of routine. The parties involved often care as much about the confidentiality of such documents as newspapers do about sources, but lawyers trust the courts to keep them in confidence. And that trust is not misplaced. Can anyone remember a judge leaking national security documents or commercial secrets? Then why should the press be exempt from a procedure that works and is applicable to everyone else?

Right of Defendant to Compel Testimony

That brings me a second doubt about the Farber case. Implicit in some of the press comments on it, I think, was an assumption that the only rights involved in the case were the rights of the press. But that was just not so.

The Sixth Amendment to the Constitution says: "In all criminal prosecutions, the accused shall enjoy the right . . . to have compulsory process for obtaining witnesses in his favor." If anyone doubts the importance of that right, its part in a civilized system of criminal justice, think of the dissenters who at their trials in the Soviet Union are often prevented from calling witnesses in their favor. It is a specific right, and American judges are sworn to uphold it. Whatever one thinks of the *Branzburg* decision that a prosecutor's needs in the grand jury override the possibility of harm to investigative news-gathering if reporters can be made to testify, surely the explicit constitutional right of a defendant to compel testimony on his behalf is weighty.

The New Jersey Supreme Court said that the defendant's constitutional rights defeated the state legislative attempt to give reporters a broad testimonial privilege. The *Wall Street Journal* reporter who detected a judicial war on the press cited this ruling as an example of unfairness. Journalists, he wrote, "are now being denied privileges commonly accorded to private lawyers, doctors, priests and so on." The New Jersey court did not explain the difference between the claimed journalist's privilege and those others, but I think there is one. The old privileges are for the benefit not of the doctor or lawyer or priest, but of the patient or client or penitent. Each of these is a defendant or prospective defendant, and the privilege is really akin to the Fifth Amendment privilege against compelled self-incrimination: it protects him from having a private confession used by the state. The journalist's privilege is designed not to protect an individual but to advance a general public interest in the free flow of information.

In the Farber case, some said that Dr. Jascalevich's lawyers could have called any witness they wanted instead of looking at Mr. Farber's old notes. But that misses the point. Not all reporters are as responsible as Myron Farber, nor all papers as the *New York Times*.

And a defendant may have good reason to see the notes of a reporter who stirred up the charges against him. The reason is that the notes may help him impeach the testimony of prosecution witnesses.

Imagine that, during the McCarthy period in the 1950s, a red-baiting magazine ran an article charging some man with Communist activity. He is prosecuted. His lawyers have reason to think that witnesses against him, in talking to the magazine writer years before, made statements that were irrational—"Eisenhower is a Red"—or that are inconsistent with what they now say on the stand. Shouldn't the defense be able to use those past comments in cross-examination?

One of the great libertarian decisions of the Warren Court, *Jencks v. United States*, held that those prosecuted by the federal government should be able to check the prior statements of government witnesses for inconsistencies. Soon after that decision in 1957, Congress wrote the principle into a statute, providing that sensitive material go to a judge first for his private scrutiny. The principle seems to me just as valid if evidence valuable for impeachment purposes is in the hands of a journalist. At the least, a judge should be able to weigh the interests: the public benefits of confidentiality for news sources and the rights of a defendant on trial for his liberty or even his life.

Argument of Press Exceptionalism

When the press talks as if no other rights than its own were involved in these cases, its premise must be that the Constitution gives it a unique status: an immunity from rules that bind others in our society. Some explicitly make this argument of press exceptionalism. And it was given considerable standing when it was articulated four years ago, in a speech at Yale, by Mr. Justice Stewart of the Supreme Court.

The speech dealt with the press clause of the First Amendment, the last words in the famous command: "Congress shall make no law . . . abridging the freedom of speech, or of the press." The press clause did not merely join with the speech clause to guaranty freedom of expression, Justice Stewart said; that would make it "a constitutional redundancy." The Framers rather intended it to protect "an institution," the organized press, in which Justice Stewart included newspapers, magazines and broadcasting. Most parts of the Bill of Rights protect liberties whoever exercises them, he said; but the press clause is "a structural provision" protecting a particular segment of the society. "The publishing business is, in short," he said, "the only organized private business that is given explicit constitutional protection."

To the Framers, he said, "the free press meant organized, expert scrutiny of government. The press was a conspiracy of the intellect, with the courage of numbers. . . ." Any member of the press would take pleasure in such words. But I think the thesis of press exceptionalism—of a preferred status for journalists—has to be judged in the market place of constitutional ideas, and judged by three tests: its roots in history, its basis in the decided cases and its practical application today.

The history that lay behind the press clause, Justice Stewart rightly said, was the repressive period with which American colonists were so familiar, when "the press in England had been licensed, censored and bedeviled by prosecutions for seditious libel." As a result of a concern over that history, several states had included guarantees of a free press in their constitutions and declarations of rights. What was new in the First Amendment, in fact, was the extension of the guarantee to speech. But it is equally clear that those eighteenth century Americans, in their concern for "the press," did not define those words to mean only newspapers. There were newspapers at that time, though they were not much like the organized press of today; they offered mostly political assault, not "expert scrutiny." But the long English and American struggle over licensing of "the press" had centered on books and pamphlets, and the freedom to publish them was just as much included in the First Amendment. In short, freedom of "the press" was meant to cover anything that came off a printing press. There is no basis in history for limiting it to the "institution" of journalism.

As to cases decided by the Supreme Court, Justice Stewart relied in particular, for his thesis, on the libel decisions beginning with *Times v. Sullivan*. They allowed the press to carry out its business boldly, he said. But "by contrast, the Court has never suggested that the constitutional right of free *speech* gives an *individual* any immunity from liability for either libel or slander."

The short answer to that argument is the opening sentence of the opinion of the Court in the *Sullivan* case: "We are required in this case to determine for the first time the extent to which the constitutional protections for speech and press limit. . . ." In cases since then the Supreme Court has in fact applied the newly-defined constitutional libel rules to protect individual rather than media defendants, including one man who wrote an accusatory letter. (*Henry v. Collins,* 380 U.S. 356 - 1965.) The American Law Institute has said that it would be "strange," in libel suits by private persons, to draw a distinction between media and individual defendants. And the leading state case on the question, from Maryland, has rejected any such distinction. (*Jacron v. Sindorf,* 276 Md. 580 - 1976.)

Justice Stewart also found some support for his thesis in the Court's close division over the press privilege question in the *Branzburg* case. No individual, he said, could possibly refuse relevant information to a grand jury on free speech grounds; the issue can arise only when a "protected institution" is involved.

But suppose a college lecturer refused on First Amendment grounds to answer a Congressional committee's questions about his beliefs and associations. In that somewhat analagous situation the Supreme Court divided 5 to 4—the same vote as in *Branzburg*—in rejecting the lecturer's claim. Or suppose a professor were called before a grand jury and asked to name the official sources for his scholarly paper on Vietnam. That case happened, too, and the professor went to prison for contempt. Should journalists be comfortable with the idea of a First Amendment that keeps them free while the scholar is imprisoned? Well, I am not.

Who Is "The Press"?

If a majority of the Supreme Court were to accept the idea that the First Amendment gives special status to the press as an institution, the first question would be: Who is "the press"? Would that concept be limited to established newspapers, magazines and broadcast stations? Or would it have to include fringe publications, underground papers, journals of sexual exploitation? In these days of the

Xerox, what about the person suddenly inspired to circulate angry attacks on some local corruption? What about a specialty publication such as a Wall Street tip sheet—could the S.E.C. regulate it without violating the freedom of "the press"?

Such questions would inevitably arise. And they would force the Supreme Court to go into the business of defining who is "the press"—of deciding who qualifies for the glorified constitutional status. Would the press be happy with that form of judicial licensing?

The idea of special status for one profession is troubling for deeper reasons. When I discuss these problems in class, some students are always "gung ho" for Justice Stewart's view. But when I put the case of the professor, or of the former C.I.A. man who wants to publish a book on Vietnam without censorship, I find that the students always want to define them as "the press," too; their cases are simply too compelling to be treated less sympathetically. Similarly, lawyers who want to take advantage of the Stewart thesis but are troubled by its narrowness are beginning to say that it should include "pamphleteers." But once you thus broaden the definition, then any publication becomes "the press" and Justice Stewart's idea loses its meaning.

In dissent from the *Stanford Daily* decision, Justice Stewart expounded his view in these words:

"Perhaps as a matter of abstract policy a newspaper office should receive no more protection from unannounced police searches than, say, the office of a doctor or the office of a bank. But we are here to uphold a Constitution. And our Constitution does not explicitly protect the practice of medicine or the business of banking from all abridgment by government. It does explicitly protect the freedom of the press."

So in Justice Stewart's view the Constitution did not allow the police to get a warrant to search the offices of an undergraduate daily for photographs of a felony, a vicious mass assault. But the Constitution would allow an unannounced search through a lawyer's files, or the files of Daniel Ellsberg's psychiatrist, Dr. Fielding.

To state the proposition is to refute it, I think. Such a mechanical concept of the Constitution would be utterly unacceptable to most

Americans, including journalists. The Constitution protects values, not particular classes of people. And there are values other than "the right to know." One is the right of an accused to defend himself effectively. Another is reputation, which Justice Stewart has convincingly said reflects "our basic concept of the essential dignity and worth of every human being"; that is why the Supreme Court has not held all libel actions unconstitutional and why I think it will continue to allow some means, whether by damage suits or some other corrective process, for those who are defamed to vindicate their good names.

Media Not Above the Law

A democratic society respects many values. They must occasionally conflict, so none can be absolute. The late Alexander Bickel, who represented the *New York Times* in the Pentagon Papers case, wrote afterward:

"There are no absolutes that a complex society can live with in its law. . . . A very broad freedom to print, and a very considerable freedom to ferret out information by all manner of means ought to be, and substantially has been, one of the chief denominations computed in our calculus as constitutional policy. But there are other denominations as well. It is the most enduring instinct of our legal order . . . to resist the assertion of absolute claims."

To say the words "freedom of the press" rapidly is not a substitute for thought. The First Amendment does not say: "The media are exempt from law." And in practice the absolute view has never been applied. Newspapers are subject to the tax laws and the labor relations laws just as other businesses are. Even sympathetic judges have made clear that they reject the notion of press exceptionalism. Justice Powell, dissenting when the Court refused to find a First Amendment right to interview prison inmates, said: "The guarantees of the First Amendment broadly secure the rights of every citizen; they do not create special privileges for particular groups or individuals. For me, at least, it is clear that persons who become journalists acquire thereby no special immunity from governmental regulation." And Justice Pashman of the New Jersey Supreme Court, dissenting in the Farber case, said: "If the ultimate evidential test had been met . . . , Mr. Farber would have had to comply with the trial court order for *in camera* inspection. No one is above the law."

To put it at a minimum, I think the press is unwise to advance the idea of special status because it is an argument that cannot be won—that will indeed outrage most of those who hear it. Judges did not respond warmly when Mr. Nixon's lawyer, James St. Clair, said that his client reserved the right to decide whether he would accept their interpretation of the Constitution. They are not likely to be any more impressed if newspapers ignore repeated judicial decisions, insist that the Constitution means what the press would like it to mean, and in effect argue that they are entitled to judge their own case. Nor is a public already skeptical about the press likely to react favorably to such arguments.

But I think the press should reject the idea of privileged constitutional status for reasons more profound than the improbability of its being persuasive. This is a country of laws, not men. The society is pervaded by law, and dependent on it to provide the social glue that others find in tradition or a homogeneous culture. I cannot put it better than Myron Farber did at one point: "Our civilization, and civility, depend on order and the rule of law." We reject the claims of law at our peril. In Watergate we have just reaffirmed the supremacy of law in the United States. Even Presidents must bow to it. And the press should not give even the appearance of claiming superiority to the law.

For the press to think of itself in such a way, moreover, would be dangerous to its own character. It would breed arrogance, a state of mind as unbecoming in journalists as in politicians. It may also encourage, ironically, excessive reliance on the law. Reporters did their job in this country for a long time without any dream of a constitutional privilege not to testify, for example; that claim was not even advanced until 1958. It is true that the press has become more probing in recent years, more determined not to take what officials say at face value; and that increases the risk of official retaliation. But serious investigative reporters in Britain operate effectively without any hope of a testimonial privilege to protect their sources; the protection is their own conscience, and sources seem to find that convincing enough. If American reporters do the same, I find it hard to believe that those with stories to tell about wrongs in society will be silenced.

Thinking of the press in exclusive terms may also keep us from recognizing the role that others may play in informing our democracy. The legal assault on Frank Snepp for publishing his book on the C.I.A. in Vietnam is just as dangerous to public knowledge as a suit against a newspaper, but the press was slow to understand that or support Mr. Snepp.

What matters is the function: the informing function. The First Amendment, Justice Powell has said, protects "the ability of our people through free and open debate to consider and resolve their own destiny. . . . And public debate must not only be unfettered; it must also be informed." Many may perform that function, and it would be foolish—self-deceiving and self-defeating—for the press to think of itself alone in that capacity. The fairer view, and the more convincing one, is that in our complex society it is usually, if not always, the press that represents the public interest in information, the press that is at the cutting edge. It acts, Justice Powell said, "as an agent of the public" in acquiring the "ideas essential to intelligent self-government." It is the function that is entitled to constitutional respect—not absolute, and not limited to one class, but respected.

The press is right to criticize judges when they speak in ignorance of the editorial process; if they knew more, I think they would lecture less. But I also believe that the press will win greater respect for its own values if it recognizes that there are others.

Shifting Values in Higher Education: From the Individual to the Ecological

by David Mathews

Two years ago in an article for *Change* magazine I listed issues in higher education deserving more attention. At the top of the list was the fact that

> the growing concern over individual and collective values has become pervasive, revealed not only in national political arenas but in local communities where concerns about shoplifting, drugs, and just basic human decency continue to swell. Equally unsettling is the prospect that our thirst for righteousness may lead us no further than the nearest scapegoat whom we use to give us an engineered sense of moral superiority. Higher education probably can't get back to its moral-religious role of the seventeenth and eighteenth centuries, but there is some serious question about whether it can maintain its twentieth-century detachment from "moral philosophy."[1]

From Moral Philosophy to Ecological Ethics

Values are valuable again in higher education. But the values we hold to now seem rather different from those we applauded just a few years ago. We will always be concerned about individual rights. But whether you and I agree or not, those rights are likely to be viewed less and less as absolute and more and more as contextual— related to and dependent upon a whole universe of values.

In order to appreciate the enormity of this shift, you have to take into account a number of changes now under way in the intellectual substrata of the country, changes in disciplines ranging all the way from biology to political science to philosophy. To absorb all that is going on is a sure prescription for indigestion but I will try to take you through the menu with a minimum of footnotes and esoteric references. What I hope you will see is a pattern in what is now emerging in American thought. Everything that I will describe has implications for individuals, for what we value about individuals, and for how we see individuals in the context of our kind of social and political structure.

I will not talk about higher education in an administrative sense; yet the matters we are dealing with could not help but affect higher education in a more substantive way.

If I were making the observation that I made in *Change* magazine now, I would have to amend it, even in spite of instructions to talk about individual rights. The focus in the country now is not on moral philosophy in the eighteenth-century sense of that term. And it is really not on individual rights, if by that we mean individual rights in a vacuum. The effort is to understand more about the individual in the context of the social order. I particularly like Amitai Etzioni's notion of the need to return to what he calls "civic ethics."

HEW sponsored a conference in 1976 on The Changing Agenda for Higher Education. We asked people not to talk about what was on the agenda now but what ought to be on the agenda in the future. This is what Etzioni had to say:

> I will deal with two questions which I hope will be included in any agenda of higher education. One concerns civic ethics and the other domestic priorities. The issue of civic ethics is one I recently began to study. If I had to summarize the issue of civic ethics in one sentence, I would define an ethical person as having the character capacity to weigh the needs of others in the community as he or she deals with their self-interests. I chose my words carefully. I am not saying that an

ethical person would always give first priority to others of the community, but he would never ignore them in his actions.[2]

Note that Etzioni speaks of the relationship of one's self-interest to the interest of others. His remarks are a good example of what I have been talking about: a trend toward a more ecological view of individuals and their rights.

It would be easy to make the generalization that the Sixties were the era of individual rights and that the Seventies and Eighties would be a time for societal rights. There is some basis for that; yet if we repeat the excesses of the Sixties at the other end of the continuum, we will have served our times very poorly. Obviously, if we protect the rights of the whole at the expense of the individual, we will simply be swapping one folly for another.

Perhaps the objective should be to do in moral and political philosophy what the ecologists have taught us to do in natural science, that is, to talk abut the whole of things without losing sight of the relationship of the individual to the whole. I think that is the direction our ethical inquiries are taking us and certainly that effort will have enormous implications for higher education.

The Individual Versus the Megastructures

Even though we will not return to the seventeenth and eighteenth centuries, there are interesting parallels between what we are contending with and what our forebears in those two centuries were about. You recall that the movement in the seventeen hundreds was away from the grasp of the body corporate, in this case the State, and toward a social system that had the individual as its central focus. Robert Filmer's defense of the divine right of kings and even Hobbes' apology for the centralization of power gave way to Locke's parliamentary democracy and eventually to the radical individualism of Henry David Thoreau. The new doctrine of natural rights gave man sanctuary that exceeded any authority of the State. And even when democratic philosophers like Bentham and Mill abandoned the doctrine of natural law for a more pragmatic philosophy, they still made the welfare of mankind the central obligation of government.

We need to remember, too, that for many in those centuries during which we had our social and political origins, the foundations of our hopes were laid in liberty and in our appreciation of the powers of the individual—as opposed to the collective power of the State. Indeed, parliamentary government and later representative government of the American sort were simply devices to ensure that individuals could control the ponderous megastructures of political life.

We are asking a lot of eighteenth-century questions again. Beyond the shrill arguments of the political right about doing away with big government and its bumbling bureaucracy, there is a re-emergence of the progressive quest to make certain that the individual is indeed in control of the now ever more massive agencies of the political system. And there is a renewed appreciation for the powers of the individual in collective enterprises that are not governmental. Perhaps this revival of eighteenth-century individualism carries with it the promise of our own version of civic ethics.

The Modern Reassessment

The issues are very basic. As Etzioni said, one is the question of how we weigh our own self-interest over and against that of all those around us. The other is the corollary: How do we shape our collective efforts so that the individual still shines through?

These questions are being debated in a variety of forums and it would be impossible to confine them to a course in moral or political philosophy or even to instruction within universities. Yet many of the disciplines basic to a university are going to be consumed with these two issues—and perhaps changed in the course of the debate. Could it be that we are about to witness the kind of revolution that replaced the quadrivium and the trivium with modern sciences and social sciences or the classics with professional subjects? I really do not know and I am not proposing that such is the case. But the social sciences and even the natural sciences are undergoing significant transformations, transformations that are related to a reexamination of the axioms of American social and political philosophy. And the shifts in emphasis within the disciplines have value-laden connotations that will affect the substance of higher education.

The current reexamination of our beliefs has been prompted, at least in part, by public discontent with the giant institutions that affect our lives. The tirades against big government have been particularly sharp. We have all heard the criticism that government is isolated from the reality of its effects, aware only of its intents not its results. Tellingly, we now refer to the "ivory tower" not of academe but of government. The average citizen has the feeling that it is very difficult to have any influence on the governmental forces that increasingly intrude in his life. Government to many seems distant, almost foreign.

And the results that government produces have not been judged to be good. For many Americans they have not been good for a long time. Vietnam and then Watergate and now affronts like the "welfare mess" are all part of a long list of grievances. In the spirit of David Halberstam's lament of the inadequacies of the "best and brightest," many Americans seem to view the last decade or so as the era when things just did not work out as we expected.

These criticisms amount to a "Great Disillusionment," a mood that seems to be giving rise to what might be termed the "Modern Reassessment."

The Natural Sciences Turn Social

Major impetus to the Reassessment has come out of a recent revolution in the natural sciences usually referred to as the "biological revolution." The focus of the revolution, however, has not been so much on biological theory as on the value connotations of biological assumptions, especially on ways of seeing the individual—not alone but in relationships. In scientific terms the revolution began with an interest in the structure and function of the most basic components of life, the molecules of deoxyribonucleic acid (DNA).

And it also took form in another branch of biology, ethology, as a reconsideration of the common traits mankind shares with animals.

In social and political terms what the biological revolution has done is return us to the most ancient mentor of the human race, Nature. And Americans, in the late 1970s, are returning to the tutelage of Nature for new instructions on everything from what breakfast cereals to buy to what social values to accept. Such a return is not surprising in a time of disillusionment and reassessment.

Pivotal figures in this revolution are scientists who are speaking to political and social questions. None has been more deliberate in this than E. O. Wilson in his trilogy, *The Insect Societies* (1971), *Sociobiology* (1975), and *On Human Nature* (1978).

In the introduction to the much talked of twenty-seventh chapter of *Sociobiology*, Wilson places mankind very much in Nature by inviting his readers to see mankind as alien natural scientists might:

> Let us now consider man in the free spirit of natural history, as though we were zoologists from another planet completing a catalog of social species on Earth.[3]

Thus endowed with this macroscopic view, Wilson lays bare a biological basis for all forms of social behavior.

Lewis Thomas, author of *Lives of a Cell* (1974), puts man even more clearly in the scheme of Nature when he ponders his own identity in a cellular cosmology:

> I did not mind it when I first learned of my descent from lower forms of life. . . . It is a source of satisfaction to be part of the improvement of the species.
>
> But not these things. I had never bargained on descent from single cells without nuclei. I could even make my peace with that, if it were all, but there is the additional humiliation that I have not, in a real sense descended at all. I have brought them all along with me, or perhaps they have brought me.
>
> It is no good standing on dignity in a situation like this, and better not to try. It is a mystery. There they are, moving about in my cytoplasm, breathing for my own flesh, but strangers. They are much less closely related to me than to each other and to the free-living bacteria out under the hill. . . . Through them, I am connected; I have close relatives, once removed, all over the place. This is a new kind of information, for me, and I regret somewhat that I cannot be in closer touch with my mitochondria.[4]

The much debated study of sociobiology, however, is not an isolated phenomenon. It is only one example of a wider use of biological insights to restructure a number of social and political disciplines.

The return to the tutelage of Nature may actually be an effort to find a new center for our society and to reform a consensus on basic social values. This new naturalism begins in science but its results are not so much scientific as philosophic, perhaps even theologic. Science's function is that of analogy,[5] even though the scientists involved take their science very seriously.

Albert Rosenfeld does an excellent job of putting the biological revolution in the context of moral and religious values. In an article for *Saturday Review* (December 1977), he finds a relationship between a current crisis in values and the ferment in the scientific community. What science discovers about the most basic life process, he suggests, inevitably raises questions that are philosophical, moral, ethical, and ultimately religious:

> The current "biological revolution," as it has rightly been called, happens to come along at the same moment we are all caught up in what has also rightly been called a "crisis in values." The two are curiously related. The biological revolution, on the one hand, contributes to the crisis but, on the other, might also help relieve it—though ethical and moral values usually fall within other provinces, notably that of religion.[6]

That these new biosocial sciences will influence our view of individuals and their rights should come as no surprise.

The New Social Sciences Turn to Old Values

But whether stimuli came from a Great Disillusionment or from a Biological Revolution or from other sources, there are also a number of scholars in the social sciences now reexamining the most sacred assumptions of their fields. They are not natural scientists but rather students of social policy or public policy or public administration. Indeed, it seems more than just coincidental that the efforts to restructure the natural and social disciplines come at the same time as a massive, multifaceted effort to reform bureaucratic structures and the agencies for carrying out social policy. Given the history of the powerful influence of naturalistic metaphors, the pervasive inclination to reestablish values, and the thrust of the new naturalists toward matters social, these two ventures are likely to influence one another.

Those concerned with bureaucratic and social reforms, "revisionists" if you will, constitute even less a movement than do the scientists looking into matters social. These revisionists are a diverse group with little conscious relation to or even knowledge of one another. But they share common themes in their writings; they often look to a Halberstamian crisis as their point of origin, and they are bound by a humanistic tenor which runs throughout their commentary. In fact, I have been tempted to describe these revisionists as humanistic. In their search for viable social and administrative structures they turn to values based in verities more ancient than those of the modern, technological eras. Like their earlier counterparts, these humanistic revisionists have put mankind at the center and have objected, in the name of humankind, to what they consider unwarranted impositions of dogma (in this case bureaucratic dogma).

It is important to note that individuals as the revisionists describe them are quite different from people as described in bureaucratic references. The distinction is well drawn in a paper delivered by Iredell Jenkins at the World Congress of the International Association for Philosophy of Law and Social Philosophy in 1975. In addressing the role of law as a cultivating influence he worries that "law is simply not an effective instrument for the formation of human character or the development of human potentialities."[7] Or, to put Jenkins' argument in other terms, the legal person is a narrow, restricted version of the human person because of the inherent limitations of law itself. The law translates human goals and values into terms with which it can deal, and in the translation loses much of what is truly human. The distinction between the legal and human person is, of course, crucial in the analysis of the dominant political form of our time, bureaucracies, because both the bureaucrat and his object, the citizen, are defined in legal terms.[8]

The revisionists abandon legalistic definitions and deal with people as they are, bound to each other in natural groupings like families and neighborhoods and clubs. Their standard for the efficacy of any political structure or program is the degree to which it sustains the natural bonding and supporting structures needed for human survival.

If you want a good example of this tendency to see the individual again in the context of the ancient structures that have sustained humankind, look at the work of Peter Berger and Richard Neuhaus. They are representatives of a group that looks at the whole of society and concentrates on the interrelations. In their work, *To Empower People*, they contend that families, communities, churches, and voluntary associations serve as mediating structures or buffers between the individual and the megastructures, "the large economic conglomerates of capitalist enterprise, big labor, and the growing bureaucracies that administer wide sectors of the society, such as in education and the organized professions."[9] They note that without the processes of mediating structures, the political order becomes detached from the values and the realities of individual life. Berger and Neuhaus would, therefore, reform public policy by making mediating structures the instruments of social action.

Another group composed of revisionists like Vincent Ostrom and George Frederickson, who are students of public administration, looks at the structures used in society to advance the public good. These men are bureaucratic reformers, working to revise the axioms about administration that we have held sacred since Woodrow Wilson and Max Weber.

In writing about the "new public administration," Frederickson points out that their scholarly effort began by challenging old administrative values. The norms of classical and neobureaucratic theory were "efficiency, economy, productivity, and centralization," but the new public administration emphasizes humanistic values that can be realized in "decentralized, democratic organizations which distribute public service equitably."[10] The central element in this reform is the application of democratic principles, normally thought appropriate only to electoral and legislative processes, to administrative processes.

Ostrom, for his part, calls for a "democratic administration" and blames much of America's malaise on the bureaucratic tradition of administration. He worries that bureaucratic centralization has "so altered the basic structure of American government that many of its benefits have been eliminated. . . ." He feels that bureaucratic structures are not sufficient for a productive and responsive public service economy. His alternative is a democratic administration that is intent upon "avoiding the presumptions of monopoly power" and concerned with enhancing "citizen participation in community development, social welfare, and public order."[11]

The new public administrators reject the Wilson value-neutral assumption that a bureaucracy can serve a democratic state as well as Frederick the Great's Prussia from which it was adapted. This group is also ecological in its view in that its members are sensitive to both client-to-organization and organization-to-organization bonds. They see themselves, too, as anti-Hobbesian and anti-Darwinian. They do not see the world as governed by mean competition; they are more like Rousseau in being optimistic about mankind, perhaps even a bit romantic about human potential. Indeed, the new public administrators are hybridizers who seem to be trying to combine the moralist tradition—in their concern with equity—with the democratic tradition of majority control.

The last group of revisionists I would like to mention are particularly concerned about the final point raised by Ostrom, that is, the point about the role of the individual citizen in the control of society's social and political machinery. Within this group there are those who want direct citizen participation in all facets of public decision making. Others extend that point and want citizen participation in the delivery of services. And there is yet another subset who wishes to see the public in control of the planning process which has become so central to modern political life.

The diverse, widespread coalition behind the participationist movement is in itself telling. Gerald E. Caiden's analysis of the supporters include:

> . . . conservatives who resent concentrated power that is not in their hands or who oppose big government in principle, southerners who want to be free of northern interference via Washington, radicals and minority groups who want to control some part of the living constitution by themselves, and liberals who still prize individualism or who are disappointed at the failure of centralization to solve societal problems.[12]

The participationists' ambitions, of course, fly straight in the face of myriad bureaucratic objections: "People are not interested"; "You can hear anything from the public you want"; "The public mind is inherently ambiguous." Both William Stewart (in *Citizen Participa-*

tion in Public Administration, 1976) and Walter Rosenbaum (in "The Paradoxes of Public Participation," *Administration and Society,* November 1976) have good analyses of these problems. My own experience has been that the form for citizen participation is the least developed of the governmental art forms. Yet, public participation is now written into most laws and it is just beginning to change, in a fundamental way, the degree of direct involvement in governmental process.

Alvin Toffler has invented the term "anticipatory democracy" for a movement that carries on his interest in "future-consciousness" and in addition ties to the more general effort to advance citizen participation. His diagnosis is that "our government and other institutions have grown so large and complicated that most people feel powerless."[13] And Toffler echoes the revisionists' characteristic conviction that bureaucracies are obsolete and do not solve but rather compound our problems. Toffler's anticipatory democrats also attack the imperfections of the existing participatory processes. They champion citizen planning groups and media feedback programs; and more, they have a good sense of the profitability of coalitions with potential allies—Community Action Programs, statewide "2000" organizations, and the like. In fact, it is the coalition of diverse groups interested in citizen participation that gives it its present influence.

The "enemy" for these latter-day Jacksonians are the social scientists and technocratic planners. Richard Applebaum, himself a social scientist, warns that "by treating human beings as if they were passive respondents to social forces. . . , the social sciences of today merely confirm in theory what exists in actuality: the impotence of the average human being before those dominant groups and the individuals that shape his or her life." Applebaum favors new modes of planning that "efface the expert-citizen distinction." He adds, "The role of the expert must be deprofessionalized—or, what amounts to the same thing, ordinary people must be given the confidence and skills required to understand the forces that mold their lives."[14] This is individual rights but of a different kind. It is the right of individuals to control their own destiny over the influence of "experts."

Are There Democratic Genes or Have Charles Darwin and Herbert Spencer Been Reincarnated?

An inevitable suspicion always follows an inevitable confusion in dealing with topics as wide ranging and as value sensitive as those I have addressed. The inevitable confusion comes in trying to see a too literal connection between all that I have described in these pages. I know of no one who would make a case for any real interrelationship between all of the new questions that are being raised in all of the disciplines. The inquiries of this decade do have in common a contemporaneous existence; that is to say, they are all a part of our times, all part of a certain history, and all part of a general response to our central dilemmas. Being basic, they will touch on much of the same type of value questions. But no one believes that the quest to understand genetic influences on behavior is directly related to the effort to promote greater citizen participation in government.

Also, we are terribly afraid that the questioning of the established consensus in social policy means that we are inevitably going back to a kind of Social Darwinism. That fear of predestination is based on an implicit assumption that our course is in fact foreordained. That is ironic, to say the least. A belief in families, a love of democracy, and a penchant for trying to understand Nature's lessons are not in and of themselves reactionary. And the people with such inclinations have been a wide assortment of liberals and progressives, radicals and reactionaries. Our reconsiderations are probably normal, possibly even healthy. And whether they are reactionary or not depends on "us," not on "them."

Civic Rights

My point in this essay, lest you have forgotten, is that a massive reassessment is under way in American thought. It is aimed at axioms we have held sacred for most of the twentieth century. Whatever the field, the individual is put back into Nature, back into families, and back into the center of our political processes. That is why I said we are moving toward an ecological perspective on individual rights. We are not too far from our eighteenth-century counterparts in wanting the individual to permeate the megastructures that carry out our collective will. And we are not above severely criticizing the forms the State has taken. The bureaucracy is perhaps our George the Third. We do not seem to be moving to a new collectivism but we do have a different view of the individual. Perhaps it is now more an issue of individual responsibilities than of individual rights; perhaps we will invent new field called "civic rights."

No reconsiderations so profound can escape having an influence on higher education. It is to be regretted, however, that intellectual currents receive less attention from professional educators than do administrative trends.

Perhaps Professor Etzioni's suggestion will be influential and universities will develop courses in civic ethics. But whether they do or not, many of the disciplines that make up a university are surely laying a basis for a new definition of the place of the individual in our society.

NOTES

1. David Mathews, "Toward a New Purpose." *Change* (October 1976), p. 62.
2. Amitai Etzioni, quoted in David Mathews et al., *The Changing Agenda for American Higher Education* (Washington, D. C.: Government Printing Office, 1977), pp. 35-36.
3. Edward O. Wilson, *Sociobiology: The New Synthesis* (Cambridge: The Belknap Press of Harvard University Press, 1975), p. 547.
4. Lewis Thomas, *The Lives of a Cell* (New York: The Viking Press, 1974), pp. 85-86.
5. *Ibid.*, p. 4.
6. Albert Rosenfeld, "When Man Becomes As God: The Biological Prospect," *Saturday Review*, December 10, 1977, p. 15.
7. Iredell Jenkins, "The Human Person and the Legal Person," *World Congress of the International Association for Philosophy of Law and Social Philosophy Proceedings* (Dobbs Ferry, New York: Oceana Press, 1975), p. 119.
8. *Ibid.*, p. 120.
9. Peter L. Berger and Richad John Neuhaus, *To Empower People* (Washington, D. C.: American Enterprise Institute for Public Policy Research, 1977), p. 2.
10. H. George Frederickson, "The Lineage of New Public Administration," *Administration and Society*, August 1976, pp. 167, 169.
11. Vincent Ostrom, *The Intellectual Crisis in American Public Administration* (University, Alabama: University of Alabama Press, 1973), pp. 19, 113, 128.
12. Gerald E. Caiden, *The Dynamics of Public Administration: Guidelines to Current Transformations in Theory and Practice* (New York: Holt, Rinehart, and Winston, Inc., 1971) p. 126.
13. Alvin Toffler, "What is Anticipatory Democracy?" *The Futurist*, 9 (October 1975): 224.
14. Richard P. Applebaum, "The Future Is Made, Not Predicted: Technocratic Planners vs. Public Interests," *Society*, May/June 1977, pp. 51-52.

Comment

John B. Orr

President Mathews has paid his audience the compliment of addressing it in generalities. It is very unfashionable to do that, yet it is precisely the risk he has taken that opens the possibility that we can begin to think about the most fundamental issues that we as a society are facing. He even opens up, through his willingness to deal in such broad generalities, the possibility that we may locate those institutions, those currents of thought that reveal new opportunities. I thank him for his daring to be somewhat unfashionable, and I want to return the compliment by casting these remarks just as much in broad generalizations.

As I understand Dr. Mathews, he puts forward for us a vision of hope in American society. His statements put him in agreement with most viewers of the American scene who claim that we are a society that is hung up, caught on the issue of who the individual is in relation to the group. One might even argue that it has become our mission to work on that problem. It has become our mission to think about, to experiment with fundamental human rights and to worry about and to experiment with the relation of these rights to collective rights and collective responsibilities. He tells us, I think, what we all feel, but what few of us are able to express. Something rather important in this great American mission is going on right now. For better or worse we do feel ourselves in a kind of watershed period, at the end of an era, at the beginning of another era. Of course, in the long run people looking back may say that we were fooling ourselves in being so impressed with the importance of this particular time. But nevertheless we feel it. We feel that something very, very important is happening; we feel that we must understand this is our project of thinking about rights of individuals in relation to the group.

President Mathews speaks of a period of disillusionment. Certainly in California, we feel ourselves to be a part of such an era of disillusionment as we lash out against what many feel to be increasing impersonalness. We lash out at big government. We lash out at the large corporations within which we work. We lash out in frustration at whether individuals can substantially sustain their environment. David Mathews sees hope. Even in the midst of what we feel to be a great disillusionment with our dream, when things are not working out in our universities and in our public life, there is ferment. The new era is opening up; there are new ways of thinking about the individual in relation to the collective. Because he is particularly interested in the university, he turns to the university context and there he finds great hope. Already in the universities, though, people are lashing out, cutting taxes, striking and expressing frustrations; already their answers are fermenting, already new ideas are entering the public mind.

It is important to remember that what President Mathews said is a guess, is indeed a guess. There are other people with other guesses at this point. Those who work in universities ought to take the more dour guesses just as seriously. We don't want to be Pollyanna in this period. If we are facing a much more serious crisis than Dr. Mathews suggests, we ought to know it. We ought to be thinking about it. And so it should be pointed out that there are some other ways that we might also go if we want, for a moment, to attempt to face what may be a much more tragic prognosis of our situation.

In his book *The Human Prospect*, Robert Heilbronner speaks about this as a new era of pessimism. He says that we are entering an era characterized by a surplus of human beings, characterized by rising unemployment and rising inflation, characterized by disillusionment with traditional American institutions. A friend of his, Richard Rubenstein, urges that maybe the United States of America is now beginning to pay the price paid by European civilization at an earlier date than we have been forced to do. He tells us that maybe now we've come to the end of our great enthusiasm associated with expanding markets and expanding institutions with various frontiers. Perhaps it is now that we must face up to the fact that our enchantment with bureaucracy, with economic mentalities, is forcing us into a new era. Perhaps Weber was right, the bureaucratic mentality has had great force in our Western culture. Perhaps he was right in saying that the bureaucratic mentality, the enchantment with economics, is taking us straight into an iron cage, a bleak future—one where whole groups of people will feel excluded from the professions; one where we will have to wonder about the fundamental health of those institutions that nurtured us morally.

If such is the case, then we cannot look toward the American universities in the next few decades for creative thinking about human rights in relation to the collective, because in fact we will be engaged in our own consuming struggle for survival. We will be having to endure in the face of the fact that people will not be looking to universities for entrance into the professions as much as they have in the past. They will be having to deal with the rising costs of higher education, and we will be worried about survival. We will also be worried, one might suggest, about protecting the privileges of those who have had the luck to make it into academe before this new era of pessimism descended. We will be protecting tenure, we will be guarding the gates against the onslaught of those who would like to approach the luxury of reasoning, the luxury of the intellectual life. In short, the university may be the least possible place for creativity and ferment.

Another guess, equally dour, we associate with those who see us now as engaged in therapeutic revolution. I think particularly of Philip Reif's book, *The Triumph of the Therapeutic,* or Richard Senna's book on *The Fall of Public Man,* and even that sparkling, beautiful dismal essay in *Harper's* magazine by Henry Fairlie on "The Absence of Heroes in American Culture." These people are telling us that if affluence is leading us out of an ability to feel a common cause, to pull together as a people, to be concerned about our collective future, we have no heroes with whom to identify. Rather, Americans are enchanted with the personalities of their politicians, their marketability as over against the great issues which in the past they were capable of bringing to the American public.

In short, we are increasingly dealing with a population devoted to its own individual self-realization, its own enchantment with therapeutic values and the expansion of intense, interesting, beautiful experience. We are dealing with a population unable to think seriously about human rights and collective responsibility because we don't think at all of those issues any more. Again, the American university looks rather bleak in that setting. It, like the churches, like the police, like the home, has been among the primary institutions devoted to the socialization of Americans in public value. It may be that if indeed we are involved in a therapeutic revolution, increasingly the mission of the university is felt to be anachronistic.

These are guesses, hopeful guesses, dour guesses. Alfred Shutes, the philosopher, tells us that there is hardly any basis for asserting which of these guesses might be correct. He says all one can do is look at various guesses and see which one drops off like a ripe pear, which one makes sense. One should cast his lot with President Mathews. I, for moral reasons, for reasons of intuition of the vitality of the American public, feel that indeed we may be entering a renaissance, that indeed in our period of disillusionment there are signs of new ferment, new thinking, new ways of moving, new ideas capable of capturing the American imagination. And that indeed these are fermenting already in American universities. I, like him, am not so sure what these ideas are. I liked his intuitions as to where in American universities one begins to see this ferment. I rather would affirm with him that the American university in this period is working. I particularly see a renaissance in professional education. The places that he sees where ferment is happening directly impinge on institutions like the University of Southern California, on how professionals get trained. I particularly see new things, new directions, new life in areas of professional education that have joined their interests with particular areas of liberal education. One can see in our law schools, for example, new concern for thinking about the law in relation to morality, and a beautiful concern for bringing the adversarial legal process to bear on issues of the new medical technology, on environmental issues. In business schools, the lashing out against the mega-corporations is giving rise to a new concern for what corporate accountability is; for, in fact, how one can bring into the mechanism, into the way of operating large corporations, a sensitivity to ecological matters.

One can begin to feel that if higher education is in a renaissance, perhaps it is in a renaissance of new linkages between liberal arts and professional education. Perhaps the grass always looks greener on the other side, but I fear, frankly, for the state of the liberal arts in this new period. In so many areas of the liberal arts now the problems are not percolating. My only hope is that this new vitality that I feel generating in professional higher education will begin more and more to be experienced in such areas as the study of literature, the study of language, the study—more broadly—of culture.

One can feel very good about the prospect of the American university in continuing its ferment about human rights because it really is the case that the university has had a deeply engrained role in American life. This last half century, when we have so self-consciously tried to make ourselves value-free, when we have been caught up in positivisms, has been an ugly metaphor and a wart on the face of American higher education. But from the day of the birth of higher education in this country until now, the dominant tradition has been its preoccupation with the training of American leadership. Obviously, the golden days of moral philosophies, the golden days of higher education in the eighteenth and nineteenth centuries, were bound to a consensus, a Protestant consensus that does not now exist. But that is not to say that we have lost that role which looks to a relatively protected intellectual elite for worry, for fermentation, about these most fundamental issues of human rights. Our social scientists in their advisement of government on public policy have continued this tradition. We see this tradition continued even in the positivist era of the natural sciences. It certainly can be seen in some places within the humanities.

In short, there is a tradition here that has never left. There is an expectation of the university that has never changed in American society, and so one can truly become, with President Mathews, very optimistic. I only hope that leadership emerges to match the optimism. I think we are suffering in American higher education today by the absence of a Hutchins, by the absence of presidents of major universities who can project for us visions of the role of American higher education in this new era. I feel almost as if, like Paul Tillich in the 1920s, I am waiting for a Fuehrer. I hope I'm not saying that. What I am saying is that the moment is right for leadership to come forward to assert again those visions of higher education as a place of moral ferment. The days are here, the possibilities are here, and one would certainly hope that the leadership of higher education in America would grasp this moment to promote new visions that can help us out of our period of disillusionment.

Comment

Charles E. Oxnard

Before I discuss the ideas that Dr. Mathews has brought before us, I would like to draw attention to some of the methods that he has used in his study of shifting values in higher education.

One of these is the matter of using history in such discussions. It certainly seems important to look at history and we can learn many things from it, but I think that historians are suspicious of watersheds. And as a historian whose period is 70 million years, I am especially suspicious of reversals. Reversals do not occur in evolution. If they did, we would not be able to distinguish them.

So I offer the warning that it is too easy to talk about "returning" to some notion or other in education. We are all very well aware of the slogan in high school education, "back to basics." That slogan is a good one as a pedagogical tool in order to try to reach a particular goal. But if we really think that in going back to the old math, we should throw out of the window everything we have learned about the new math, then we must think again.

In the same way, when we look at college education, "back to structure" seems an attractive slogan. But in adopting it, we should not think for a moment that we are also rejecting some of the developments of recent years that bring much needed flexibility into the college curriculum. And yet again, although it can be very useful to refer to history to point to the notion of returning to ideas like "back to individual rights and civic ethics" in higher education, it should be clear to us that we are not, in fact, returning to those eighteenth and nineteenth century concepts. The educational system today is far more complex, and if in fact we try directly to return to the past, we do ourselves a great disservice.

A second kind of device that Dr. Mathews has used to expand on the subject of education is analogy—that is, looking at other areas to find to what extent we can draw upon them in order to gain insights into education. It turns out that with educational matters, as with many others in the social sciences, biology is often examined as a source of analogy. Let me point to one of these.

Biological Darwinism was discovered, invented, created, whatever it is that we think happened; soon after, social Darwinism came along, partly as a result of sociologists seeing the explanatory power of biological Darwinism. Sociologists were obviously looking at other analogues too, but biological Darwinism was an especially convenient one on which to build. It turns out, as we now know, that the original biological Darwinism was very incomplete. And it turns out that social Darwinism was destructive. I therefore suggest that we should be careful when using these analogies. If the analogy is purely for expository purposes, that's fine. But if we think we are actually going to learn something new from it, we have to be very cautious.

Yet it does seem reasonable to explore if recent ideas in biology have anything to say in our present social situation. There *is* a new idea that is current in biology, one that is—I hesitate to call it the conventional wisdom because there is still a great deal of argument about it—immensely respected. It is an idea that has so powerful a grip on the imagination that Nobel prizes have been awarded to its practitioners. This is the idea that understanding human behavior depends very largely on understanding animal behavior. Animal behavior is seen as the determining factor; human behaviors are merely glosses upon animal behavior. This is one of the concepts of sociobiology, and is something that can, like biological Darwinism in a prior century, be readily used by social scientists, by educators, by anyone who is interested in these problems. And indeed it has so been used today.

I think that we have to be careful about using this analogy for the following reason. It is rather likely that the next twenty years will show that this concept in biology is misunderstood and requires much modification. I do not say it is totally wrong; I do suggest it is rather likely that new work will modify it enormously. Some ideas suggesting this stem from the discipline (human evolution) in which I am especially interested, and they are the following.

It is attractive to see elements of human behavior that appear to correlate with animal behavior, e.g. human aggression as a parallel to animal aggression. This superficial similarity is why this kind of discussion first started. But one point that really gives great strength to the notion of the close dependence of human upon animal behavior is the idea that man as a genus is very young. Only a short time ago, and certainly at the time that sociobiology emerged, man was thought to be only a few hundred thousand years old. It thus seemed reasonable to believe that human behavior was a very thin veneer on top of an enormously thick bedrock of animal behavior.

New findings now appearing show that this is not correct. Man has been around ten times longer, perhaps twenty or thirty times longer than previously guessed. Man is not five hundred thousand years old but five million years old; maybe even older. That alone means that the evolution of those behaviors that are human (through psychosocial evolution, if we use Huxley's phrase) is something that has occurred over a much longer period of time. Because we know that psychosocial evolution is very fast, compared to biological evolution, it therefore follows that what we see in human behavior today is an enormously thick sludge of human behavior lying upon a very thin bedrock of prior animal behavior.

Human aggression proceeds, for instance, from such minor phenomena as fights in the playground or home to child-beating and family violence. It proceeds further to murder in an emotional state, through deliberate murder, through torture, warfare, attempted genocide, to genocide itself. As I look at this enormously complicated set of things that make up human aggression, I see almost nothing of animal aggression in it; I see something that is not animal.

In a similar way, as I view human creativity, or human society, or human mysticism—I can easily multiply the examples—I see very little in the form of animal precursors. These are fundamentally human developments. And so I am enormously suspicious of using this analogy in education. Our speaker agrees that he does not believe there is a direct transfer, but I am even suspicious of using the analogy at all because we may well find out, in the next decade-and-a-half, that the basic idea is wrong.

At this point, then, I would like to move more directly to the matters that we are talking about, and I would like to do it from the viewpoint of education and its outcome for individuals.

What for me is the first and foremost outcome is something that I think is designated by the word "fun" or by the word "pleasure": the pleasure of seeing the enormous and complex structure of knowledge, the fun of seeing beyond that normal structure into a foggy, misty area where we do not know. This is the real outcome of education, and an outcome that goes with us for a lifetime. If I point this out to students, they nod their heads wisely, and disbelieve every word of it. But for me it is true, and I think it is true for most of us.

A second outcome that we expect to see from education speaks directly to the human condition, and that is the concept of the concerned citizen. Now this, of course, is a very old idea and very important; but it is one from which we have departed in the last few years. It is slightly more complex than it appears on the surface. It is not just a question of taking a course in government or civics. It is certainly not simply a "return to basics."

It is being aware of what goes on in our own country and understanding it. And although, surely, learning something about our laws and our society has something to do with being a concerned citizen, I think, for America, it is something more, something with which all Americans are familiar, but exciting to me because I come from a different culture. It is that aspect of education in America that allows each one of us to "rub elbows with the President." It is that aspect of education that means that almost all of us have shared a similar educational milieu and, therefore, shared a common spread of ideas that help us understand what's going on. This is in contrast to England where 25 years ago 80 percent of the members of Parliament came from four schools and two universities, and where, even only twelve years ago when I left, only six percent of the children actually shared a common (University) education with the leaders of the country. It is clear to me that this is a very important notion. This is something that universities have to preserve strongly over the next period of time.

Yet a third outcome is one on which students *will* agree with me, and it is that education includes training for a career. In some senses this has had unforeseen and unfortunate results. It is the process that produces our "experts," and so we can say that not only have students decided to become physicians at the age of about 21 when they apply to medical school, we can really say that they have decided to become physicians just as they enter college at the age of 18 when they realize that they must take those pre-medical courses. In fact, they may have actually decided that they are going to be physicians when they were 14 years old as they determined to get straight A's over the next four years. (In my own case, the decision was made overtly at the age of six, when on one occasion, instead of saying "engine driver" in answer to the traditional question about careers, I said "doctor." Thereafter, I was never allowed to answer the question myself; my mother answered it for me. I suspect that the narrowness of this education actually started before conception, for my mother was a nurse. More seriously, I want to suggest that this emphasis on early professional training is one of our major problems, one of the major reasons why we are in serious difficulties with our individual rights and our social responsibilities. It emphasizes *an* immediate career. It forgets that today we must educate broadly enough to provide a basis for the *several* careers of each of our students as their lives change—and they surely will, over the years.

In recent years a fourth outcome has emerged that relates to the recognition of the individual. We have had described to us the plight of the lonely individual trying to lash out against the bureaucracy. But this is not the situation now although it was so a decade or two ago. Since those times, we have had a distinct change. Individuals have organized themselves into groups. We no longer have powerless individuals arrayed against groups, we have groups against groups.

This is displaying itself very much in the adversary nature of individual rights and social responsibilities. I believe that this is bad; but let me first say that I do not denigrate adversary relationships. It is clear that adversary relationships are enormously important. In a civil court, the outcome may be $10,000 for X or $10,000 for Y, and there is no way that we can look at it but that the award of $10,000 for X is good for X, and $10,000 for Y is good for Y. It is even more pointed in the criminal courts where a decision that the individual be freed is surely good for the individual. And many people believe that the opposite decision, that the individual be fined, incarcerated or even killed, is, depending on what has occurred, good for society. These, then, are situations where adversary relationships are absolutely essential to obtaining a proper decision.

But I submit that in matters related to those kinds of individual rights within society that we are discussing, this way of working it out is bad. Consider the situation where one group wishes to have an oil refinery somewhere because of what it will do for the economy in that area (A). Individuals organized as another group wish not to have the oil refinery because of what it will do to the environment (B). It sounds as if an adversary relationship is a good thing in that situation. Certainly if we have an adversary relationship, we will get either A or B or some intermediate consensus.

The point that I'm driving at is that whatever result is arrived at by that adversary relationship, it is not necessarily the best result for both of those groups. The group that thinks the environment is important may suddenly discover, if it "wins," that it was wrong— the environment may actually suffer because a reduced local economy has other deleterious effects. And another equally unexpected and harmful result may be the case if the second group "wins." The optimum answer may well be some third possibility that is foreclosed by the very existence of the adversary model.

I think we have come to this situation because of the presence of the narrow "expert" who can be "used" by the group. Here we come back to career education. We have been educating people for a long period of time to be experts. And experts are not others, as has been indicated today; experts are "us." We are the enemy. I submit that a major problem today is that we have narrow experts working in false adversary relationships.

Let me turn again to medicine for an example. There are clearly many societal problems in relation to medicine at the present time, and one suspects that they are far too important to be left to the doctors. The medical profession certainly does seem to be one of the groups that should be involved in solutions. But to set such experts against other experts, against economists if it's a medical economics problem or against ethicists, if it's a medical ethics problem, and so on, is likely to be counterproductive. We should in fact be looking to the understanding that results from collegial involvement of the experts in these various areas.

I think that the future of the universities in dealing with these complex cases may be the following. It may be vitally important to produce the kinds of people that have been educated in both modes, or in several. Lawyers may no longer be educated as lawyers alone, but know something about fields other than law. A few law schools, our own especially, have already realized this. Medical schools are notoriously rigid in this regard. (I can say this because I come from a medical school and so I am free to cast the stone.) However, a few medical schools have realized it is really rather important to know something more than medicine, to have some other aspect to one's education as a physician in addition to being trained in medicine. It seems to me that it is extraordinarily important that this notion come much more quickly than it has.

I'd like to take this a little further. It is not a question simply of adding knowledge in additional areas. It is something also having to do with "rubbing elbows," with a new form of socialization. The medical profession has long been a secret guild. You may have knowledge if you are a medical student or doctor, but you may not if you aren't. And many aspects of the law and of some of our other professions have fallen into that situation. It is about time not only that we trained physicians to know something about economics and ethics and sociology and so on, but also that some people going into those non-medical fields should be given something of the training of the medical student and, therefore, start to rub elbows with the potential physician. Then, when all come to look at common problems it is no longer in an adversary mode, nor yet in a patting-on-the-back mode, but in a mode where there is genuine understanding on all sides of the case.

I think this can go even further. It is not just a question of educating for the professions of law or medicine—I have merely been using them as examples. Let us consider the purely academic side of education, and talk about that much-maligned person, the Ph.D. There is a need to do something about the education of the Ph.D. because, although it is frequently said that there is an overabundance of these individuals, one thing I know for certain: there is no overabundance of bright people, of intelligent people, of good people; there certainly is no overabundance of those.

It seems to me that society needs something here. Society needs the person who really understands how to discover problems and how to solve them. But with a traditional doctoral education, even bright persons may fail because their education may have been too narrow and their abilities to transfer problem-solving to other areas absent. Some appropriate modifications in academic graduate work are thus required. This is not the place to discuss what they might be.

Though we see some early steps being taken towards many of these ideas, I am not yet sanguine enough to believe that they will happen to the degree and at the speed that our current problems demand. Nor am I entirely satisfied that my own profession (of higher education) is yet flexible and creative enough to promote them.

The Relationship of the Rights and Responsibilities of the Individual to Public School Education— Its Meaning for the Nation

by Wilson Riles

"Four score and seven years ago, our fathers brought forth on this continent a new nation, conceived in liberty and dedicated to the proposition that all men are created equal." Lincoln might well have added to those words spoken at Gettysburg, "and endowed by their creator with certain inalienable rights."

Five score and fifteen years later, as we begin America's third century, we need to reexamine our commitment to those principles of liberty, equality and inalienable rights. We need to pause, as Lincoln paused on the battlefield at Gettysburg, to consider the import of those principles in a nation beset by doubts, confused by criticism, torn by disagreement and threatened by those of little faith. We need to pause and ask ourselves, "What of the rights and responsibilities of the individual—rights which descend from the blessings of liberty, responsibilities which accompany citizenship in a nation dedicated to freedom and equality?"

273

We, as educators and concerned citizens, must pause to ask ourselves, "What of publicly suported schools—are they fulfilling the hopes of those who saw education as the keystone in the arch of self-government? Have they contributed to fulfillment of the promise that all men 'have certain inherent rights, among which are the enjoyment of life and liberty, with the means of acquiring and possessing property, and pursuing and obtaining happiness'?"[1]

This conference on the "Rights and Responsibilities of the Individual" seems an appropriate place to ponder these questions. The faith of the people in the efficacy of organized education is indeed humbling. The responsibility placed upon education to preserve democracy and human rights is indeed awesome.

Historical Tradition: Education for Democracy

Those who composed the Declaration of Independence and those who shared the framing of the Constitution eleven years later believed, as Jefferson wrote, "that man was a rational animal, endowed by nature with rights. . . , that men habituated to thinking for themselves and to follow their reason as guide would be more easily and safely governed than by minds nourished in error and vitiated and debased . . . by ignorance."[2]

Habituated to thinking for themselves, able to follow their reason—such capabilities demand not only universal public education, but *effective* education. It is little wonder that most of the men who officiated at the birth of a nation conceived in liberty argued for the establishment of publicly supported schools. As Jefferson pointed out, "By that part of our plan which prescribes the selection of genius from among the classes of the poor, we hope to avail the state of those talents which nature has sown as liberally among the poor as among the rich, but which perish without use."[3]

"Any nation," Jefferson wrote, "that expects to be ignorant and free expects what never was and never will be."[4]

The promotion of universal education was not limited to Jefferson. Washington in his Farewell Address urged establishment of institutions for the general diffusion of knowledge. "In proportion," he said, "as the structure of government gives force to public opinion, it is essential that public opinion be enlightened."[5]

John Adams, who feared the excesses of democracy, was firm in his conviction that, "The whole people must take upon themselves the education of the whole people, and must be willing to bear the expense of it."

There is little need to belabor the point—the founders of this nation supported education for all those who would inherit the rights of free men, for all those who would enjoy the blessings of liberty. They knew that freedom and ignorance could not exist side by side. They knew that rights to liberty, property and happiness couldn't long endure if minds were nourished in error and debased by ignorance.

Even before the Constitution was framed, Congress wrote into Article Three of the Northwest Ordinance of 1787 an endorsement of education and an implicit delegation of the responsibility to state and local government to provide it. The language of Article Three may not be explicit as to *means,* but it leaves no doubt as to intent: "Religion, morality, and knowledge being necessary to good government and to the happiness of mankind, schools and the means of education shall be forever encouraged."

Under the Bill of Rights in the Constitution of the United States, framed that same year, the establishment of schools and encouragement of the means of education were rights and responsibilities left to the states and, through them, to local governments.

As the nation grew and new communities were formed, the school, the churches and the general store became symbols of America's priorities. The general store represented the forces of individualism; the churches represented the forces of factionalism; and the school represented the forces of joint responsibility. Only the school crossed all lines and bound the community together; established by the community, supported by the community, governed by representatives chosen by the community, the school served all of the children. In those simpler times, the common school had an accepted purpose—to train future generations to carry on the responsibilities of free men. Nation building required a common language, a common loyalty and a common heritage. Where better to ensure those ends than in the common school?

Local citizens joined to build the school, select the teachers and determine what should be taught. Local control of education was virtually unhampered by state law or professional expertise. There was general community acceptance of its responsibility for the right of the individual to secure a basic education, and community involvement in the management of schools reflected that responsibility.

For nearly half our nation's history, schools operated on the dual premises of local responsibility and political purpose. Immigrants were turned into Americans, the poor became supporters and participants in the nation's industrial growth. From the roots of society, through the efforts and the efficacy of the common school, came the middle class—the inventors, entrepreneurs, politicians, scientists, writers and artists who made real the dreams of Jefferson, Washington, Adams, Franklin and their fellow revolutionaries.

As society became more complex, as communities grew to urban centers, full local control and support of schools became unmanageable. Ward politics turned the schools into opportunities for graft rather than for education. The pendulum swung full arc, pushed by public outrage.

Before long, responsibility for education was divided between the state government and a rapidly emerging new professional—the educator. Parents and taxpayers furnished the raw material and the resources, and the public school system, governed primarily by state legislatures and managed by professionals, made educational decisions for the local community. Most individuals still had the right to a free public education, but responsibility for the educational process, content and result was taken away from the lay public and the parents. If Johnny can't read, it is hard to find anyone today who will accept responsibility for his failure.

Our challenge now is to develop new mechanisms so that those who provide the raw materials and the resources have some voice in what is happening within the education system and some feeling of responsibility for results.

Education Today: Where Are Individual Rights?

In school districts serving thousands of youngsters, there is no way for every parent and taxpayer to be heard at the district level. In a society where professionalization builds an impenetrable barrier around our institutions, it becomes very difficult to find people who are both sensitive to the rights of the individual and who have the authority to make the system responsive to those rights. That problem is not limited to schools, of course, but it is most critical in the field of education, because there the victim—the child—is powerless.

If we, as parents and concerned citizens, sit by, limiting expression of our discontent to talking back to our television sets, nothing will change. We are deluding ourselves if we think that our representatives in legislative bodies will read our minds and do what is best for the children. Of course we have faith in education. Of course we want public schools to be adequately funded. Of course we don't mean that public schools are to be crippled when we stage taxpayer revolts and demand that the fat be cut from government. Yet we let the lobbyists for special interests influence the distribution of increasingly scarce public resources. Such a failure to speak out leaves legislative bodies free to respond only to the voices they hear.

We are *not* powerless. We have a responsibility to ourselves, our children and the future of this nation to make certain that educational systems are adequately funded and responsive to the rights of each individual.

We have the power to bring the locus of educational decision making down from the halls of Congress, down from the halls of state legislatures, down from the administrative offices of the school district to the place where student and teacher meet, to the point where learning takes place, to the school itself. We have the power, in spite of the growth of massive bureaucracies, in spite of voices concerned only with special interests, in spite of those who would de-school America, to affect the educational process. It is our responsibility to use that power to make our schools what they must be if they are to continue as the keystone in the arch of self-government.

Let me hasten to add that I do not count myself among the critics of the American educational system. I do not join the pack of detractors who would have us believe that our schools are failing. America's schools aren't failing—for the majority of the nation's children they are highly successful.

A century ago, one American in five was illiterate; today, only one

American in a hundred over the age of 14 is unable to read or write. In 1910, only 13.5 percent of the country's adult population completed the twelfth grade; today, nearly 24 percent have completed four or more years of college, and 84 percent of the adult population have completed high school.[6]

When a major television network asked recently, "Is Anybody Out There Learning?" the investigative reporters found that 15 percent of the millions of students attending our schools aren't doing too well. If this is true, it means that 85 percent of those students are doing just fine, but the reporters failed to acknowledge that.

Figures are cold symbols of the personal progress of millions of Americans along the path of education. Statistics give little indication of America's shift during the twentieth century from an agrarian economy to a position of leadership among industrial and scientific communities everywhere. Literacy rates and grades of schooling completed are only proxies for a standard of living and an opportunity for upward mobility which are the envy of the world.

In the face of the progress and the prosperity that are the norm for the majority of American families regardless of color or ethnic origin, how can one doubt the success of American education in achieving economic and social purposes?

In the light of our political stability, despite recent crises of leadership, how can anyone doubt the success of American education is achieving its political purpose?

No, American schools have not failed. Education has not been limited to some elite group, leaving the rights of the poor and minorities unmet. Our public school system has worked hard to fulfill the dream of the founders of this nation *and* the mandate of the Supreme Court in *Brown v. Board of Education* to provide equal educational opportunities for all children. But that doesn't mean that we're relieved of our responsibility for its continued success.

Responsive Education Through Individual Responsibility

As successful as schools are, they can and must be made better. To stop improving, to stop searching for better methods, is to condemn schools to certain obsolescence. No one who cares about the rights of the individual, no one who cares about the future of our 200-year-old experiment with self-government, no one who shares the faith of the founders of America in "reason, progress and common humanity" would tolerate the destruction of our public school system.

But—how can we improve education so that we may continue to discharge our responsibility to protect the rights of the individual and to preserve liberty and freedom?

First, we must make certain that those who exercise the franchise, those who draft initiative measures, those who sit in the halls of the legislatures and Congress understand the *true purpose* of education. We must make certain that those who would sacrifice the future for a tax cut today understand that the true purpose of education is to educate man*kind*, not man*power*—to unlock the vast potential of our most fundamental resource, the human mind.

We can survive as a nation with less energy, with depleted natural resources, with less of almost everything—but *we can't survive without creative minds, without participating and productive citizens, capable of self-government in the face of all odds.* That means we must with single-minded determination be champions of the rights of the individual. We must see every child as a potential solver of world problems, as a potential Einstein or Madame Curie, as a potential finger on the nuclear trigger.

That is our primary responsibility—educator, parent, concerned citizen alike.

Second, we, as champions of the rights of the individual, must see that those rights are protected and enlarged. We must see that each child's unique needs are met and that no public school system is permitted to grow into a bureaucratic monster that forces the child to fit the system or fail.

We must continue to work until we're certain that we are fulfilling the true purpose of education, that we are, in truth, unlocking the potential of each human mind. We must not turn aside until we are certain that the schools are teaching children not only how to use the basic tools of learning proficiently, but also how to think creatively and critically; how to solve problems and get along well with others;

how to make decisions and accept the consequences of actions; how to listen as well as to speak; how to value the diversity of others and to cherish and nurture their own self-esteem.

If the schools are to achieve these purposes, they must be more than a collection of classrooms and courses. They must be filled with opportunities for real-life experiences and with practical application of acquired skills, just as Benjamin Franklin advocated more than two centuries ago.[7]

Schools must be places where proficiency, not merely competency, is the primary criterion for achievement. They must be places where learning, not simply the accumulation of units, seat hours or grades, is the desired objective. Schools must be places where tests are given, not to prove what a youngster knows or doesn't know at the end of a course, but what he needs to know in order to attain proficiency in a skill essential to "perform basic public responsibilities. . . ; to awaken him to cultural values. . . ; to prepare him for later professional training. . . ; to help him adjust normally to his environment. . . ; to succeed in life" to quote from the decision of the learned justices of the Supreme Court of the United States in *Brown v. Board of Education.*

We have a responsibility in this regard to insist that a school encompass the whole community in the learning process. We must insist that parents be included as partners of the school, rather than its adversaries. We must insist that there be no moat filled with the sharks of educational jargon or the piranhas of educational process separating the school from the lay community.

Let me give you an example of the kind of barriers that exist between parents and schools in all too many communities.

> A Houston, Texas, father recently received a message from the principal of his son's high school—a man who, no doubt, had at least one advanced degree from an institution of higher education. The message read: "Our school's cross-graded multiethnic, individualized learning program is designed to enhance the concept of an open-ended learning program with emphasis on a continuum of multi-ethnic, academically enriched learning using the identified intellectually gifted child as the agent or director of his own learning. Major emphasis is on cross-graded, multi-ethnic learning with the main

objective being to learn respect for the uniqueness of a person."

The father, speaking for all parents everywhere, replied: "I have a college degree, speak two foreign languages and four Indian dialects, have been to a number of county fairs and three goat ropings, but I haven't the faintest idea as to what the hell you are talking about. Do you?"

We must insist that there is some apparent relationship between what is taught and the right of each and every individual to develop to his/her full potential.

Finally, we have a responsibility to see that the needs of minorities in the school population are met—not with token response, but with effective programs.

Robert Maynard Hutchins said a half-century ago, "Education is an act of faith and I have faith that no child is ineducable. . ."[8]

Translating that faith into reality is our responsibility as educators and concerned citizens of a nation "conceived in liberty and dedicated to the proposition that all men are created equal."

Every child, rich or poor, minority or majority, advantaged or disadvantaged, has a right to an education that meets his/her unique needs and develops his/her full potential. Every individual has a right to an education that provides an equal opportunity to compete for places in the world of work or the world of higher education.

To offer double standards for admission to colleges and universities on the mistaken premise that only by such acts of charity can minorities qualify, to offer minorities a "back door" entry to future success, is to shirk our responsibility to respect the rights of the individual.

To perpetuate an underclass that can gain employment only through "affirmative action programs" because its members, through little fault of their own, are "qualifiable" rather than qualified is, again, to evade our responsibilities to the rights of the individual.

To exclude the severely handicapped from education because we aren't prepared to meet their needs is an equally serious avoidance of our responsibility to respect the rights of every individual—a denial of the basic premise of equality.

Too frequently, as we follow the beacon of democracy, we shape our course to satisfy the needs and the will of the majority and neglect those whose needs are greatest.

We have a responsibility to heed the caution given us by Jefferson in his first Inaugural Address:

> All . . . will bear in mind this sacred principle that though the will of the majority is in all cases to prevail, that will, to be rightfull, must be reasonable; that the minority possess their equal rights, which equal laws must protect, and to violate would be oppression.[9]

In Lincoln's time our nation couldn't survive half free, half slave. It can't survive now, as we face the potential social, economic and political crises of the world, part educated and part ignorant. Every individual has an equal right to an education that allows the full development of his/her potential. Anything less is a denial of rights and a guarantee that the individual will be less able to fulfill his/her responsibilities as a citizen.

Ahead to Basics

If there is any doubt about the grave import of our responsibilities for the future welfare of the nation, we have only to look back a decade. In the 1960s, riots in our major cities and assassinations of national leaders aroused serious doubts about the viability of the faith of our founders in the individual as a rational animal, a creature capable of self-government. Out of the turmoil and doubt came questions concerning the value of education. Students rebelled and rioted, tearing down educational fortresses, defying our well-intentioned efforts to mold them into the citizens of yesteryear. They demanded courses relevant to their time and to their future needs. In too many instances, we gave them not better, but easier, courses; not relevant, but ridiculous, responses; not intellectual nourishment, but mental junk food. We, in our panic, heard their cries but misread their meaning.

Now, all across America, irate taxpayers are echoing almost the same demands. They are demanding that we go back to basics; the taxpayers of tomorrow are demanding that we go *ahead* to basics, that we give them proficiency not only in the basic tools of learning but in the essential skills they will need to participate in and contribute to the world of the twenty-first century. In short, the tax-payers of today *and tomorrow* are demanding that we respect their rights—including the right to *effective* education.

If we are going to meet those demands, citizens, parents and educators must cease to be critics and adversaries and come together in a constructive partnership designed to bring our schools to standards of excellence, to make certain that schools achieve their public purpose as keystone in the arch of self-government:

- Nothing less will brighten the image of the public school system.
- Nothing less will restore education to its rightful place in the list of public priorities.
- Nothing less will preserve the rights and liberties of the individual.
- Nothing less will keep the dream of freedom and equality alive in these United States.

NOTES

1. "Virginia Declaration of Rights," quoted in Henry Steele Commager, *Empire of Reason*, Garden City, N.Y.: Anchor Press/Doubleday, 1978, p. 242.

2. Thomas Jefferson to Justice Johnson, *ibid.*, p. 44.

3. Thomas Jefferson in "Notes on Virginia," *ibid.*, pp. 135-36.

4. Thomas Jefferson in a letter to Colonel Charles Yancey, quoted in John Bartlett, *Familiar Quotations* (14th ed.), Boston: Little, Brown and Company, 1968, p. 473.

5. George Washington, "Farewell Address," *An American Primer*, Daniel J. Boorstin (ed.), New York: New American Library, 1968, p. 222.

6. U.S. Department of Health, Education and Welfare, *Annual Report of the Commissioner of Education, 1976*, pp. 233-34.

7. Carl Van Doren, *Benjamin Franklin*, New York: Viking Press, p. 191.

8. Robert Maynard Hutchins, *Education and the Social Order*, Los Angeles: Modern Forum, 1936, p. 12.

9. Thomas Jefferson, "Inaugural Address," *An American Primer*, Daniel J. Boorstin (ed.), New York: New American Library, 1968, p. 232.

Comment

Benjamin DeMott

Obviously, I admire Dr. Riles' optimism and his hostility to jargon. I admire his understanding of the mandate of the founding fathers, and most of all, I admire his rejection of the impotence syndrome that touches not only this state, but many others. I have one or two minor carps—who would not, being a professor and earning his living by carping?

Certainly I would want to ask about college and the increasing numbers of people who have the advantages, as we say, of college education. What exactly does a college education mean? In connection with that, I put a question about whether we are indeed more knowledgeable than our fathers and our grandfathers. I am not certain that there has not been a significant degradation of the skills of the worker over the past 150 years and I think that point has to be given some weight.

I'd also say that while I share the sense that we should talk more often about the 85 percent who succeed, should talk more often about the three out of four who learn to read and have passed the test, we should be more worried now about the other 15 percent. I think a great deal has been learned over the past fifteen years about learning problems. One of the most troubling things for someone who teaches my subject, English, is that a good deal of the best work that has been done in the last fifteen years has suffered terribly from failure of dissemination. All the work of Goodman in the teaching of remedial reading; the work of Professor Myra Shaughnessy at the City University of New York in the teaching of writing, represent extraordinary breakthroughs in these fields and yet, if you do as I've been doing, if you move about through the lower schools of the country, you find that scarcely anyone is even aware that such work has in fact been done. Hardly anyone is aware of how much more can be done with a person who is confronted with learning difficulties than is presently being done.

These are, as I said, minor carps. The theme that most mattered in Dr. Riles' talk, was the notion of seeking to reinvigorate the relationship between the community and the school. Dr. Riles spoke of the need for new mechanisms to permit parents to have a voice in schooling, a more significant voice than they have had for some time. He tells us that we have the power to bring the decisions about schooling down from the state legislature into the community, down to, as he says, the school itself. We have the power to make parents partners in the schooling process. We could, he says, make the school capable of encompassing the community. I happen to agree with all this, but I also happen to feel that there is a significant commonality between this theme and a great many other themes involving rights and responsibility.

Something has to be done, not only about parents' participation in the school, but workers' participation at work and citizens' participation generally in the government. We seem to see ourselves as troubled by a kind of national psychosis of passivity. We see ourselves as needing to recover some awareness of our own power, some awareness of our own capacity to affect the course of events. In some instances, when we search for the mechanisms that Dr. Riles speaks of, we have to look to the future. We have to be inventive, we have to imagine, we have to be—despite Mr. Horowitz's counsel against being anything of this sort—futurologists. But I believe there is a sense in which, in relation to schools and in relation to work, we don't need to be futurologists; we need to be historians. We need to understand that when there was community, when there was a sense of responsibility, when rights and responsibilities were profoundly and significantly linked, it was because certain circumstances maintained or obtained in the culture of the time. We do not want to go back to all of those circumstances.

Those who are students of labor history know the difference between seventy-hour work weeks at ten cents an hour and present wages; but they also know that labor historians will seek to learn what the life circumstances and worker satisfactions of the period of seventy-hour work weeks and ten cents an hour wages were. They will be astonished at the range and number of satisfactions people still alive recall—some to be sure, in a spirit of nostalgia, some to be sure, enjoying the halo effect of being interrogated by historians long after their work lives have ended. Those satisfactions often include the making of the workplace into a familial or ethnic enclave. They involve close relationships, familiar relationships on the job. They involve a sense on the part of the worker that he is engaged in the making of a product that is the best of its kind, a sense that the paternalistic employer would never put out thirds or seconds as firsts, and so on. The period to which Dr. Riles alluded when the community did indeed participate in the life of the schools is a period about which much more can be known.

If we but go back to our older knowledge, then we seem at present to see what I think is most known and most visible and most significant about the time when a genuine relationship between parent and school existed. It was that schooling did not take place only in the school. What we need, I think, more than anything else, if we are going to reinvigorate that relationship which matters so much to Dr. Riles and to me, is a sense that the school has too long dominated schooling. The school itself and the public school system are not adequate as the agency of schooling in the whole society. It is not a matter of de-schooling the society. It is a matter of understanding that education is ultimately too important a matter in the whole life of the community to be left to teachers, to be left to the system as it presently stands.

Comment

Stephen J. Knezevich

I understand Wilson Riles to say that indeed the relationship between rights and responsibilities of the individual and a system of public school education is a very basic relationship. It is difficult in any society dedicated to and truly concerned about the rights of individuals to have these attitudes exist in reality without a system of public education. Obviously, this is simply more than creating awareness that individuals have rights. If this were the sole task, we could accomplish it very much as we do with the *Miranda* cards that are read by officers prior to an arrest. We could do this with other rights as well.

But there are things that are more basic, that go beyond simply generating an awareness that in our culture rights are there to enjoy. We recognize the importance, as well, of the balance wheel, that there are responsibilities that an individual must demonstrate lest his right become merely a license, lest it become confused with a privilege rather than something made available to all individuals living in a particular culture. Education is so important that no one is to be deprived of it either by personal choice or because of the manner in which we structure our school system. Education is a social good, not simply an individual consumption good that one may choose to accept or to reject because he is too busy, say, making money and, therefore, ignores societal demands. We have a system of education available to all at least through a certain period of life. So an educational system is basic, starting with elementary and secondary schools and then with a university system, both public and private, as a capstone.

Because this is true, we can have certain ways of using the school system beyond simply developing toward rights the attitude that these are something an individual enjoys and protects. We can teach their protection by teaching the reponsibilities that go with rights. It is not by accident that we find rights being talked about rather fervently with a great deal of emotion on university campuses. We witnessed this in the United States during the Vietnam days when people felt keenly about certain issues and their rights. We see it today in countries such as Iran. It is not unusual to find that universities are closed when emotions reach a certain pitch, when people feel so keenly about rights. An educational system can nurture and develop rights, and it can be used as a platform for demonstrating the importance of those rights.

In the United States today, we see yet another thing with reference to rights and a school system. We find our school system caught in a social turmoil in which many of the great social problems of our time are being brought to the doorsteps of the schoolhouse and most have walked right in. Education is caught in the argument as to whether an individual's right is being curtailed because of discrimination against some resulting from the manner in which our education systems are organized or structured. Presently, we have a great debate with reference to what is called desegregation or integration; that equal access to education is an important right and no system of education can be organized to modify that right in any way. We have almost come to the point where the very system that is basic and is dedicated to the promulgation of rights and responsibilities of all individuals may be threatened by the fact that it is caught in a rather serious dispute.

The most interesting case I have seen of this is in Cleveland. The Cleveland Public Schools are being run by the courts to such a degree that the courts appointed an administrator responsible directly to the court. This individual's authority, for all practical purposes, superceded that of the Superintendant of Schools and of the Board of Education. This led to the resignation of one superintendent and of the Board of Public Education in the city of Cleveland. Today, the United States Supreme Court is really the national school board. Why? Because the rights of individuals are so important that no one is allowed to operate in a manner that would suggest that certain rights may be abrogated. We have come full circle to where the school systems are so essential to the development and protection of rights. This system has often been used as a platform for discussions with reference to these rights. Now this system is caught in the middle of a conflict over the manner in which society may be organized for purposes of residence, or for whatever other purposes. And the schools are now being accused of depriving individuals of some rights because of social arrangements traditionally outside the scope of the schools.

I feel optimistic that we'll work our way out of this one and that once again the schools will be able to perform their primary role, namely that of helping individuals to understand and to enjoy their rights but at the same time to protect these rights by recognizing the responsibilities that go along with them.

Comment

Frederick Rudolph

It would have been staggering news if the Superintendent of Public Instruction of the State of California had come out against the public schools. He has, of course, done no such thing. His robust assertion of faith in the schools, his confident readiness to accept "the responsibility upon education to preserve democracy and human rights," are in the best tradition of American public life.

Yet, while I congratulate the people of California for possessing in Dr. Riles a guardian of the true faith, I urge on him and on his fellow Californians a caution, a healthy skepticism, a sense of balance that I find missing in his paper, as indeed they have generally been missing in the way we Americans have looked at our schools.

We too often act as if the schools alone are the sources of guidance and instruction in our society, as if they alone possess the means and the potential to set things right when they go wrong. A young lady of my acquaintance recently forcefully demonstrated to me how easily we forget the powerlessness of the schools in the presence of stronger competing educational forces. The four-year-old of whom I speak had had her nap and her juice and was told by her nursery school teacher that it was "demonstration time" and that it was her turn to show her classmates how to do something. "I'll need some toothpicks, some white paper, and some Scotch tape," the young lady informed the teacher, and after they were provided and distributed among her classmates, she went ahead. "And now," she said, "I will show you how to roll a joint." More recently her family awoke to the discovery that they had been robbed of most of the portable technological equipment that defines the well-situated contemporary American home. Into the dismay and confusion being registered by her parents she hurled a question: "And *where* was Wonder Woman?"

So, like Professor DeMott, I remind us of those other agencies of education—the family, church, elected officials, courts, the media (or should I say "communications technology"?)—and urge us to break loose from the tradition of unbounded faith in the power of the schools that has, in the words of one historian, "led all of us to make unwarranted, unrealistic, and harmful demands upon them."

I am grateful to Dr. Riles, as I know we all are, for so ably clarifying the subject of this morning's panel and for defining the relationships between the individual and society as revealed in the American experience with public schooling. I have no trouble with his concern for the rights of students. I too would have every student regarded with respect, love, and a tentativeness appropriate to an unopened birthday present: as something mysterious, perhaps breakable, and with good luck wondrous to behold—a human being. I would have every student acknowledged as an equal and as an individual, moving through the system of public education in a way that recognizes individual needs and talents and in a way that does not assign anyone, because of sex or race or ethnic origin, to an experience in prejudged expectations. (May I add that among the bits of news encouraging to freedom that came out of the November 1978 elections was the decision of California voters not to infringe the right of students to smoke in public with homosexual teachers.)

As for student responsibilities, I would be willing to try to spell them out and to argue that a student's first responsibility is *to try*, even if there is no encouragement from home or teacher, because to try is essential to self-respect; a second responsibility might be to accept the various dogmas of the American myth, all of its credos, all of its tenets—i.e., Carmen Gonzales *can* be president of the United States—and yet at the same time subject them to critical inquiry and the saving cure of laughter.

Where I have trouble with Dr. Riles is in his almost uncritical acceptance of the burdens, even the contradictory purposes, that have accumulated around the schools. I wish that his faith had limits. From the time when the Puritans went about setting up their first schools—in large measure in order to ward off incipient juvenile delinquency—to the present, we have asked too much of the schools. We have thrown them every problem for solution, every fantasy for fulfillment. All of us may not go as far as did Lyndon Johnson, who remarked, "The answer for all our national problems comes down to one single word: education." But in one way or another most of us have asked too much of the schools or expected too much from them, so that of course we are led from time to time to think that they have failed. When a society pours a quarter of its population into public education—and that is where we are, as student, teacher, or administrator—someone is bound to be disappointed.

I do not think that we can accurately undertake an assessment of the "relationship of the rights and responsibilities of the individual to public school education" or clarify "its meaning for the nation" without being sensitive to the contradictory expectations that are imbedded in its history. Schooling in America began as an exercise in social control. A 1729 Massachusetts sermon summed up the argument with which New England ventured into public schooling: "The education of youth is a great benefit and source [of safety] to the public. This is that which civilized them, takes down their temper, tames the fierceness of their nature, forms their minds to virtue, learns 'em to carry it with a just deference to superiors; makes them tractable or manageable; and by learning and knowing what it is to be under government, they will know the better how to govern others when it comes to their turn . . . Yea, good education tends to promote religion and reformation as well as peace and order."

You will recognize in this 1729 rationale for the American school much that is familiar, but if the American school were to be only what is suggested by this sermon, it would not develop into a popular institution nor become an agency for transforming society. That Massachusetts clergyman did not anticipate a world that needed Wilson Riles. He did, however, have a keen sense of how the future would use the schools in an effort to confirm the present, to tame the young if not break them, to discipline them, and to a remarkable degree make going to school often one of the most unpleasant experiences exacted of the young by a free society.

What is missing in his formula is any sense of the promises that American life would hold out to the young, or any recognition of social and economic mobility as one of the dynamic facts and myths that would define American life.

Benjamin Franklin, as Dr. Riles has reminded us, understood what was going on, and in 1749 and 1751 he proposed in two papers addressed to the Philadelphia governing class that they open a school that would turn out young men "fitted for learning any business, calling, or profession." Franklin's school was intended to serve the needs of a society where careers were open, where status was achieved rather than ascribed. Franklin, moreover, in his own life epitomized the qualities of American life that were intended to find support in his proposed school—pluralism, versatility, multiplicity, change, discontinuity, and experiment (the very essence of individualism and freedom), and these of course were the very qualities that would collide with efforts to make the American school a rigid instrument of social control.

This is neither the time nor the place for a capsule history of public schooling in the United States, but as the society fell into the habit of turning to the schools as agencies of social purpose, and as the people themselves looked to the schools as instruments of individual aspiration, the American school became in myth and in fact that most engaging paradox—a mechanism of social control responsive to the wishes of those with power *and* a mechanism of individual liberation responsive to the dreams of the people, an instrument for teaching men and women their place *and* for liberating them from the place they find themselves in. In the schools society lays claim to the young, but also in the schools the young lay claim to the future.

Schooling in America has not been simply a quiet process of acculturation, as that Massachusetts clergyman clearly expected. It has also been the instrument by which a dominant culture (once white, Anglo-Saxon, and Protestant) has dealt with various counter cultures and has itself been modified and transplanted. The school, then, is not only burdened with the responsibilities consciously assigned to it in the present and accumulated from the past. It also has an independent life of its own as the place where successive generations redefine the values, the promises, and the performance of American life.

The weight of these contradictory yet inescapable burdens must be acknowledged. The school must be recognized as but one of many agencies of education in our society. And we must understand that the school has a meaning beyond instruction as an arena where we as a people have been engaged in defining who we are and where we want to go. In other words, unless we proceed with a great deal of humility and caution and sensitivity, the challenges and responsibilities so ably defined by Dr. Riles will surely lead to another round of disappointment, disillusionment, and disenchantment with our schools.

Biographical Notes

David H. Bayley is Professor of International Studies at the Graduate School of International Studies of the University of Denver. He is the author of numerous books and articles, including *Forces of Order: Police Behavior in Japan and the United States* and *Public Liberties in the New States*.

Gordon M. Berger is Associate Professor of History at the University of Southern California. He is the author of *Parties Out of Power in Japan, 1931-1941* as well as several articles on Japanese history.

Ross N. Berkes is Professor of International Relations at the University of Southern California where he was for many years Director of the School of International Relations. Dr. Berkes is co-author of the highly-regarded *Diplomacy of India*. A founding member of the International Studies Association, he was its president in 1963-64.

Adda B. Bozeman is Professor Emeritus of International Relations at Sarah Lawrence College and was recently the Benedict Distinguished Visiting Professor in Political Science at Carleton College. Dr. Bozeman is the author of a number of important works, including *Politics and Culture in International History* and *The Future of Law in a Multicultural World*.

Carl Q. Christol is Professor of International Law at the University of Southern California. His research interests have been in legal and political problems associated with the oceans, outer space, the world's environment, human rights, and United States constitutional law. These interests have resulted in six books and numerous professional articles.

Alexander DeConde is Professor of History at the University of California, Santa Barbara, specializing in the diplomatic history of the United States. His two-volume work *A History of American Foreign Policy* has just appeared in a third edition.

Benjamin DeMott is Professor of English at Amherst College. Dr. DeMott has been a consultant to many educational foundations and has served on the editorial boards of a variety of important national journals. His published works include several novels and volumes of essays on life and letters.

Robert S. Ellwood, Jr. is the Bishop James W. Bashford Professor of Oriental Studies at the University of Southern California. He is the author of ten books on religious and spiritual groups in America and on religious culture and traditions in East Asia.

Timothy Fuller is Associate Professor of Political Science at Colorado College, where he specializes in political philosophy and particularly Thomas Hobbes, J. S. Mill, and Michael Oakshott as well as modern political philosophy and the philosophy of history. These interests are reflected in his publications in professional journals.

Alan Gilbert is Assistant Professor in the Graduate School of International Studies at the University of Denver and a visiting scholar in Cornell University's Department of Philosophy. His book, *Marxist Politics: Communists and Citizens*, is being published simultaneously in the United States and England.

William J. Goode is Professor of Sociology at Stanford University. Previously he was Franklin H. Giddings Professor of Sociology at Columbia University. Among his numerous publications, the most recent is his book *The Celebration of Heroes*.

Irving Louis Horowitz is Hannah Arendt Professor of Sociology and Political Science at Rutgers University. His most recent works are *Science, Sin and Scholarship* and *Dialogues on American Politics* (with S. M. Lipset).

Barbara C. Jordan is Lyndon B. Johnson Professor of Public Affairs at the University of Texas. She received her law degree from Boston University. She was a member of the Texas State Senate from 1966 to 1972 and Member of Congress from the 18th district of Texas from 1973 to 1979.

Stephen J. Knezevich is Dean of the School of Education at the University of Southern California. He is the author of nine widely-used texts on school administration.

Henry Koeppler was Director of the Institute for the Study of the Interaction of Foreign and Domestic Affairs at Baylor University at the time of his death in 1979. He was founder and first Director of Wilton Park, an international interdisciplinary discussion center in Sussex, England. In addition to a distinguished career of service to the academic world, he was Under Secretary of State in the Foreign and Commonwealth Office of the United Kingdom, 1975-77.

Andrzej Korbonski is Professor and Chairman of the Department of Political Science at the University of California, Los Angeles. A specialist in East Central European Affairs, he has published numerous books and articles on these subjects. He was a member of the United States Delegation to the Conference on Security and Cooperation in Europe held in Belgrade.

Ernest W. Lefever is Director of the Ethics and Public Policy Center which he founded at Georgetown University. For many years he was on the senior foreign policy studies staff of the Brookings Institution. His most recent book is *Nuclear Arms in the Third World*.

Anthony Lewis is author of a twice-weekly column in the *New York Times*, and a two-time winner of the Pulitzer Prize. He is the author of *Portrait of a Decade*, a study of changes in race relations. In addition to his journalistic duties, Mr. Lewis teaches at the Law School of Harvard University and is considered an expert on the constitutional rights and duties of the press.

David Mathews is President of the University of Alabama. From 1975 to 1977 he was Secretary of the U.S. Department of Health, Education, and Welfare. He is the author of several papers on higher education.

John B. Orr holds the John R. Tansey Chair of Christian Ethics and is Director of the School of Religion at the University of Southern California. He is the author of several books and articles in his special fields of religious ethics, the sociology of values, education and public policy, and ethical rhetoric.

Charles E. Oxnard is Dean of the Graduate School and University Professor of Anatomy and Biological Sciences at the University of Southern California. Originally trained as a physician, Dr. Oxnard also earned the Ph.D. and D.Sc. degrees from the University of Birmingham. He is the author of many articles and books in the areas of functional and evolutionary morphology, morphometrics and biomechanics of mammals, especially the Primates.

E. Raymond Platig is Director of the Office of External Research for the Bureau of Intelligence and Research in the United States Department of State. Before joining the Department of State, Dr. Platig taught at the University of Denver and was Director of Studies for the Carnegie Endowment for Peace.

Wilson Riles is the elected Superintendent of Public Instruction and Director of Education for the State of California. Before his election, Dr. Riles served in several high-ranking capacities within the California State Department of Education. A graduate of Northern Arizona University, he is the recipient of several honorary degrees recognizing his contributions to public education.

Frederick Rudolph is the Mark Hopkins Professor of History and Chairman of the American Civilization Program at Williams College. A distinguished authority on the history of higher education, Dr. Rudolph is author of the classic, *The American College and University: A History*.

Mark L. Schneider is United States Deputy Assistant Secretary of State for Human Rights. Before accepting this post in 1977, he was a legislative assistant to Senator Edward M. Kennedy with special responsibility for foreign policy, including Latin America, human rights, and arms control.

Kenneth W. Thompson is the White Burkett Miller Professor of Government and Foreign Affairs at the University of Virginia where he is also Director of the White Burkett Miller Center of Public Affairs. He was for many years Vice President of the Rockefeller Foundation. He is author or co-author of nineteen books on international politics and foreign policy.

Vernon Van Dyke is Carver Distinguished Professor at the University of Iowa where he teaches international politics. His many books and articles include *Human Rights, the United States, and World Community* and *International Politics*.